Lecture Notes of the Institute for Computer Sciences, Social Informatics and Telecommunications Engineering 138

T0212716

More information about this series at http://www.springer.com/series/8197

Giovanni Vincenti · Alberto Bucciero
Carlos Vaz de Carvalho (Eds.)

E-Learning, E-Education, and Online Training

First International Conference, eLEOT 2014
Bethesda, MD, USA, September 18–20, 2014
Revised Selected Papers

 Springer

Editors
Giovanni Vincenti
University of Baltimore
Baltimore
USA

Carlos Vaz de Carvalho
Instituto Sperior de Engenharia do Porto
Porto
Portugal

Alberto Bucciero
IBAM - Istituto per i Beni Archeologici e
    Monumentali
Italian National Research Council
Roma
Italy

ISSN 1867-8211   ISSN 1867-822X (electronic)
Lecture Notes of the Institute for Computer Sciences, Social Informatics
and Telecommunications Engineering
ISBN 978-3-319-13292-1   ISBN 978-3-319-13293-8   (eBook)
DOI 10.1007/978-3-319-13293-8

Library of Congress Control Number: 2014956515

Springer Cham Heidelberg New York Dordrecht London

Printed on acid-free paper

Springer International Publishing AG Switzerland is part of Springer Science+Business Media
(www.springer.com)

Preface

The First International Conference on e-Learning, e-Education and Online Training, or eLEOT 2014, was held during August 18–20, 2014 at the Bethesda Marriott Hotel in Bethesda, Maryland, USA. This conference has been in the works for many years, with its original date set for 2010. After a few delays, some changes in aims, location, and circumstances, we are happy to report on its success! This year's goal was a simple one: presenting a cross-section of educational technologies and practices that spans over multiple disciplines.

The work was coordinated by our Organizing Committee, which is reported later in this publication. The program was composed of 26 technical papers, which were presented in six sessions over the span of 2 days. The Technical Program Committee Chair, Dr. Alberto Bucciero, managed a team of 30 scholars and practitioners who carefully reviewed the 76 submissions that we received. The final program included three tracks: the main track, dedicated to affirmed researchers, the online track, which extended the boundaries of eLEOT 2014 to include those who could not join us physically, and a student track, which gave ample space and resonance to the work of those just getting started. Overall, eLEOT 2014 included collaborators and participants from Europe, North America, Asia, Africa, and Australia/Oceania.

The highlights of the conference included three main events. This year's edition was kicked off with a keynote address by John "Pathfinder" Lester, a pioneer of online education, evangelist of virtual worlds, and constantly working as a connector between research and practice. His past experiences range from Linden Lab (Second Life), to Massachusetts General Hospital and Harvard Medical School, leading him to his current position as Chief Learning Officer at ReactionGrid. Then we opened our TechTalk series with Stefano Santo Sabato, of MediaSoft, S.r.l.. This group has become one of Italy's premier private endeavors in bridging the gap between industry and academia in the area of distance education, among other fields. As the TechTalk is aimed at "looking under the hood" of technological solutions, MediaSoft offered the perfect palette for audiences of all levels of expertise. They also represent our first industry sponsor, which is supporting the Best Student Paper award. We also would like to thank Daniel Bliton and his colleagues at Booz Allen Hamilton, who prepared the pre-conference workshop.

The Organizing Committee is grateful to each member of the Technical Program Committee, and I am grateful to each member of the Organizing Committee for their tireless support of this idea that has finally completed its first edition. I would like to also thank the European Alliance for Innovation (EAI) as our primary sponsor and organizer, with a special mention of Sinziana Vieriu, who kept us all sane, synchronized, and (somewhat) on schedule. Lastly, I would like to thank all the presenters, who have been the true protagonists of this event.

See you in Italy for eLEOT 2015!

Giovanni Vincenti

Organization

Steering Committee Chair

Imrich Chlamtac   Create-Net, Italy

Steering Committee Member

Giovanni Vincenti   University of Baltimore, USA

Organizing Committee

General Chair
Giovanni Vincenti   University of Baltimore, USA

Technical Program Chair
Alberto Bucciero   Italian National Research Council (Consiglio Nazionale delle Ricerche, CNR), Italy

Local Chair
James Braman   Towson University, USA

Workshops Chair
Gabriele Meiselwitz   Towson University, USA

Panels Chair
Greg Walsh   University of Baltimore, USA

Special Sessions Chair
Ali Wolf   University of Baltimore, USA

Publications Chair
Carlos Vaz de Carvalho   Instituto Superior de Engenharia do Porto, Portugal

Eai Conference Coordinator
Sinziana Vieriu   European Alliance for Innovation, Italy

Web Chair

Marco Zappatore   University of Salento, Italy

Tpc Members

Nicoletta Adamo-Villani   Purdue University, USA
Nan Adams   Southeastern Louisiana University, USA
Jamshid Beheshti   McGill University, Canada
Davide Bolchini   Indiana University, USA
Melody Buckner   University of Arizona, USA
Victor Callaghan   University of Essex, UK
John Carfora   Loyola Marymount University, USA
Mark Chrisman   Amazon, USA
Michelle Crosby-Nagy   International Business School, Hungary
Nicoletta Di Blas   Politecnico di Milano, Italy
Alfreda Dudley   Towson University, USA
Luca Ferrari   University of Bologna, Italy
Nick Flor   University of New Mexico, USA
Anna Lisa Guido   University of Salento, Italy
Markus Helfert   Dublin City University, Ireland
Maria Grazia Ierardi   CNR-IMATI, Italy
Amruth Kumar   Ramapo College of New Jersey, USA
Chiara Laici   University of Perugia, Italy
Daniel Laughlin   Morgan State University, USA
Sabrina Leone   Università Politecnica delle Marche, Italy
Dario Maggiorini   University of Milan, Italy
Gerry Mulligan   Education Management Corporation, USA
Andrea Pandurino   University of Salento, Italy
Laura Ripamonti   University of Milan, Italy
Sujan Shrestha   University of Baltimore, USA
Blair Taylor   Towson University, USA
Aldo Torrebruno   Politecnico di Milano, Italy
Minjuan Wang   Shanghai International Studies University, China,
                           San Diego State University, USA
Denise Wood   Central Queensland University, Australia,
                           University of the Western Cape, South Africa
Marco Zappatore   University of Salento, Italy

Hands-On Play and Redesign of a Leadership Game from Analog to Digital

Daniel Bliton, Jamie Catania, Aimee Norwood, and Trey Reyher
Booz Allen Hamilton, Inc.,
8283 Greensboro Drive, McLean, VA 22102, USA
{bliton_daniel, catania_jamie, norwood_aimee, reyher_trey}@bah.com
Abstract. Although serious games are an effective approach for learning higher-level cognitive skills, there is an ongoing challenge to design and verify instructional effectiveness without incurring significant coding expenses. This workshop explores the design and development considerations for analog and digital games. Join us for a lively discussion, engage in hands-on play of a sample analog game, and wrap up with the development of a plan for moving the game from analog to digital. The initial portion of the workshop includes discussion of: general game mechanics; reasons for 'analog first' prototyping prior to digital development; considerations for analog and digital games; factors that make any learning experience effective; and the process used to convert an analog game to a digital simulation for leadership development. During the second portion of the workshop, participants will play a quick board game (Leaders of Innovation) and then small groups will work together to apply the concepts discussed previously by creating an initial design of a digital game. The workshop will culminate with design pitches from all of the small groups. Designers and developers will leave this workshop with a reusable, but powerful, 5-step framework for designing/evaluating conversion efforts for training (instructor-led training to eLearning) and games (analog to digital) that you can apply to your own projects.
This workshop is intended for anyone designing, developing, or testing simulations and other serious games. It is intended for instructional designers, game designers, and project managers. To gain the maximum benefit from this workshop, participants need only to have a passion and interest in using serious games to improvement learning and performance. The workshop learning objectives are:

- Identify tenets of serious game design that apply to an 'analog first' approach
- Perform an analog to digital conversion, given an example game
- Apply tenets for 'analog first' design to your own situations and needs
- Apply a reusable 5-step framework for designing/evaluating conversion efforts

Workshop Facilitators

Daniel Bliton is a learning strategist with Booz Allen Hamilton. He is a passionate learner and has been designing computer-based and web-based training solutions for over 24 years. Dan is a casual game designer and he has been deeply engaged with research on effective learning transfer. He is the creator of the documentary film "The Machinima Primer" which showcased the use of video game technologies for storytelling and the rapid production of movies. One of his favorite projects was the creation of a web comic for the Smithsonian National Museum of Natural History.

Jamie Catania is a learning experience designer with Booz Allen Hamilton. A lifelong advocate of problem-based learning, he has been designing and developing immersive, web-based training solutions for over 5 years across several industries, including K-12, higher education, high-tech, and government. Jamie's current work emphasizes the application of user-centered design and rapid prototyping methodology in a context of learning. He partnered with the Leadership Development team at Booz Allen to redesign a successful leadership simulation to be delivered in a mobile, networked environment.

Aimee Norwood is an immersive learning strategist with Booz Allen Hamilton's Strategic Innovation Group. Having been engaged in learning and technology for over 24 years, she continues to partner with organizations to improve performance through holistic learning solutions. She is currently a Program Manager, creating virtual and face-to-face learning for both civil and defense health agencies focused on health information technology.

Trey Reyher is an immersive learning expert with Booz Allen Hamilton. Since 2007, he has managed the development of games, virtual environments, and novel user interfaces for research, educational, and entertainment objectives. He currently serves as the chair for the Washington, D.C. chapter of the International Game Developers Association. Before joining Booz Allen, he developed games and neurofeedback systems at the Massachusetts Institute of Technology.

Contents

Scripted Animation Towards Scalable Content Creation for eLearning—A Quality Analysis

Nicoletta Adamo-Villani[1(✉)], Jian Cui[2], and Voicu Popescu[2]

[1] Department of Computer Graphics Technology, Purdue University,
401 N. Grant Street, West Lafayette, IN 47907, USA
nadamovi@purdue.edu
[2] Department of Computer Science, Purdue University, 305 N. University Street,
West Lafayette, IN 47907, USA
{cui9,popescu}@purdue.edu

Abstract. The success of eLearning depends on the broad availability of educational materials that provide a high-quality delivery of high-quality content. One approach for high-quality delivery is to rely on a computer animated instructor avatar that not only speaks, but that also gestures to elucidate novel concepts and to convey an engaging personality that captures and maintains the learners' focus. The traditional approach of manual key frame animation does not scale, as it requires a substantial time investment as well as artistic talent. We have developed a system that allows animating an instructor avatar quickly and without the prerequisite of artistic talent through a text script. In this paper we quantify the speed/quality tradeoff made by our scripted animation by comparison to manual animation.

Keywords: Instructor avatar · Instructor gesture · Scripted animation · Manual key frame animation · Effective online learning materials

1 Introduction

The proliferation of inexpensive yet powerful internet-connected computing platforms such as laptops, tablets or even smartphones creates opportunities for eLearning to supplement, and, in some cases to supplant, traditional classroom education. The success of eLearning depends not only on the quality of the content of the online learning materials, but also on the quality of the delivery. This is even more important for young learners whose language skills are still developing. For such learners, text is not enough, nor are verbal explanations from an invisible narrator. The lesson is best delivered by an online instructor, which evokes teacher-student and parent-child interactions that are known to work with young learners. One solution is to deliver the lessons through videos. A skilled instructor is videotaped giving the lesson to the camera and the video is placed online to be accessed by learners from school and from home. The skilled instructor gives a good lesson that is captured faithfully by the video camera yielding great results. However, the approach has important limitations.

Lack of interactivity. Instructors cannot ask questions, they cannot provide feedback to students, and they cannot adapt the lesson pace and content to each particular student or group of students.

© Institute for Computer Sciences, Social Informatics and Telecommunications Engineering 2014
G. Vincenti et al. (Eds.): eLEOT 2014, LNICST 138, pp. 1–9, 2014.
DOI: 10.1007/978-3-319-13293-8_1

Constrained delivery. Asking the instructor to follow a script and to give the lesson in front of the camera can result in an unnatural delivery, with the instructor being worried about following the script and about staying in the field of view of the camera as opposed to simply being a teacher; moreover, in a studio setting there is no audience to connect with, and the delivery can become an unenthusiastic monologue.

Lack of scalability. Making videos is a tedious process and covering all the ways in which a concept can be explained, all concepts, for all disciplines, for all student age groups requires a huge investment.

A promising alternative is computer animation, which has long shown that it can tell stories convincingly. Computer animation characters could serve as believable and effective instructor avatars, alleviating the challenges enumerated above.

Interactivity. Computer animation is more amenable to *interactivity* than video. The instructor avatar can request input from the learner, analyze the correctness of the answer, and react accordingly. The instructor avatar has perfect memory and infinite energy, which, paradoxically, could result in a more natural *delivery*.

Scalability. What is needed is a fast and accessible method for creating e-lessons delivered by instructor avatars; the entertainment industry uses two main approaches for animating characters—manual animation and motion capture; in manual animation the character pose is defined by a digital artist through a graphical user interface for each key frame; for complex animations one needs multiple key frames per second; key frame animation is slow and requires artistic talent; it is simply not feasible to manually animate the delivery of the world's ever-expanding knowledge base. Motion capture requires expensive specialized hardware and talent to perform the animation to be captured and thus it does not scale to our context either.

Scripted animation—a promising solution. We have developed a system that provides a computer animation instructor avatar that is animated quickly and effectively based on a text script [21]. The script is created by the eLearning content creator with a conventional text editor. The script specifies what and when the avatar does and says. The script is executed automatically to obtain the desired animation. The animation is obtained quickly, and without the requirements of artistic talent, of familiarity with complex animation software, and of programing expertise.

We have used the scripted animation system in two studies on research instructor gesture. The first study investigates which instructor gestures make the instructor avatar appear to students as having a more engaging personality [21]. The second study investigates whether deictic and embodied cognition gestures improve student learning [21]. The system of scripted instructor avatars enabled the efficient creation of tens of high-quality and precise stimuli for these studies. Creating the stimuli for these two studies relying on manual animation would have been prohibitively slow.

In this paper we examine the questions of whether the efficiency of scripted animation compared to manual animation comes at the cost of a loss of animation quality, and, if yes, of how much this cost is. We have chosen a 1 min mathematical equivalence lesson sequence, and we have animated the sequence with both the scripted animation and the manual animation methods. The scripted animation was created with our system in 1 h and it is available via YouTube at the following

URL: https://www.youtube.com/watch?v=rgSq5lm7yY0. The manual animation was created by a computer animator in 23 h and is available via YouTube at the following URL: https://www.youtube.com/watch?v=s-a0FUytpNQ.

Fig. 1. Frames from the scripted animation (*left*) and from the manual animation (*right*).

As can be seen in Fig. 1, the two animations are similar but not identical. For example, in the scripted animation the pointing to the equal sign is more precise, in the manual animation the right hand rests on the hip as the left hands makes the pointing gesture, and the balance gesture indicating equality is more evocative of physical equilibrium in the scripted animation compared to the manual animation. The animator decided that the answer "13" should appear at the end of the lesson.

The two animations were then shown to computer animators, computer science researchers working in graphics and visualization (and not in animation), and psychology researchers working on gesture. After each animation, the viewer was asked three questions regarding the quality of the animation, regarding the quality of the synchronization of gestures with speech, and regarding the perceived personality of the instructor avatar. Computer animators were asked seven more questions regarding the quality of the motion, the quality of the poses, and the degree to which the animation adheres to each of five principles of animation. The overall score for the scripted vs the manual animation was 3.0 vs 4.1 on a 1 to 5 scale. Psychologists, for whom the animations are intended, liked both animations (4.2 vs 4.6).

2 Background

Computer animated characters have been used in e-learning environments to teach and supervise. Early examples of pedagogical avatars are Cosmo [1], a cosmonaut who explains how the internet works, Herman [2], a bug-like creature that teaches children about biology, and STEVE [3] who trains users in operating complex machinery using speech, pointing gestures, and gaze behavior. PETA is a 3-D computer animated human head that speaks by synthesizing sounds and conveys different facial articulations [4]. PETA allows children to acquire a new language in a spontaneous, unconscious manner. A similar example is the "Thinking Head" [5], a virtual anthropomorphic software agent able to speak and to display emotion through complex facial expressions, vocal prosody, and gestures. Gesturing avatars have also been used to teach sign language, mathematics, and science to young deaf children using sign language, e.g. Mathsigner and SMILE [6]. The ASL software system [7] allows educators to create and add animated signing avatars to e-learning materials.

Rigorous empirical testing was used to assess the contributions of pedagogical agents to learning, and the affective impact on students. Many studies confirm the intended positive influences on education by systems using these agents [8, 9]. Studies also suggest that teaching avatars could be employed in e-learning environments to enhance users' attitude towards online courses [10]. Agents interacting using multiple modalities appear to lead to greater learning than agents that interact only in a single channel [11]. A comparative study of three e-learning interfaces suggests that e-learning materials incorporating full-body teaching agents that speak and gesticulate are the most efficient, effective and engaging [12].

Animating a 3D character is a challenging task that has been approached from various directions. In manual 3D animation, a skilled animator uses a 3D animation software package (e.g. Maya) and a variety of techniques, such as keyframe animation, to craft the character poses and motions by hand. Manual animation is time consuming, has a steep learning curve and requires artistic talent. In data-driven animation (e.g., motion capture), live motion is recorded directly from an actor, digitized, and then mapped onto a 3D character. Motion capture animation requires highly expensive equipment and the recorded data often needs to be manually refined by a skilled animator.

In automated (or scripted) animation the character's speech and gestures are automatically generated from input text. BEAT [13] is an example of fully automated character animation system which takes plain text as input, runs a linguistic analysis and generates speech intonation, facial expressions and gestures. GESTYLE [14] annotates text with hand/head/face gestures based on "style" definitions. "Style" determines the gesture repertoire and the gesturing manner of the animated character. Virtual Presenter [15] is an animation system in which gestures can be added to input text manually, or can be automatically generated with keyword-triggered rules.

In addition to fully automated systems, to facilitate the development of embodied agent applications, software toolkits have been created that allow people with no animation expertise to produce and add animated characters to e-content (we call these systems "partially automated"). While these tools do not generate the animations automatically from text, they provide an easy-to-use interface and do not require any training in animation. Examples include Character Builder [16], NOAH virtual instructor technology [17], Codebaby [18] and Gesture Builder [19]. Although the characters produced using existing fully or partially automated systems speak and gesticulate, their gesture repertoire is limited and generic and the occurrence of facial and manual gestures in concurrence with speech is not driven by research-based rules on the relationship between verbal and non-verbal behavior.

3 Scripted Animation

We have developed a system of computer animation avatars that are controlled with a text script [21]. The input to the system is pre-recorded audio of what the avatar has to say and a text script. The system bypasses the need for digital artistic talent by animating the avatar either automatically or using pre-generated animation stored in a database. The automatic animation relies on lip-syncing and inverse kinematics algorithms to have the avatar utter words and to perform deictic gestures, which include pointing, circling, and underlining at any location on the whiteboard. More complicated gestures, such as the balance gesture used to indicate the equality of the left and right sides of a correctly solved mathematical equivalence problem, are pre-animated by a digital artist, stored in an animation database, and invoked using the script. The script specifies which gestures have to occur and when in relation with the audio file. The script is executed automatically, creating the avatar animation.

The script for the sequence used in the comparison consists of 66 lines, organized according to 17 audio sentences. The partition of the audio into sentences facilitates script writing by allowing quick previews of the part currently edited and by simplifying time references. The script from Fig. 2 plays the audio sentence Lesson9. At 1.2 s in, a pause is inserted to allow for

PlayAudio Lesson9
@ 1.2 **Pause** 1.5
@ 0.2 **Deictic RightUnderline** 6 9
+ 0.0 **Move** B
+ 0.0 **Deictic LeftUnderline** 0 4 **SPEED**=0.8
+ 0.0 **Move** A

Fig. 2. Script for one audio sentence.

the completion of the gestures up to that point. The ability to insert pauses greatly simplifies the audio recording process, which can proceed without concerns for allowing enough time for gestures to complete. At 0.2 s, the avatar is instructed to make a right hand underlining gesture, spanning characters 6 through 9 on the whiteboard (i.e. the right side of the equation in Fig. 1, left). As soon as the underlining gesture finishes, the avatar is instructed to move to position B. We use three positions: facing the students (A), profile, looking at the board (B), and extended profile, reaching for the right edge of the board (C). After reaching B, the avatar underlines the left side of the equation, at a slower speed, and then turns to face the students again.

Writing the initial script takes about 60 min. Changing gestures to obtain a different experimental condition takes 10 min, with most of the time spent to rework the synchronization. Switching from gesture to control (i.e. no gesture) condition takes less than a minute, as does creating an exercise for a different mathematical equivalence. The script is executed in real time using interactive rendering techniques, therefore the animation is available as soon as the script is written.

4 Manual Animation

The manual animation was created by a digital artist with 4 years of experience in 3D animation. The artist was given a video of the scripted animation sequence, the computer animation character of the instructor, and the lip synch animation used to generate the scripted animation. He was asked to reproduce the sequence in a professional grade computer animation software system (Maya) using traditional animation techniques. He employed key frame animation to set the character's main body poses and used various interpolation types provided by the software to generate the in-between frames. Then he manipulated the animation curves by hand to attain realistic timing and fluid motions. Because of the limitations of the character's facial rig, facial articulations could not be animated.

The artist took 9 h to complete the animation. The sequence was rendered using a high-quality offline rendering engine (Mental Ray); the rendering process took 14 h. Whereas removing gestures as needed to transform a gesture stimulus into a control (no-gesture) stimulus is straightforward, changing the animation for a different mathematical equivalence problem takes approximately 2 h and changing the type of charisma gestures takes approximately 4 h.

5 Results and Discussion

We conducted a survey to compare the two animations. We drew respondents from three groups of experts: psychologists working in gesture research (3), computer scientists working in graphics and visualization research (7), and computer animators (16). Each respondent was shown both animations. The order in which the animations were shown was randomized. The respondents were asked the same questions after each animation. All questions were answered on a five point scale: strongly disagree (score of 1), disagree, neutral, agree, and strongly agree (score of 5). We first present the survey questions and answers and we then discuss the results.

The survey had three parts. The first part had three questions addressed to all respondents (Table 1). The second part contained questions that depended on expertise. The psychologists were asked whether they would use the animation in their research on gesture. The mean scores were 4.33 for both animations. The computer animators were asked about specific aspects of animation (Table 2), including whether the motion is fluid and realistic, whether the quality of the animation poses is high, and whether the animation adheres to five fundamental principles of animation (i.e. a subset of the 12 Disney principles of animation [20]). The third part of the survey consisted of an essay question posed to all respondents. The respondents were asked to comment on the animation they had just seen, and to point out and explain the subsequences they liked/disliked the most.

Two of the computer scientists liked the scripted animation for its rendition of the balance gesture, two liked the animation overall; two computer scientists complained of the quality of the audio file, including the high background noise during the speech compared to the perfect silence (of the inserted pauses). The computer scientist who

Table 1. General questions about the scripted (S) and manual (M) animations addressed to computer scientists (CS), psychologists (Psych), and computer animators (CA).

Questions	Mean scores							
	CS		Psych		CA		Avg	
	S	M	S	M	S	M	S	M
Animation is of high quality	2.4	3.0	4.3	4.7	1.9	4.3	2.9	4.0
Gestures well synchronized with speech	3.2	3.8	4.3	4.7	2.5	4.5	3.3	4.3
Avatar has engaging personality	2.8	3.0	4.0	4.3	1.7	4.4	2.8	2.9

liked the scripted animation the least complained about the appearance of the character, about the unenthusiastic voice, and about the simplicity of the mathematical problem. The psychologists liked the scripted animation overall, lauding the balance gesture and the body movements. The only complaint mentioned was that the avatar says "11" and points to "8", which is the choice of the psychologist who designed the lesson—11 is the total so far, up to and including the addend 8. Whereas psychologists occasionally disagree, their disagreement should not blemish the record of the system. The computer animators were much more critical of the scripted animation. The main complaints were about the lack of adherence to the principles of animation and about the poor quality of the rendering.

Regarding the manual animation, the comments of CS respondents were slightly more positive. The CS respondent who was most disapproving of the earlier animation sees progress, but only marginal, limited to improved lighting that is "less gloomy"; the character was still perceived as "ugly", and with a monotonous voice. Two CS respondents liked that the answer is only revealed later, and one respondent thought that the reflection of the character in the whiteboard was distracting. The psychologists thought that the avatar was engaging, but reported "superfluous" arm gestures at the beginning, and uncertainty about the "body movement toward [the viewer]". The computer animators strongly preferred the manual animation noting the adherence to the principles of animation and superior rendering quality. The negatives noted include the lack of facial expressions, an occasional "stiffness".

Table 1 shows that, on average, the scripted animation was perceived of lower quality, with scores roughly one point below the scores for the manual animation. For the psychologist respondents, who are the users for whom these animations are intended, approve of the scripted animation and give it virtually identical scores to the manual animation. The computer animation respondents were the most critical of the scripted animation, noting the lack of adherence to animation principles (Table 2) and the lower rendering quality. As discussed in the earlier sections, the scripted animation was completed in a fraction of the time it took to put together the manual animation, and real time rendering was used, which are facts not disclosed to the animators. Moreover, some of the features added during manual animation and that increased the score from the computer animation respondents were judged by the psychologists as harmful to the experiments (e.g. reflections, superfluous gesture).

Table 2. Animation-specific questions addressed to computer animators.

Motion quality high		Pose quality high		Anticipation		Arcs		Slow in & slow out		Secondary action		Stretch and squash	
S	M	S	M	S	M	S	M	S	M	S	M	S	M
2.0	4.3	1.9	4.7	2.0	4.1	2.2	4.1	2.2	4.3	1.8	4.1	1.8	4.0

6 Conclusions and Future Work

Although falling short of the highest quality manual animation, scripted animation is of sufficiently high quality to provide a scalable option in support of research on education and eLearning. Another important conclusion of our work is that the animation quality is application and user dependent—whereas computer animators consider animation principles and highest quality rendering non-negotiable, education researchers and eLearning applications might be willing to tradeoff in favor of authoring efficiency.

We have addressed the issue of eLearning scalability by simplifying the task of animation. As future work we will pursue scalability by adding more gestures to our animation database, and by adding support for more concepts, disciplines, and student age groups (e.g. more avatars, more whiteboard drawing capabilities, more types of math problems). Finally, we will investigate extending the system in two divergent directions: to bridge the gap between scripted and manual animation by adding adherence to animation principles, and to further reduce the animation authoring time by scripting. The latter effort will first focus on developing a graphical user interface for editing the script, which promises to lower the script language learning curve and to avoid the possibility of syntax errors. Then, we will investigate automating the animation based on instructor gesture rules, which eliminates scripting altogether.

References

1. Lester, J., Voerman, J., Towns, S., Callaway, C.: Cosmo: a life-like animated pedagogical agent with deictic believability. In: Notes of the IJCAI '97 Workshop on Animated Interface Agents: Making Them Intelligent, Nagoya, Japan, pp. 61–70 (1997)
2. Lester, J., Stone, B., Stelling, G.: Lifelike pedagogical agents for mixed-initiative problem solving in constructivist learning environments. User Model. User-Adap. Inter. **9**(1–2), 1–44 (1999)
3. Johnson, W.L., Rickel, J., Stiles, R., Munro, A.: Integrating pedagogical agents into virtual environments. Presence: Teleoper. Virtual Environ. **7**, 523–546 (1998)
4. PETA – a pedagogical embodied teaching agent. In: Proceedings of PETRA08: 1st International Conference on PErvasive Technologies Related to Assistive Environments, ACM Digital Library, Athens (2008)
5. Davis, C., Kim, J., Kuratate, T., Burnham, D.: Making a thinking-talking head. In: Proceedings of the International Conference on Auditory-Visual Speech Processing (AVSP 2007), Hilvarenbeek, The Netherlands (2007)
6. Adamo-Villani, N., Wilbur, R., Eccarius, P., Abe-Harris, L.: Effects of character geometric model on the perception of sign language animation. In: IEEE Proceedings of IV09 -13th International Conference on Information Visualization, pp. 72–75 (2009)

7. Hayward, K., Adamo-Villani, N., Lestina, J.: A computer animation system for creating deaf-accessible math and science curriculum materials. In: Proceedings of Eurographics 2010 – Education Papers, EG Digital Library, Norrkoping, Sweden, May 2010
8. Lester, J., Converse, S., Kahler, S., Barlow, T., Stone, B., Bhogal, R.: The persona effect: affective impact of animated pedagogical agents. In: Proceedings of CHI '97, pp. 359–366 (1997)
9. Lester, J., Converse, S., Stone, B., Kahler, S., Barlow, T.: Animated pedagogical agents and problem-solving effectiveness: a large-scale empirical evaluation. In: Proceedings of the Eighth World Conference on Artificial Intelligence in Education, pp. 23–30 (1997)
10. Annetta, L.A., Holmes, S.: Creating presence and community in a synchronous virtual learning environment using avatars. Int. J. Instr. Technol. Distance Learn. 3, 27–43 (2006)
11. Lusk, M.M., Atkinson, R.K.: Varying a pedagogical agent's degree of embodiment under two visual search conditions. Appl. Cogn. Psychol. 21, 747–764 (2007)
12. Alseid, M., Rigas, D.: Three different modes of avatars as virtual lecturers in elearning Interfaces: a comparative usability study. Open Virtual Real. J. 2, 8–17 (2010)
13. Cassell, J., Vilhjalmsson, H., Bickmore, T.: BEAT: the behavior expression animation toolkit. In: Proceedings of SIGGRAPH, pp. 477–486 (2001)
14. Noot, H., Ruttkay, Z.,: Gesture in style. In: Camurri, A., Volpe, G., (eds.) GW 2003. LNCS (LNAI), vol. 2915, pp. 324–337. Springer, Heidelberg (2004)
15. Noma, T., Zhao, L., Badler, N.: Design of a virtual human presenter. IEEE Comput. Graph. Appl. 20(4), 49–85 (2000)
16. Character Builder (2011). http://www.mediasemantics.com/
17. NOAH Animated Avatar Technology (2011). noahx.com/index.asp
18. Codebaby (2010). www.codebaby.com/products/elearning-solutions
19. Gesture Builder (2010). www.vcom3d.com/index.php?id=gesturebuilder
20. Johnston, O., Thomas, F.: The Illusion of Life: Disney Animation. Disney Editions, New York (1995)
21. Cui, J., Popescu, V., Adamo-Villan, N., Cook, S., Duggan, K., Friedman, H.: An animation stimuli system for research on instructor gestures in education. Technical reports, Department of Computer Science, Purdue University. doi:http://docs.lib.purdue.edu/cstech/1771/

E-Learning Repository System for Sharing Learning Resources Among Saudi Universities

Ayidh Alanazi[(✉)] and Maysam Abbod

Electrical and Computer Engineering, School of Engineering and Design,
Brunel University, London, UK
{Ayidh.Alanazi,Maysam.Abbod}@brunel.ac.uk

Abstract. This paper discusses the status and diversity of needs for building a centralized e-learning repository system for Saudi Universities. The study is based on surveys that were distributed to faculty members in various Saudi Universities. The purpose is to provide an analytical overview of the current needs for a unified e-learning repository system among Saudi Universities for sharing learning objects and materials. Moreover, the primary aim of the study is to give an evaluation of the needs of faculty members by gathering facts about the current demands and future adoption among Saudi Universities. To achieve this, the services needed by each part in the universities were analyzed.

Keywords: E-learning · Saudi Universities · Repositories · Unified E-learning

1 Introduction

The concept of learning objects repositories has become more prevalent in the field of teaching as the demand for e-learning applications has steadily increased. In order to meet the growing need for e-learning content and to save developers' time and efforts, learning objects repositories have been created as means of storing units of information which are used as building blocks for developing e-learning content in accordance with the requirements of a given discipline. The repositories provide various benefits such as the speed of developing content and the reduction of cost through the possibility of sharing learning objects among different e-modules.

Learning objects have existed long before e-learning itself became common. Within the traditional classroom, a teacher may utilize cardboard cutouts, maps and images to serve educational purposes. Then another teacher may choose to use some of these very objects alongside others in a different context to serve different teaching purposes. Later, the student may borrow some of these resources from a library or a learning objects centre in order to do homework assigned by the teacher. Nowadays, with the advent of the age of digital learning environments, educational designers have replaced traditional centers of learning resources with digital libraries or what was initially termed "learning resources banks". These banks store multimedia resources of information which can be used in various contexts to serves different teaching purposes [1].

© Institute for Computer Sciences, Social Informatics and Telecommunications Engineering 2014
G. Vincenti et al. (Eds.): eLEOT 2014, LNICST 138, pp. 10–18, 2014.
DOI: 10.1007/978-3-319-13293-8_2

2 Literature Review

Several studies have stressed the possibility of using digital learning objects repositories in developing various skills. For example, the study by Boskic at The University of British Columbia concluded that reusing learning objects already available in repositories benefits curriculum designers who can choose the objects which suit the design of their curriculums and determine the interaction level that matches the leaner's comprehension abilities [2].

Another example of the benefits can be seen in the study by Catherine Caws and Norm Friesen. Researchers at Victoria University and Alberta University in Canada designed an e-repository called (FLORE) for teaching the French Language in the post-high school stage. The repository stores 900 learning objects and allows its users to search for objects by entering the title, author, description or URL, thus providing ease of access. The study concluded that there was an increase in the learning skills for those who used the repository to learn French [3]. Furthermore, the study by Ambe-Uva aimed to evaluate the long-distance learning programs at the Open University in Nigeria. The study concluded that their open-learning students exhibited a lower quality of learning than their counterparts who relied on e-repositories [4].

Different initiatives have been implemented to streamline e-learning repositories across organizations and educational institutions, and each has a different approach [5]. The concept of UER is to offer a system that is accessed by a web portal for the purpose of managing learning contents in the repository. In such systems, system administrators first approve the method of interaction with the objects; administrators grant specific privileges to users with respect to their different roles. Therefore, instructors, course compilers and multimedia designers, on the one hand, are given the privileges of using, reusing and updating the repository's contents. On the other hand, students are often allowed only to view and interact with the course materials, drills and activities. Every UER differs in approach and policy towards learning materials. Some UER systems grant users the privilege to copy the learning materials onto their own LMS or LCMS, while other UES systems put active limits on the use of their materials to their own learning network [6].

3 Functions of Learning Object Repositories

Although the published studies have agreed on a definition for learning object repositories, they disagree on specifying their functions because most repositories have been built within certain organizations to fulfill their specific needs and requirements, and most streamlining efforts among these repositories have mainly focused on facilitating the transfer and exchange of learning objects. After surveying the various studies available, the following shared functions have been identified:

- Storing learning objects metadata and providing interface panels which suit the users.
- The ability to search for and reproduce learning objects using the metadata.
- Linking learning objects to each other through analyzing the metadata.

- Organizing learning objects according to shared characteristics.
- Linking to digital learning environments.
- The ability to review learning objects directly through the website of the repository.
- Providing help and technical support to the users.
- Sharing and exchanging learning objects with other repositories
- Providing tools for authoring and editing learning objects.
- Creating a cooperative environment which allows content developers to interact with each other [7–11].

4   Learning Object Materials

Different studies have compared the currently available forms of repositories as well as the predicted future forms. The study by Clifford Lynch and Joan Lippincott starts by surveying the repositories which are managed by educational institutions in the USA. Then, it compares the currently available types of learning objects in these repositories with the future types which the repositories intend to produce. The study is based on an analysis of the future plans adopted by these repositories based on user feedback. However, the published studies have not agreed on recommending specific forms for learning objects since this issue is often decided by the various needs of the course designers. By reviewing the different studies in this regard, Lynch and Lippincott agreed the following types of learning objects available in repositories in university education [11–14]: (1) Text Materials, (2) Dynamic Texts, (3) Digital Images and Pictures, (4) Moving Pictures and Video, (5) Digital Audio Files, (6) Utility Files and Software, (7) Templates and (8) Open Source Files.

5   Classifications of Learning Objects

There have been various attempts to classify learning objects. Some classify them according to type, while others have classified them according to the delivery method such as Susan Smith Nash, who designates the following classification [15]: (1) Online Learning Objects, (2) Learning objects stored on digital optical storage disks, (3) Multiple-delivery learning objects. Although this classification seems logical and convenient, it is not the only one available. Churchill [14] classifies learning objects according to their intended function in the learning content, thus favoring the principles of educational design and function. The classification includes the following categories: (1) Presentation and Practice Objects, (2) Simulation and Information Objects, (3) Conceptual Models and contextual Representation.

6   Statement of the Problem

The institutions of higher education in Saudi Arabia are keen to provide the best e-learning systems, thus leading to the increased use of digital repositories. These repositories facilitates the storage and redistribution of e-content from a centralized location; however, it is only the teaching staff who are capable of utilizing the full potential of repositories and enriching them with e-content covering all modules across the various specialties. Therefore, there must be a shift in the role of the teaching staff from merely providing expertise on academic disciplines into becoming full-fledged experts, mentors, designers and developers of e-content and its related software. E-content constitutes the cornerstone of their modules. Consequently, the opportunities and the needs of the use of digital repositories must be explored from the vantage point of the teaching staff in Saudi universities because they are essentially the developers content in these repositories.

7 Methodology

The methodology followed in this study is descriptive survey using a questionnaire.

Study Sample: The study sample consisted of 189 male and female lecturers in Saudi universities who were randomly chosen.

Study Tool: The researcher has prepared a questionnaire as a tool, by making use of the tools in the previous studies and by reviewing the related literature. The tool consisted of 23 paragraphs spread over two domains: the needs for e-learning materials on the repository (10 paragraphs), and the needs for services and functionality on the repository (13 paragraphs).

Validity of the Tool: The tool was presented to 7 experienced arbitrators in the domain of e-learning of university lecturers in Saudi Arabia. They were asked to define the appropriateness of the paragraphs in the tool and suggest any amendments. The amendments were made. The tool after arbitration consisted of 23 paragraphs in two domains.

Reliability of the Tool: The tool was applied to 25 lecturers in Saudi universities from outside the samples. The reliability of the tool was verified by using Cronbach's alpha formula for internal consistency (Table 1).

Table 1. Reliability of internal consistency

Domain	Reliability coefficient
The needs for e-learning materials on the repository	0.85
The needs for services and functionality on the repository	0.81
Total	0.84

The response to the tool was designed as per quintet grading as follows: strongly agree (5), agree (4), neutral (3), disagree (2), strongly disagree (1).

  *For the purposes of this study, the researcher calculated the degree of the Lecturers, evaluation of the type of e-learning materials they would like to be available on the repository, and the type of services and functionality should the repository provide, according to the range equation, as the follows:

1. Range = largest value of response alternatives − smallest value of the response alternatives = 5 − 1 = 4.
2. Category length = (range / number of categories) = 4 / 3 levels (high, moderate, low) = 1.33. Therefore it will be:

   - Minimum limit = 1 + 1.33 = 2.33
   - Moderate limit = 2.33 + 1.33 = 3.66
   - Maximum limit = more than 3.66

Thus the weights of paragraphs become as follows: (5.00–3.67) is high, (3.66–2.34) is moderate and (2.33–1.00) is low.

8 Results

The results relate to answering the first question which says: "What type of e-learning materials you would like to be available on the repository?" To answer this question, the arithmetic mean, standard deviation and the ranking of the lecturers' estimates for each of the tool paragraphs. Table 2 shows that lecturers have high perceptions about the type of e-learning materials to be available on the repository, as the arithmetic mean of their estimate of the total tool is 3.95 and SD = 0.29. Their estimates on item 7 were high. The highest estimates were related to the material in item 9 "open source materials" which ranked first with an arithmetic mean of 4.33 and SD = 0.83. Their estimates on item 3 were moderate. The material in item 4 "templates" ranked last with an arithmetic mean of 3.54 and SD = 0.92. The results relating to answering the second question which reads: "what type of services and functionality should the repository provide?" To answer this question, the arithmetic mean, standard deviation and the ranking of the lecturers' estimates for each of the tool paragraphs.

Table 2. Mean, standard deviation and the ranking of the lecturers' estimates.

Items	M	SD	Rank	Importance
1. Electronic text	3.88	0.95	6	High
2. Graphics and pictures	3.95	0.92	5	High
3. Video	4.29	0.88	3	High
4. Templates	3.54	0.92	10	Moderate
5. Sound files	3.85	0.89	7	High
6. Flash files	4.32	0.84	2	High
7. Dynamic maps	3.65	0.85	8	Moderate
8. Quizzes	4.08	0.92	4	High
9. Open source materials	4.33	0.83	1	High
10. Past exam papers	3.58	0.91	9	Moderate
Total	3.95	0.29		High

Table 3 shows that lecturers have high perceptions about the type of services and functionality which the repository should provide, as the arithmetic mean of their estimate of the total tool is 4.16 with SD = 0.34. Their estimates on item 12 were high. The highest estimates were related to the service in item 6 "connect similar subject materials to benefit the teaching staff" which ranked first with an arithmetic mean of 4.48 and SD = 0.79. Their estimates on item 8 "Teaching staff can evaluate others teaching materials" were moderate, and ranked last with an arithmetic mean of 3.63 and SD = 0.92.

Table 3. Means, standard deviation and the ranking of the lecturers' estimates about (type of services and functionality should the repository provide).

Items	M	SD	Rank	Importance
Riposte the materials	4.27	0.81	6	High
Classify the materials according to subject	4.22	0.87	7	High
Search engine for subject, module, course	3.96	0.92	10	High
External links to other repositories	4.15	0.92	9	High
Security (members only)	4.31	0.83	5	High
Connect similar subject materials	4.48	0.79	1	High
Tag the materials so it can be recalled easily	4.40	0.81	3	High
Teaching staff can evaluate others materials	3.63	0.92	13	Moderate
Teaching staff can add materials to the repository	3.79	0.85	12	High
Copyright marks for the downloaded materials	4.47	0.78	2	High
Connection to external sources such as u-tube	3.88	0.89	11	High
Video and audio files can only be live streamed	4.19	0.85	8	High
Link to existing external teaching materials	4.32	0.78	4	High
Total	4.16	0.34		High

The results relating to answering the third question which says: Are there statistically significant differences at the level of ($\alpha \leq 0.05$) among lecturers' perceptions due to the Faculty variable? For answering this question, the means and standard deviations of lecturers' estimates were calculated in both tools, depending on the Faculty variable, and the results were as in Table 4.

Table 4 shows that there is a difference between the means of lecturers' estimates in both tools depending on faculty variable. To detect if the differences in the means of lecturers' estimates are of statistical significance at level ($\alpha \leq 0.05$), depending on the faculty variable, (ANOVA) test was used and the results were as in Table 5. The results show the existence of differences with statistical significance at level ($\alpha \leq 0.05$) between the means of lecturers' estimates, depending on the Faculty variable in booth tools. To determine the source of the differences between the means of lecturers' estimates, depending on the Faculty variable, the researcher used multiple comparisons (Tukey HSD) method.

The results in Table 6 shows that the source of statistical significance differences was between the means of lecturers' estimates in faculty of medicine, and between the

Table 4. Means and standard deviation of the lecturers' estimates for different faculties.

Faculty variable	M1	SD1	M2	SD2
Medicine	3.69	0.32	3.82	0.44
Engineering	3.93	0.29	4.18	0.36
Science	4.01	0.18	4.20	0.40
Education	3.96	0.35	4.24	0.30
Law	3.99	0.24	4.27	0.33
Management	3.98	0.14	4.15	0.13
IT	4.03	0.24	4.16	0.21
Total	3.95	0.29	4.16	0.34

M1 ** SD1: type of e-learning materials should be available on the repository.
M2 ** SD2: type of services and functionality which the repository should provide.

Table 5. ANOVA results depending on Faculty variable differences.

Tool	Source	Sum of squares	df	Mean square	F	Sig.
Type of materials available on the repository	Between groups	1.830	6	0.305	4.015	0.001*
	Within groups	13.821	182	0.076		
	Total	15.651	188			
Type of services and functionality should the repository provide	Between groups	2.936	6	0.489	4.757	0.000*
	Within groups	18.724	182	0.103		
	Total	21.660	188			

* Statistically Significant

Table 6. Multiple comparisons (Tukey HSD).

Tool	Faculty variable	Medicine	Engineering	Science	Education	Law	Management	IT
Type of e-learning materials would like to be available	Medicine	–	0.24*	0.32*	0.28*	0.31*	0.29*	0.34*
	Engineering	–	–	0.08	0.03	0.06	0.05	0.10
	Science	–	–	–	0.04	0.02	0.03	0.02
	Education	–	–	–	–	0.03	0.02	0.07
	Law	–	–	–	–		0.01	0.04
	Management	–	–	–	–	–	–	0.05
	IT	–	–	–	–	–	–	–
Services and functionality should the repository provide	Medicine	–	0.35*	0.38*	0.41*	0.44*	0.32*	0.34*
	Engineering	–	–	0.02	0.06	0.09	0.03	0.01
	Science	–	–	–	0.04	0.06	0.05	0.04
	Education	–	–	–	–	0.03	0.09	0.08
	Law	–	–	–	–	–	0.12	0.10
	Management	–	–	–	–	–	–	0.01
	IT	–	–	–	–	–	–	

estimates of lecturers in other faculties (Engineering, Science, Education, Law, Management, IT) in favor of estimates of lecturers in other faculties. This result means that lecturers in faculty of medicine estimate their needs of type of e-learning materials and services and functionality should the repository provide less than lecturers in other faculties.

9 Conclusion

The lecturers in Saudi universities have urgent needs for e-learning materials on repository. Teaching at a university level requires several materials in order to enrich the teaching process and provide multi-learning sources for learners such as "open source materials", "flash files", "video". However, some materials have moderate importance for teaching, like "templates", "dynamic maps" because their less frequent use in teaching. Moreover, the lecturers in Saudi universities express strong needs for several types of services and functionality which the repository should provide. These include "connecting similar subject materials to benefit the teaching staff", "Tagging the materials so they can be recalled easily" and "linking to existing external teaching materials". In this regard, the function "teaching staff can evaluate others teaching materials" was not important enough perhaps because evaluating the teaching materials is not an essential part of the teaching process. Finally, it appears that the lecturers' of the faculties of medicine have less urgent needs for e-learning materials and several types of services than lecturers in other faculties. The reason may have to do with the fact that teaching medicine depends mainly on the practical application field rather than on virtual learning and e-learning. The proposed repository is innovative and will enhance the e-learning experience in Saudi Universities.

References

1. Geissinger, H.: Re-use of current teaching resources at a dual-mode university. Campus-Wide Inf. Syst. **18**(3), 120–124 (2001)
2. Boskic, N.: Faculty assessment of the quality and reusability of learning objects. Dissertation, Athabasca University (2003)
3. Caws, C., Norm, F., Beaudoin, M.: A new learning object repository for language learning: methods and possible outcomes. Interdisc. J. E-Learn. Learn. Objects **2**(1), 111–124 (2006)
4. Ambe-Uva, T.N.: Interactivity in Distance Education: The National Open University of Nigeria (NOUN) Experience (2006). http://eric.ed.gov/?id=ED494376
5. Peters, M., Araya, D.: Networks, information politics and the new paradigm of social production. Educ. Res. Netw. Technol. **2**, 33–42 (2008)
6. El-Saddik, A., Hossain, M.: LORNAV: Virtual reality tool for navigation of distributed learning objects repositories. In: Pierre, S. (ed.) E-Learning Networked Environments and Architectures: A Knowledge Processing Perspective. Springer Book Series Springer, Heidelberg (2007)
7. Lehman, R.: Learning object repositories. New Dir. Adult Cont. Educ. **113**, 57–66 (2007)
8. MacLaren, I.: New trends in web-based learning: objects, repositories and learner engagement. Eur. J. Eng. Educ. **29**(1), 65–71 (2004)

9. Kaczmarek, J., Landowska, A.: Model of distributed learning objects repository for a heterogenic internet environment. Interact. Learn. Environ. **14**(1), 1–15 (2006)
10. Griff, R., McGreal, R., Hatala, M., Friesen, N.: The evolution of learning object repository technologies: portals for on-line objects for learning. J. Distance Learn. **17**(3), 67–79 (2002)
11. Lynch, C.A., Lippincott, J.K.: Institutional repository deployment in the US as of early 2005. D-Lib Mag. **11**(9), 1–11 (2005)
12. Lim, C., Lee, S., Richards, C.: Developing interactive learning objects for a computing mathematics module. Int. J. E-Learn. **5**(2), 221–244 (2006)
13. Lee, G., Su, S.: Learning object models and an E-learning service infrastructure. Int. J. Distance Educ. Technol. **4**(1), 1–16 (2006)
14. Churchill, D.: Towards a useful classification of learning objects. Educ. Technol. Res. Dev. **55**(5), 479–497 (2007)
15. Nash, S.: Learning objects, learning object repositories, and learning theory: preliminary best practices for online courses. Interdisc. J. E-Learn. Learn. Objects **1**(1), 217–228 (2005)

Lecturers' Attitude to Social Network Media: Implication for Accessibility and Usability Need in Open and Distance Education

Apata Funke Susan[✉]

School of Education, National Open University of Nigeria,
Victoria Island, Nigeria
funke.apata@yahoo.com

Abstract. An attempt was made to determine the level of lecturers' attitude to social network media, the factor which is paramount to accessibility and usability need of the learners in Open and Distance Learning (ODL). A multi-stage, stratified and simple random sampling techniques were used to select 80 lecturers that constituted the study sample. Fifty of these lecturers came from single mode University while, the remaining 30 were from dual mode university. The instrument used for data collection was adapted from an eclectic integration of previous instruments developed by some researchers, with a reliability coefficient of 0.75 using test-retest method. Five research questions and three hypotheses guided the study. Descriptive statistics was used to analyse the research Questions. The hypotheses formulated were analyzed with t-test and Analysis of variance. It was discovered that the general attitudes of lecturers towards social network media were positive. It was therefore recommended that awareness programme that promote attitude towards social network media should be organized, for ODL lecturers to further increase their interest in their participation in good accessibility and usability exercise in ODL. Also, ODL lecturers should be given training that is e-learning oriented in social network media through, workshop and conferences to further improve their contribution to accessibility and usability needs of the learners.

Keywords: Lecturer · Attitude · Social network media · Accessibility · Usability · Distance education

1 Introduction

Open and distance learning focuses on removing barriers to accessing learning. National Policy on Education [1] emphasizes on the uses of a variety of media and technologies to provide and/or improve access to good quality education for large members of learners wherever they may be. Open and Distance Learning, (ODL) refers to the form of study where students are not in direct physical contact with their lectures. Distance education has the goal of providing access to quality education and equity in educational opportunities for those who otherwise would have been denied. Also, most ODL system has a philosophy that aims to remove barriers to education and allow learners to study what they want, when they want and where they want (Common

© Institute for Computer Sciences, Social Informatics and Telecommunications Engineering 2014
G. Vincenti et al. (Eds.): eLEOT 2014, LNICST 138, pp. 19–29, 2014.
DOI: 10.1007/978-3-319-13293-8_3

Wealth Learning [2]). Therefore ODL is about increasing educational access and increasing educational choice.

Laudable as the objectives are in ODL, the successful implementation of information and communication technologies to achieve the objectives depend largely upon the accessibility and usability of the learning resources to meet the needs and preferences of all users. According to Cooper [3] usability can be defined as the effectiveness, efficiency and satisfaction with which user can achieve specified learning goals in a particular environment with a particular learning resources, while accessibility is defined as the ability of the learning environment to adjust to the needs of all learners [4]. Thus accessibility and usability are intrinsically linked. Milken [5] had earlier reported that information and communication technologies under the right conditions have the potential to accelerate, enrich, and deepens knowledge acquisition. Example of such is Web 2.0 technologies which include social networking sites, blogs, wikis, video sharing sites, hosted services web applications and others. Social network media is an unmatchable and essential channel through which meaningful knowledge, skills and ideas could be imparted and, or transmitted to the learners [6]. According to Brag [7], social networks has been defined as a body of applications that augment group interaction and shared spaces for collaboration social connection, and aggregates information exchanges in a web-based environment. Social networking tool are more diverse and some are better fit for a particular purpose. The specific applications that are devised to be used as a teaching tool are often referred to as e-learning platforms. The sites where students can participate, create his own studying schedule, exchange information with other students and interact with the instructor in real-time, while teachers are privilege to monitor the performance of their students in specific tasks, and can give them support, feedback and assistance [8].

The importance of teachers' quality in education has been emphasized in the national policy of Education [1], it is stated that no education system can rise above the quality of its teachers. Therefore, it is worthwhile to know that attitude of lecturers' remains the key factors for any strategy put in place to ensure students' success in education. This is because successful integration of the media is possible where lecturers display reasonable positive and acceptable attitude towards a thing. Also, lecturers' attitude and believe are known to influence their teaching and management strategies and thus, directly influence students' outcome [9]. In the same vein, Yusuf [10] stressed that belief or attitude about the use of any material or tool may determine the extent to which the teacher is willing to make adjustment in the teaching methods, curriculum or instructional mode. Therefore, right attitude will propel lecturers to be conversant with educational innovations, new media and their application in learning process, also, it will help him present the courses learning materials in a meaningful manner, and foster the communication environments require which encourage and facilitate the students' accessibility and usability needed for meaningful learning.

Furthermore, Darling-Hamond [11] opined that what lecturers know and do have positive influence on what the learners achieve. As such there is need to consider the area of specialization of lecturers while assessing the lecturers' knowledge of and attitude to social network media. Also, it takes a skillful lecturer to produce high levels of students through quality instructions that are taught using an appropriate medium.

In addition, the quality lecturers provide an environment that allows students reach their potential.

Researchers have found that lecturer become more efficient and more effective as he stays longer on his profession by learning more and more on the job, learn more about the difficulties learners encounter while learning [12, 13]. His grooming experience help students gain insight into how to overcome. In a study conducted by Adeyemi [14], he found that institutions having more lecturers with 5 years and above teaching experience achieve better results than those having more teachers with less than 5 years teaching experience. Similarly, Rice [15] reported that lecturers become more skilled with experience.

In addition, the mode of University might also influence lecturers' knowledge of and attitude to social network media, which in turn could have implication on the media accessibility and usability exercise. Study has revealed that Nigeria has one single—mode Open University, the National Open University of Nigeria as well as six dual—mode Universities (conventional Universities with Distance Learning Institute) recognized by the National Universities Commission. These are the Universities of Ibadan, Lagos, Abuja, Maiduguri, Obafemi Awolowo, Ile—Ife and Federal University of Technology, Yola [16].

2 Statement of the Problem

Removing barriers to access learning in Open and Distance Learning (ODL) requires a deep knowledge about the complex interrelation between lecturers' attitude to accessibility and usability need of learning resources for learners. The difficulty in achieving such knowledge might result in pedagogy ineffectiveness. Thus, surveying the lecturers' attitude to social network media as a prerequisite to effective accessibility and usability development in distance learning is a topic worth researching.

Research Questions

1. What are the lecturers' attitudes towards social media?
2. What type of social media do lecturers in Open and Distance Learning (ODL) have the most knowledge of?
3. Do areas of specialization of ODL lecturers influence their attitudes towards social media?
4. Do years of experience of ODL lecturers influence their attitudes towards social media?
5. How does institutional mode influence lecturers' attitude to social media?

Hypotheses

Ho_1 There is no significant difference in the attitude of lecturers' of different areas of specialization towards the use of social media.

Ho_2 No significant difference exists between the attitude of experienced and less experienced lecturers in their attitude towards the use of social media.

Ho$_3$ There is no significant difference between attitude of lecturers in single mode and dual mode ODL toward the use of social media.

Methodology

Research Design. A descriptive survey employing the ex-post factor design in which none of the variables used was manipulated, but was utilized as they occur.

Population and Sample. The population of the study was made up of all lecturers in Open and Distance Learning Universities in Nigeria. A multi-stage, stratified and simple random sampling techniques were used to select 80 lecturers that constituted the study sample. The first stage was to stratify the lecturers in ODL on the basis of their faculties. Using the simple random sampling technique, the representatives of each of the faculties were selected: 19, 10, 19, 16, and 16 of these lecturers were drawn from school/ faculty of Education, Law, Management Science, Art and Social Sciences, and Science and Technology respectively. The second stage was to stratify the selected 80 ODL lecturers on the basis of their institutional mode: 50 lecturers drawn from the only single mode distance University—National Open University of Nigeria (NOUN) and 30 lecturers from one of the oldest dual mode Universities (The Distance Learning Institute—DLI in University of Lagos). Among the sample were 40 experienced lecturers and 40 less experienced lecturers.

Instrument and Data Collection. The instrument used for data collection was adapted from an eclectic integration of previous instruments developed by Beatie, Andeson and Antonak [17], Christensen and Knezek [18], Yusuf [19] and Issa [20]. The instrument comprises of three sections. Section A deals with demographic information including Institutional mode, name of school/faculties, lecturers' teaching experience and area of specialization. Section B contains items that elicit information from lecturers on attitudes to social network media using a 4-point likert type response format (4 = strongly agree, 3 = agree, 2 = disagree, 1 = strongly disagree). Section C contains items that elicit information from lecturers on their use of social network media, using a close ended questions regime, YES/NO answer. The questionnaire instrument was validated by colleagues at school of education, National Open University of Nigeria. The reliability of the instrument was determined through a test–retest method, and value was found to be 0.75. The research assistants ensured questionnaires were collected in person, this ensure 100 % rate of return. The data collection took two weeks.

Data Analysis Procedures. Data collected for the study were analysed using descriptive to statistics (Frequency and percentages) for research questions, to ascertain the level of lecturers' attitude to social network media. The bar charts were drawn to represent extent of attitude to social network media among ODL lecturers. The three hypotheses were tested using t-test and Analysis of variance.

Results and Discussion

1. **Research Question 1:** What are the lecturers' attitudes towards social network media?

Table 1. Lecturers' attitude to social network media

S/N	Items	Agree (%)	Disagree (%)
1	I enjoy doing things on the Social Network Media for teaching	73 (91.3)	7 (8.7)
2	I am tired of using Social Network Media for teaching	9 (11.3)	71 (88.7)
3	I would work harder if I could use Social Network more often	65 (81.3)	15 (18.7)
4	I can learn many things when I used Social Network Media	74 (92.6)	6 (7.4)
5	I believe that is very important for me to learn how to use Social Network Media to assist students	76 (95)	4 (5)
6	Social Network Media would improve the education of the students	76 (95.1)	4 (5)
7	Knowing how to use Social Network Media to assist students is a worthwhile skill	73 (91.3)	7 (8.8)
8	Learning Social Network Media to assist the students is boring to me	11 (13.8)	69 (86.2)
9	Social Network Media would increase my productivity in teaching the students	71 (88.8)	9 (11.2)
10	The challenge of learning about Social Network Media to teach the students is exciting	80 (100)	0

From Table 1, it is observed that responses in each of the ten items were in favour of positive attitude to social network media in distance learning by the lecturers. This was also supported by the favourable frequency counts and percentages recorded under the agree column. For instance, enjoying doing things on the Social Network Media for teaching (N = 73, % = 91.3), Social network would increase my working pace (N = 65, % = 81.3), Knowing how to use Social Network Media to assist students is a worthwhile skill (N = 76, % = 95).

1. **Reseach Question 2:** What type of social network media do lecturers in Open and Distance Learning (ODL) have the most knowledge of?

From Table 2, most ODL lecturers generally use Facebook (N = 64, % = 80) among all the types of social network media, followed by Messenger (N = 50, % = 62.5), Youtube (N = 48, % = 57.5) and Google Plus (N = 45, % = 56.3) in that order. The least ones are Tagged (N = 2, % = 1.3), Propeller (N = 2, % = 2.5) and Technorati (N = 3, % = 3.8).

Table 2. The social network media the majority of lecturers had knowledge most

S/N	Social network media	Yes (%)	No (%)
1	Flickr	32 (40)	48 (60)
2	Diigy	4 (5)	76 (95)
3	Xanga	13 (16.3)	67 (83.8)
4	Twitter	41 (51.2)	39 (48.8)
5	Tumble	8 (10)	72 (90)
6	Friendster	9 (11.3)	71 (88.8)
7	Twiki	14 (17.5)	66 (82.5)
8	Messenger	50 (62.5)	30 (37.5)
9	Stumbler	13 (16.3)	67 (83.8)
10	Technorati	3 (3.8)	77 (96.3)
11	Najialonge	9 (11.3)	71 (88.8)
12	Facebook	64 (80)[a]	16 (20)
13	Linkedin	30 (37.5)	50 (62.5)
14	Fresqui	8 (10)	72 (90)
15	Hi5	15 (18.8)	65 (81.3)
16	Skype	38 (47.5)	42 (52.5)
17	Myspace	27 (33.8)	53 (66.3)
18	Yigg	9 (11.2)	71 (88.8)
19	Live.journal	8 (10)	72 (90)
20	Google Plus	45 (56.3)	35 (43.8)
21	Orkut	15 (18.8)	65 (81.3)
22	Twacle	5 (6.3)	75 (93.7)
23	Propeller	2 (2.5)	78 (97.5)
24	Reddit	4 (5)	76 (95)
25	Bebo	3 (3.8)	77 (96.3)
26	Tagged	1 (1.3)	79 (98.8)
27	Cafemom	5 (6.3)	75 (93.8)
28	Meetup	9 (11.3)	71 (88.8)
29	Youtube	46 (57.5)	34 (42.5)

[a] The Social Network Medium that the majority of the lecturers use.

1. **Research Question 3:** Do areas of specialization of ODL lecturers influence their attitudes towards social media?

From Fig. 1, it is clear that attitude of ODL lecturers towards Social network media is slightly influenced by their area of specialization, since all the five schools have almost the same mean. However, Science and Technology lecturers have the highest attitude.

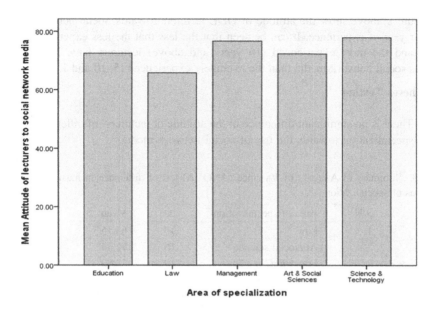

Fig. 1. The influence of area of specialization on lecturers' attitude to social network media.

1. **Research Question 4:** Do years of experience of ODL lecturers influence their attitudes towards social media?

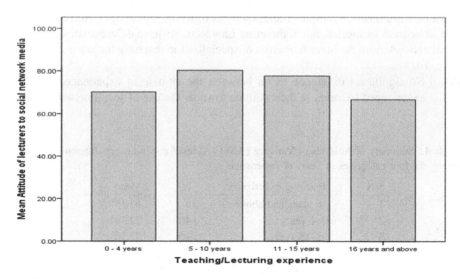

Fig. 2. The influence of experience on lecturers' attitude to social network media

Figure 2 above show the attitude of ODL lecturers towards Social network media by their year of experience. It can be seen that the less that the less experienced (0–4 years) and the most experienced (16 years and above) lecturers have less attitude towards social network media than the averagely experienced (5–10 and 11–15 years).

Hypotheses Testing

Ho$_1$ There is no significant difference in the attitude of lecturers' of different areas of specialization towards the use of social network media.

Table 3. Summary of Analysis of Variance (ANOVA) test of difference in means among the five areas of specialization

S/N	Area of specialization	N	Mean
1	Law	10	65.75[a]
2	Art/social science	16	72.34[b]
3	Education	19	72.50[b]
4	Management	19	76.71[b]
5	Science/technology	16	77.97[b]
	F-value = 4.124, df. = 4, 75 p-value = 0.004		

From Table 3, the Calculated F-value is 4.124 (degrees of freedom, df. = 4, 75) with p-value of 0.004, it is therefore concluded that there is significant difference in the means of attitude (in percentage) of lecturers among the five areas of specialization. This implies that area of specialization has significant effect on attitude of lecturers to social network media. From the Table, Law has different superscript (letter a) from the other four areas of specialization, therefore Law lecturers have different attitude toward social network from the other four areas of specialization that have the same superscript (letter b).

Ho$_2$ No significant difference exists between the attitude of experienced and less experienced lecturers in their attitude towards the use of social network media.

Table 4. Summary of Analysis of Variance (ANOVA) test for significance difference in means among the four categories of years of experience

S/N	Teaching experience	N	Mean
1	16 years and above	6	65.75[a]
2	0–4 years	40	72.34[a]
3	11–15 years	15	72.50[b]
4	5–10 years	19	76.71[b]
	F-value = 10.228, df. = 3, 76 p-value = 0.000		

From Table 4, the Calculated F-value is 10.228 (degrees of freedom is 3 and 76) with p-value of 0.000, since the p-value (0.000) is less than 0.05 (level of significance) the null hypothesis is rejected and it is therefore concluded that there is significant difference in the means of attitude (in percentage) of lecturers among the four categories of experience. This implies that years of teaching experience has significant effect on attitude of lecturers to social network media. From the Table, 16 years and above and 0–4 years have the same superscript (letter a) and they are different from the other two categories (11–15 years and 5–10 years) with different superscript (letter b). Therefore lecturers with 16 years and above and 0–4 years of experience have different attitude toward social network from the other two categories (i.e. 11–15 years and 5–10 years).

Ho_3 There is no significant difference between attitude of lecturers in single mode and dual mode ODL to of social net work media.

Table 5. t-test of attitude of ODL lecturers in single mode and dual mode towards Social network media

Variable	N	Mean score	Std dev.	Std. Error	DF	T-cal	P
Single mode	50	73.100	10.22	1.45	78	−793	0.430
Dual mode	30	74.750	6.47	1.18			

Significant at 0.05 level

Table 5 showed that the mean attitude of lecturers in single mode is 73.10 while that of those in dual mode ODL is 74.75. The t-calculated is −0.793 (degree of freedom is 78) with p-value of 0.430. The hypothesis is accepted at 0.05 level of significance (p-value > 0.05). It is therefore concluded that there is no significant difference between attitude of ODL lecturers in single mode and dual mode towards Social network media.

3 Discussion of Findings

Distance education's focus on opening access to education for those who otherwise would have been denied is mostly achievable through lecturers who have right attitude to media technologies.

From this study, ODL lecturers have been found to have positive attitude towards social network media. This is in agreement with the finding of Issa [20] who reported lecturers' positive attitude towards assistive technologies. This might be possible because of the popularity that social network media have gained in removing time and space barriers in education.

Finding on area of specialization on ODL lecturers' attitude showed that area of specialization influenced their attitude. This is contrary to the report of Winogrod [21] who asserted that the role of media technologies in various areas of specialization is like the role of mathematics to the physical sciences. This is because of the variation found in lecturers' attitude as it regards their areas of specialization, towards social network media.

Experience on lecturer's attitude revealed that the less experienced (0–4 years) and the most experienced (16 years and above) lecturers have less attitude towards social network media. The reason might be because the young lecturers are yet to realize the need to remove barriers in distance education, while the older ones are still finding it difficult to change from the orientation which they had in conventional institutions (where face to face teaching is the main thing) before transferring their services to ODL institutions. Also, lack of training through seminars and workshops that is e-learning oriented might be responsible for the results.

The importance of training was further underscore by these researchers. Swarts [22], supports the need for teachers to be adequately and appropriately trained through pre-service and in-service education programmes. In a similar manner, Desimone [23] asserts among others that high quality professional development of teachers exhibits the characteristics: focus on core content and modeling of teaching strategies for the content, and inclusion of opportunities for active learning of new teaching strategies. Also, Coggshall and Ott [24] discovered that professional training through staff programmes improves teachers' effectiveness.

Findings on attitude of lecturers in single mode and dual mode institutions towards social network media showed no significant difference between the two. The reasons might be because of the central objective of ODL, which is to provide access to quality education and equity in educational for those who otherwise would have been denied. Therefore, lecturers in the two both have obligations to do things that will facilitate this objective.

4   Conclusion and Recommendations

It can be concluded that ODL lecturers' positive attitude towards social network media can position them to have understanding of its specific standards and thereby, provide huge contributions to accessibility and usability needs of the learners, through feedback offered to the soft ware developers.

It was recommended that:

1. Awareness programme that promotes ODL lecturers' attitude towards social network media should be organised, to enhance their move for good accessibility and usability exercise in ODL.
2. ODL lecturers should be given training that is e-learning oriented in social network media through, workshop and conferences, to further increase their interest in effort towards success of accessibility and usability needs of the learners.

References

1. Federal Republic of Nigeria (FRN). National Policy on Education, 4th edn. Abuja NERDC Press, Lagos (2004)
2. Commonwealth of Learning (COL): An introduction to open and distance learning (2000). http://www.col.org/ODL.Intro/introODL.htm
3. Cooper, M.: Assessing the usability of online instructional materials (2013). http://academia. edu/174026/Assessing_the_usability_of_online. Accessed 6 May 2014

4. Global Learning Consortium: Guidelines for developing accessibile learning applications (2002). http://www.imsglobal.org/accessibility/accvlpo/imsace_guideevlpO.html. Accessed 24 May 2007
5. Milken Exchange in Educational Technology. Will new teachers be prepared to teach in a digital age? Santa Monica Milken Fmily Foundation (1999). http://mff.org/pubs/me154pdf. Accessed 13 Jan 2004
6. Omoniyi, T.: Principles and Applications of Educational Technology, pp. 23–31. Ibadan BASH-Moses Publishers, London (2009)
7. Bragg, A.: Reflections on pedagogy. Reframing practice to foster informal learning with social software (2006). http://www.dream.sdu.dk/uploads/files/Anne%20Bartlett-Brag.pdf. Accessed 10 Feb 2008
8. Merril, M.D.: A task-centered instructional strategy. J. Res. Technol. Educ. **40**(1), 33–50 (2007). ISSN (printed): 1523–1539
9. Smith, M.G.: Secondary teachers' perception towards inclusion of students with severe disabilities. NASSP Bull. **84**(613), 54–60 (2000)
10. Yusuf, B.L.: Secondary school teachers' attitude to and use of community resources in social studies teaching. M.Ed Project, University of Ilorin (2000)
11. Darling Hammond, L.: What Matter Most: Teaching for America's Future. National Commission on Teaching and America's Future, Washington, D.C. (1996)
12. Olokoba, A.A.: Teachers' biographic factors as correlates of teachers' productivity. M.Ed dissertation. University of Ilorin (2002)
13. David, C.B.: The Wonder of Exemplary Performance. Creating Powerful Thinking in Teachers and Students. Holt: Rinehart and Wiston, New York (2004)
14. Adeyemi, T.O.: Teachers' teaching experience and students' learning outcomes in secondary schools in Ondo State, Nigeria. Educ. Res. Rev. **3**(6), 204–212 (2008)
15. Rice, J.K.: Teacher Quality: Understanding the Effectiveness of Teacher Attributes. Economic Policy Institute, Washington D.C. (2003)
16. Okebukola, P.: Open Education and the March to 2020: Can Nigeria Make It? Second Pre— Convocation Lectures. National Open University of Nigeria, Victoria Island (2013)
17. Beatie, J.R., Anderson, R.J., Antonak, R.F.: Modifying attitudes of prospective education towards students' with disabilities and their integration into regular classrooms. J. Psychol. **131**(3), 245–259 (1997)
18. Christensen, R., Knezek, G.: Parallel forms for measuring teachers' attitude towards computers. In: McNeil, S., Price, J.D., Boger-Meail, S., Robin, B., Willis, J. (eds.) Technology and Teacher Education annual Charlottesville: Association for the Advancement of Computer Education (1998)
19. Yusuf, H.T.: Secondary School Teacher's Attitude to and use of Community Resources in Social Studies Teaching in Ilorin, Nigeria. An M.Ed project University of Ilorin (2004)
20. Issa, A.I.: Teachers' Awareness of and Attitude to Assistive Technologies for Special Education in Nigeria. Ph.D. thesis, Science Education Department, University of Ilorin (2009)
21. Winogrod, T.: Understanding Natural Language. Harper and Row Publishers, New York (2000)
22. Swarts, J.: Information technology as discursive agents: methodological implications for the empirical study of knowledge work. J. Teachers Writ. Commun. **38**(4), 301–329 (2008)
23. Desimone, L.M.: Improving impact studies of teachers' professional development: toward better conceptualizations and measures. Educ. Res. **38**(3), 181–199 (2009)
24. Coggshall, J.G., Ott, A.: Retraining Teacher Talent: Conversance and Contradictions in Teachers' Perceptions of Policy Reform Ideas. Learning Point Associates, Naperville and Public Agenda, New York (2010)

Introducing Online Learning in a Small Organization: The Case of the Diplomatic Institute of the Italian Ministry of Foreign Affairs

Stefano Baldi[✉]

Ministero degli Affari Esteri, DGRI – Istituto Diplomatico,
Via di Villa Madama, 250, 00135 Rome, Italy
stefano.baldi@esteri.it

Abstract. The Diplomatic Institute (ISDI) - the structure of the Italian Ministry of Foreign Affairs dedicated to internal training of the personnel – has started several experiments in the field of online learning. Tools such as Blogs, online learning modules, webinars and Netvibes have been developed and have contributed to enrich the training offer of the Institute. This paper illustrates the challenges that this small structure has faced and the results that have been accomplished so far. It also shares seven lessons learned from this experience.

Keywords: Ministry of foreign affairs · Diplomacy · Training · Online learning

1 Introduction

Being appointed Director at the Diplomatic Institute of the Ministry of Foreign Affairs of Italy, the structure of the Ministry dealing with training of personnel has been for me a great privilege as well as an opportunity to explore new approach to diplomatic training and test some ideas developed over a long period. Working as a diplomat. I learned the importance of training in a profession where people change "job" every four years, moving from an Embassy to another Embassy or back to the Ministry of Foreign Affairs.

The Diplomatic Institute (ISDI) was founded in 1967 and is part of the Ministry's General Directorate for Resources and Innovation as this confirms the close relationship between training and management of human and financial resources.

To put the training challenges of the Diplomatic Institute in context, it may be appropriate to provide a few details about the structure of the Italian Ministry of Foreign Affairs: The Ministry is responsible for the State's functions, tasks and duties in matters concerning Italy's political, economic, social and cultural relations with other countries and International Organisations.

The Ministry operates through a network of more than 300 offices around the world: embassies, permanent missions to international organizations, special diplomatic delegations, consular offices and Italian cultural institutes. If we consider only the 127 embassies abroad, 26 are located in the European Union, 23 in Asia and Oceania,

© Institute for Computer Sciences, Social Informatics and Telecommunications Engineering 2014
G. Vincenti et al. (Eds.): eLEOT 2014, LNICST 138, pp. 30–40, 2014.
DOI: 10.1007/978-3-319-13293-8_4

21 in the Americas, 21 in Sub-Saharan Africa, 18 in non-EU countries in Europe, and 18 in the Mediterranean and Middle East.

At the beginning of 2014 the Ministry of Foreign Affairs counted about 6,900 people. Of these, 4,200 permanent staff and 2,600 non-permanent (local) staff.

Therefore one of the challenges of the Director of the Institute is to find the best sustainable way to train a potential population of 4,200 staff, half of which are not working in the headquarters in Rome, but in different places in the world (plus the 2,600 local staff all of whom work abroad).

The internal demand (and the need) for training keeps increasing while the resources, not surprisingly, fail to keep pace and are, in fact, falling. This paradox affects many people responsible for training. While there is no magic hand in the real world, it is best to see opportunities in those challenges rather than consider them as traps.

When I arrived at the ISDI in 2011, the development of an online learning system compatible and sustainable with the structure of the Institute and of the Ministry itself was identified as a key opportunity. These two concepts (compatible and sustainable) are particularly relevant in order to understand the initiatives that have been setup and the success (and some failures), The lessons learned in doing this are the subject of this paper.

2 Why Online Learning

The terminology "Online Learning" covers a range of different things and solutions. When deciding to develop Online Learning facilities in a small structure I had the advantage of understanding the complexity of the issue.

As far ago as 2003 I published (together with my friends Jovan Kurbalija and Ed Gelbstein) a booklet entitled "Online learning for professionals in full time work" (DiploFoundation, 2003), which makes a distinction with online learning in the academic world. Both may use the same technologies, but with significantly different objectives.

Online learning is based on several premises and promises – essentially that it can be particularly effective for professionals, that it is easy to implement and quick to deliver results, that it is cost-effective and that online learners love it. These are all true, but not all the time and not for everyone.

Some of the benefits of successfully implemented online learning identified more than ten years ago are still valid and have been applied to the experience described in this paper:

- The ability to deliver learning opportunities to anyone, at any-time, almost anywhere;
- A learning experience that is often perceived as being "better" than classroom instruction;
- Easier access to experienced professors, lecturers, facilitators and mentors;

- Access to massive information resources through the World Wide Web, including commercial information service providers (such as, for example, Lexis-Nexis or the Economist Intelligence Unit);
- The possibility for learners to actively participate in the learning process, in particular shy learners who may hesitate to participate fully in a more traditional learning environment;
- Access to online learning and technical support;

The planning and implementation of ISDI's Online Learning strategy has taken into account all these principles. The action has been articulated in several phases which has led to the use of a wide range of tools and services available online. In this way a new innovative training offer has been created to complement (not substitute) the traditional one.

The tools used include the Moodle Platform for developing and hosting self-paced online modules and the Wordpress platform for the development of a Blog. We also used Survey Monkey for experimenting with the evaluation of the courses and Webex and Adobe Connect for online webinars.

Other experiments looked at non-traditional activities such as Webradio programming (diplomaziaedintorni.wordpress.com), the organization of a Pecha Kucha contest and the creation of a calendar with visuals.

(www.slideshare.net/ArturoToscanini/cybersecurity-guidelines-for-diplomats).

Some of the characteristics of the Ministry of Foreign Affairs that affect the training offer support the choice of the Online Training trials:

1. High turnover of personnel – Staff and managers rotate regularly (every 3–5 years) moving back and forth from headquarters to Missions abroad or from Mission to Mission.
2. Low level of knowledge sharing – There is no formalized internal system to ensure internal knowledge sharing of micro-procedures or practices established by practitioners.
3. Increasing average age of personnel – Due to restrictions in recruitment the age profile of staff is continuously increasing. The current average age is 50 years.

On this last point it is important to note that in future new staff will be recruited by the Ministry of Foreign Affairs in limited numbers due to legal provisions concerning the Civil Service. This limitation makes it very important that the future requirements, for newly recruited staff at all levels include a good understanding of IT, and knowledge of social media platforms. This will enable the Administration to exploit the opportunities offered by the Internet and by the e-tools available.

3   The Blog as a Training Tool

The need to reach a wide number of users (we should call them "learners") located in the four corners of the world is an issue for considering the use of blogs as a training tool. This could be defined as "soft training", by making available selected useful sources for particular topics.

A couple of years ago (in 2012), we experimented with a blog focusing on the knowledge of "soft skills" relevant for diplomats when acting as managers.

The blog, called ISDI Learning corner (istitutodiplomatico.wordpress.org), is based on the experience of the Institute in terms of training needs for this specific topic. The sources used for the blog postings are focused on professional and personal growth and reflecting the training needs of a Ministry of Foreign Affairs. The blog is in English, and uses the free Wordpress platform. It can be consulted by the personnel of the Ministry of Foreign Affairs of Italy as well as by other interested people.

The Wordpress platform gives the possibility to set up a subscription service through which subscribers can receive in their email every newly published post. People can subscribe using the "Follow" function, available on the blog, simply providing their own Email address. The Administrator can also "invite" new potential subscribers who will have to accept the invitation. According to our experience the "unsolicited" action ("Follow") is less effective in terms of gaining new subscribers than the invitation by the administrator.

This "push" service is a great asset and makes the post more effective than the simple publication on the site. For this reason much effort has been put in increasing the number of subscribers amongst Ministry personnel which remains the first and main target of the Blog.

The number of subscribers has progressively increased thanks to the subscription campaigns launched through the invitation function. The progression of the subscriptions is as follows:

May 2012 – 250 subscribers
March 2013 – 850 subscribers
March 2014 – 2100 subscribers

Before setting up the Blog, no other tool had been used to make training material easily available and simple to consult. In particular this was the first time that a Blog had been used by a Ministry of Foreign Affairs for sharing internally knowledge related to soft skills. In the past training on soft skills was limited to some traditional seminar done in a face-to-face format. By definition, this kind of activity, however effective, could only reach a limited number of officers.

In order to ensure the continuity of blogging, having started with two weeks when posts were published more or less at random, it was decided to establish a timetable that provides at least three posts of different types every week.

These types include articles about books, videos and other content considered suitable for the development of "Soft Skills".

Users can comment on every post. The comments are moderated and published only if they specifically relate to the post. Each post can be easily shared on the main social networks. The number of replies has been limited and this is probably due to the limited familiarity of staff with these tools as well as a tendency not to express opinions or to engage in a public domain. On the other hand one the objectives of the initiative was to familiarize personnel with the new tools available in the web 2.0.

The Wordpress platform gives the possibility to monitor access to the blog and daily statistics provide, for example, the number of accesses and where they come from.

Information concerning this blog has been provided to homologous institutions of the European Union. Invitations to use this blog have been extended during coordination meeting of Training Directors of MFAs training institutions. This kind of action has not yet produced the same encouraging results that have been reached at our internal level. Further action is needed to explain the effectiveness and usability of the tool.

4 The Online Learning Modules

Starting from scratch can be an opportunity but it also means that you have no previous experience to refer to. This was the challenge the Institute faced for developing Online learning modules. The first modules produced by the Institute were introduced two years ago. The steps to achieve this were:

(1) Selecting a Learning Management System: ISDI decided on the Moodle platform because of its flexibility, simplicity of use and wide adoption by small and medium-size organizations.
(2) Procurement of bandwidth: The procurement of a fiber connection was considered a priority in order to ensure the adequate performance of external connections to the Online Learning system.
(3) Development of Content: The Institute mainly provides training on the specific activities and responsibilities of the Ministry of Foreign Affairs. Therefore the personnel of the Ministry were the best qualified people that could develop learning material. We started by involving those most willing and open and we

also adapted some available published material. While this is not the best solution, it is the only one available to build a culture of online learning in an environment where this is completely. In a way, is a confidence-building exercise.

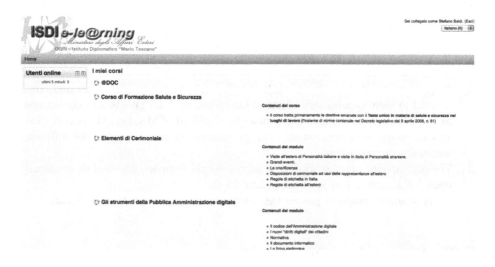

The first module to be developed concerned the essential knowledge of rights and obligations of the Ministry of Foreign Affairs Personnel. It was a very short self-paced course that gave the opportunity to test the system and gain reactions from the first group of participants. This first trial identified the need to link the completion of the course to an automatic (or semi-automatic) system to issue the certificate of participation and register it in the electronic personal records. It is important to recognize and/ or reward those who complete the courses and a certificate is a good "motivator" for many participants. The certification system took a few months to be completed by the IT Department of the Ministry that worked closely with the IT staff of the Institute (alas, composed by only two very able people).

Other modules have been developed taking into account the lessons learned with the first trial. The main difficulty in developing new self-paced modules is to find internal experts to develop the text and related quizzes. Persuading people to spend time to share their knowledge and put it in writing is not always easy. One factor is the difficulty of explaining the benefits of this effort. A strong point remains that these modules allow reaching staff abroad that would otherwise not have access to face-to-face training.

The modules that have been developed so far are:

(1) Obligations and Rights of Civil Servants
(2) Protocol practice
(3) Human Rights
(4) Visas Management
(5) Consular assistance to Italian nationals abroad

The wide range of topics reflects our attempt to cover different sectors (and potential beneficiaries) to validate this kind of online training. The variety can also be explained by the availability of qualified internal staff to develop the modules. Many other people were asked to work at new modules but have not yet provided any contents.

The short online (self-paced) module on "Consular Assistance to Italian nationals abroad" is a good example for showing the way these courses are currently organized. The stages and results obtained in the first edition of the module were:

(1) Request to the diplomatic network (in this case limited to embassies and con-sulates) to identify who should attend the online module. This is also considered as an authorisation to attend the courses by the Head of Mission (312 participants 154 of which were local staff). The participants were working in 99 different embassies or consulates
(2) The participants were authorised to access the platform and the module remained open for a defined period of time (four days);
(3) 83 % of the participants passed the verification test (and got the certificate).

5 The Distance Learning Experiment

The initial good results experienced with self-paced modules led to the decision to experiment another type of online learning not self-paced but based on a series of live streaming with the possibility to interact using the chat. The Distance Learning approach was particularly suitable for specific courses to virtual classrooms composed of people working in different Missions located all over the world (what internally is defined as "decentralized training").

The equipment that has been adopted for the implementation of Distance Learning experiment is LifeSize (www.lifesize.com).

This kind of equipment provides:

(1) Videoconferencing System (over IP)
(2) Live streaming facilities
(3) Creation of Video Library

In the case of the Diplomatic Institute:

– Videoconferencing has been used for video sessions with specific locations abroad and with Universities. Interactive video seminars have been organized and this has allowed time and travel expenses savings.
– Live streaming has been a key feature for implementing and broadcasting spe-cialized courses (in administration, accounting and consular matters) for Embassies, Consulates and Italian Cultural Institute all over the world. This approach has led to the creation of virtual classrooms located in our missions abroad selected for the participation to the courses.
– Most of the videos have been recorded and they now constitute a unique internal video library that is used for continuous learning purposes.

The quality of videoconferencing and live streaming is affected by the bandwidth available at the end point. Taking into account the limitations experienced in some remote countries and thank to the opportunities offered by the equipment, we have reduced the bandwidth usage while maintaining an acceptable quality of the live streaming.

6 The Diplomatic Webinars

In collaboration with the DiploFoundation (www.diplomacy.edu), in 2013 the Institute organized a cycle of jointly developed webinars (online seminars using Internet) on advanced diplomatic topics.

(www.diplomacy.edu/capacity/onlinediplomacy). Each webinar included a short background document and an interactive video presentation.

The basic idea behind this experiment was that time is limited and people lead busy lives. Diplomats also need to stay current with what is happening in the world and take time to reflect on changes and developments.

In the series organized we addressed the challenges of modern diplomacy from two perspectives: evolution of diplomacy and technology - looked into history in order to see what we can use in addressing modern diplomatic problems; social media and diplomacy – focused on the use of modern social media tools in diplomacy (e.g. Twitter, Facebook, blogs, wikis).

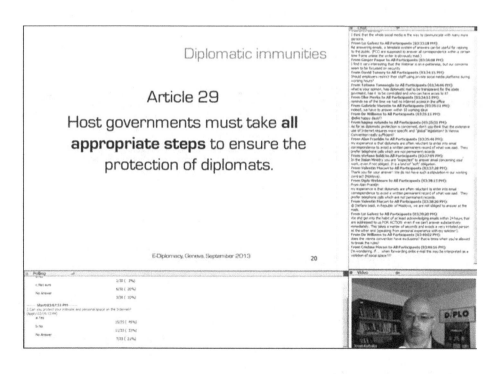

The results were encouraging, but only when these webinars were included in formal training courses where attendance was compulsory. The few webinars that were offered for voluntary participation had relatively low attendance (even if feedback from participants was good). This could be explained with the fact that the use of new technologies and tools, even when they are simple and short, need time and practice before becoming part of a "corporate culture" and therefore being part of the accepted normal training programme.

7   Netvibes

The Institute also trialed the use of Netvibes (www.netvibes.com) for training. Netvibes is an easy-to-use online dashboard that, in the case of diplomats, can be particularly effective for aggregating information provided by many online sources.

Taking advantage of the positive experience I had gained using Netvibes (free of charge in its basic offer), basic training and practice were introduced in the programme of the "Innovation Lab" series of workshops for diplomats attending courses at the Institute (mostly junior diplomats and mid-career diplomats).

The examples for the courses were based on two pages I had previously created, both in the public domain and freely accessible;

(1)   a page concerning information sources of general interest for diplomats with a couple of subsections dedicated to the European Union and to training (www.netvibes.com/diplosor)

(2)   a page concerning Science diplomacy (www.netvibes.com/sciencediplomacy)

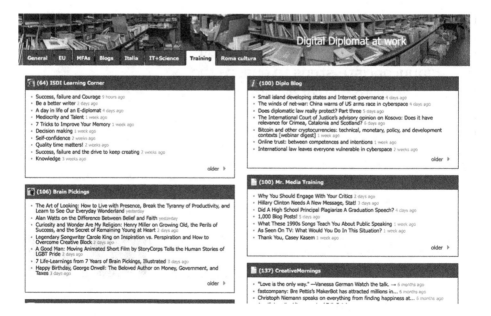

The Institute staff was encouraged to use Netvibes for training purposes and this led to the creation of an original Netvibes page dedicated to learning English. The page (www.netvibes.com/englearn) is structured in several subsections dedicated to various aspects of language training.

The feedback of those who attended the workshops was good and this kind of tool was perceived as useful for professionals, like diplomats, who have to manage large amounts of information. Nevertheless the follow up in terms of implementation of new public pages by those who attended was relatively modest. One example, though, is the page concerning EU information (www.netvibes.com/dgue03#GLS).

8   The Seven "Lessons Learned"

(1) *It takes time* – Rome was not built in one day and the same apply to introducing and developing even the simplest form of Online Learning in an Institution. It also takes time before the OLL becomes part of the learning culture.

(2) *It takes a team* – No matter how good and knowledgeable a leader is, it takes a team of motivated people to set up online learning. The more they know about the organisation, the easier it will be to develop a sustainable system.

(3) *People before content* – Reasonable content can only be developed by the right experts. This is particularly true in the case of an MFA given the specificity of their activities and knowledge. Persuading people to collaborate with and contribute to the OLL project is vital to its success.

(4) *Simplicity ensures sustainability* – Complicated systems and procedures can be discouraging in an environment not used to new technologies. Therefore simplicity of use and access should prevail on the temptation to have the "perfect" tool (which, by the way, does not exist).

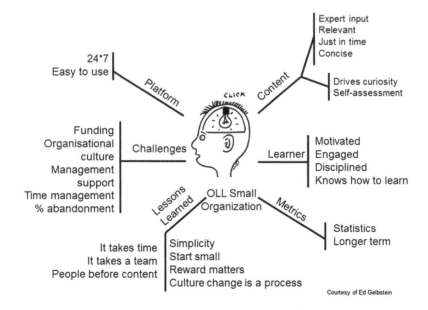

Courtesy of Ed Gelbstein

(5) *Start small* – Projects and objectives must be sustainable. In a small organization it is better to have a limited project up and running than the pursuit of the "grand design" that will always be in the "feasibility study" phase. It is even more so in an organization with a high level of turnover.

(6) *Reward is part of the game* – In adult learning there must be a concrete objective to justify training. The simple appeal to the need for continuous learning will not work if not accompanied by some kind of reward and/or recognition. This can be a certificate, career progression or new career opportunities or anything else that can motivate the individual.

(7) *Creating a new professional culture is a process* - The ability to use new tools for professional purposes is not only related to training but also to an individual's sensitivity, willingness and readiness to put into practice what is being taught. Making people aware of opportunities is only the first step of a much longer process aimed at creating a new professional culture.

Building a Mobile Collaborative Learning Environment for the Identification and Classification of Real World Objects

Otto Borchert$^{(\boxtimes)}$ and Brian M. Slator

Computer Science Department, North Dakota State University, Fargo, ND, USA
{otto.borchert,brian.slator}@ndsu.edu

Abstract. This paper describes the theoretical framework and in-progress implementation of the Collaborative Identification, Retrieval, and Classification Learning Environment (CIRCLE). CIRCLE uses recent research findings in collaboration, constructivism, mobile development, and retrieval learning to develop a multi-user tool for the identification and classification of real world objects. CIRCLE supports group efforts at taxonomy building by providing a framework for data gathering in the field and scientific hypothesizing and debate in a virtual laboratory. Future plans include a pilot usability study and classroom experiments to determine the effectiveness of the approach towards learning the identification of rocks and minerals (in a geology lab), weeds (in a weed identification course), and animals (in an ecology class).

Keywords: Collaborative learning · Constructivism · Mobile application · Identification and classification games

1 Introduction

Identification and classification games are not new. Classification games abound on the Internet and in mobile app stores [3–7]. Rather than socially-mediated, actively constructing knowledge, as in Vygotsky's social constructivism [8], these identification games provide a method for retrieval learning. This theory suggests that the act of retrieving knowledge in multiple different ways results in better learning outcomes [9].

Pervasive and location-based mobile gaming serves to harness the locative functionalities of mobile devices to supplement the real world with virtual information. Pervasive games "pervade" the user's life, in contrast to games that occur at one particular time and place. Montola defines a game as an activity that involves a certain set of individuals that occurs at a particular place and at a particular time [10]. He further states that a pervasive game expands on this definition along social, spatial, or temporal dimensions. Social expansion means that people not playing the game can still participate within the game structure. Spatial expansion means that a pervasive game can be played anywhere, while temporal expansion means that a pervasive game can be playing at any time.

Even before computers, students were memorizing "things" using flashcards. A number of studies have been performed to determine effective ways to improve

© Institute for Computer Sciences, Social Informatics and Telecommunications Engineering 2014
G. Vincenti et al. (Eds.): eLEOT 2014, LNICST 138, pp. 41–48, 2014.
DOI: 10.1007/978-3-319-13293-8_5

learning while using flashcards [1, 2]. In addition to physical artifacts for learning identification tasks, students handle actual physical specimens in a lab or real world setting. This project seeks to enhance even these highly effective methods of learning by putting the gathering and organization of content in users' hands.

Location-based games are a subset of pervasive games, where a fixed location is used within the mechanics of the game itself. Location-based games use the environment to augment the players' experience. For example, MicroBlog [11] asks players to take pictures of their environment to share them with other users, using the environment as part of the game. In these games, a parallel world is created in virtual space. Individuals interact with this virtual world by going to real world locations. Other location based games that use user-generated content include Gopher [12] and Indigator [13].

Within this discipline, distinctions are made between designed activity and user-generated activity in mobile settings [14]. Designed activities are developed by programmers, designers, and experts with a specific pedagogical plan in place. User-generated activity is content and structure spontaneously created by users to meet their own learning needs.

A number of designed activities have been created for a variety of different subjects and situations including games for geometry learning in an outdoor setting [15], as museum guides [16], in college orientation sessions [17], in biology topics including genetics, protein synthesis, evolution, and food webs [18], and in weather forecasting [19]. While designed activities are important to provide guided opportunities for learning, the Internet allows individuals to guide and create their own learning affordances. This self-directed learning is intrinsic to this research project.

The combination of social constructivist principles that guide collaborative, user generated, multiplayer mobile games and retrieval learning that inform identification games provides an opportunity to create a new application for concept learning. We call this application CIRCLE, the Collaborative Identification, Retrieval, and Classification Learning Environment.

2 Implementation

CIRCLE is composed of five different activities: content acquisition, trait elaboration, hypothesis formation, tree construction, and game play. Students will be tracked to observe their use of the system and identify the amount of time they spend during each activity. Within the application, students can take on various collaborative roles, each correlated to one of the five activities.

2.1 Content Acquisition

First, students go out into the field using a mobile device to collect identifiable objects from the real world. The student will collect photographs, video, and audio where appropriate for the object under study. These multimedia artifacts are uploaded to a central server, where other users will be able to interact with them in real-time.

Students performing this role will be identified as gatherers. An example task for a gatherer would be to take a photograph of the interesting trees or rocks in their neighborhood.

2.2   Trait Elaboration

Second, students look at acquired content from their group and offer suggestions on traits to observe or experiments to conduct to further refine a potential identification. The originating student then performs the requested experiments and observations to elaborate on the content either by performing them immediately, if feedback is prompt, or return to the object under study. As experiments provide attributes for features (traits) these will be stored for use by future students. For example, the first person to suggest a 'hardness' experiment using a 'glass plate' to classify a mineral will have those items stored in the system. Or a player might just observe from the photographic evidence the tree is covered with sharp needles, not leaves, and store that information in the system. Later players will be able to choose these observational or experimental results from the inventory. Students in this stage will be identified as elaborators. Continuing the rock example, an elaborator would suggest an acid test be performed on the neighborhood rock specimen.

2.3   Hypothesis Formation

Third, students offer hypotheses about the general classification or precise identity of the unidentified object. Eventually, an expert (typically the teacher) will verify the hypothesis. In absence of an expert, hypotheses could be voted upon, where more votes could be measured as a confidence in an identification. Students in this role would be called identifiers, and would offer the category "Conifer" in the tree example, or suggest "Limestone" in the rock example.

2.4   Taxonomy Construction

Fourth, students build versions of identification trees together. Traits and experiments will be shown graphically as potential branches, while the content collected by students will be the leaves. Students will move the nodes and leaves around in real time, seeing how other students are arranging the tree and offering suggestions for node placement. Players in this role will be called constructors. After enough identifications have been made in the hypothesis formation stage, constructors can build dichotomous keys of the trees or rocks.

2.5   Game Play

Finally, games are automatically created by the system based on gathered content. Students are given multimedia, traits, observations, and experiments and are asked to identify the object in game form. Students in this role will be called players. These students will play identification games similar to flashcards to help them retrieve knowledge they have gained from working in the other four stages.

Observing students in each of these stages may result in the identification of roles that are motivating or act to increase student learning. Ideally, students of all roles will:

(a) Learn how to identify objects in the real world within their discipline of interest
(b) Determine the observations and experiments necessary to accurately identify these objects
(c) Classify these objects for faster identifications
(d) Use retrieval learning to strengthen their knowledge
(e) Gain collaboration skills

Ultimately, CIRCLE is an innovative approach to identification and classification that combines successful attributes of other environments into one. CIRCLE will utilize effective learning science principles, harness the advantages and inherent motivation of user generated content, including images, videos, sound, and text, allow for synchronous and asynchronous collaborative interactions, create a system of juried peer review of results and hypotheses, and finally create computationally generated "flashcard" games to strengthen student learning.

3   Rationale for Implementation

According to constructivist theorists, students combine their prior understanding and new information to actively construct new knowledge [20]. This learning is created within a social context. A person's culture, environment, and social context combine to affect the construction of knowledge. This idea lies at the heart of social constructivism [21]. Individuals create new knowledge mediated by interactions with other human beings and with the environment. These interactions can be structured so that learning is indifferent, compromised, or supported by the efforts of other individuals. Social interdependence theory describes these interactions as being individualistic, competitive, and cooperative, respectively [22–25].

Individualistic behavior is characterized by people working towards their own personal goals. The success or failures of others do not matter to the successful completion of their goals. While this approach towards learning can be effective, it has a number of negative side effects. People working individualistically tend to have lower psychological health, including lower self-esteem and higher anxiety [26]. They also do not gain the benefits of cooperative learning listed below.

Competition is characterized by the requirement that other people must fail in order for one to achieve personal goals. Competition increases self-acceptance based on meeting external standards and expectations [27], reduces effort in lower achieving students (to reduce negative self-worth), decreases effort in high achieving students when they realize they'll always "win" [28], marginalizes weaker, lower achieving members, and moves student focus from the process of the task to the end result [29]. Because of these drawbacks, CIRCLE focuses on cooperative learning.

Cooperative learning provides many benefits to students including: an increase in academic skills [30–33], misconception identification and repair [34–36], collaborative work skills [34], the insight that the sum of individual knowledge is greater than the parts [37], the development of social skills [38], and the strengthening of inter-group relations [33].

These many benefits do not come simply by placing individuals into a group and giving them a task. Certain conditions must be met to create the most effective group dynamic. The ideal cooperative group fosters 5 primary conditions: positive interdependence, individual accountability, promotive interaction, social skills, and group processing [25, 39].

Positive interdependence is achieved when group members depend on each other for skills, talents, and knowledge to advance shared group goals. All group members believe that all other members are needed to succeed in the task at hand. Positive interdependence in CIRCLE will be enforced using game rules. For example, a certain number of people in the group will need to offer evidence on the identity of an object.

Individual accountability means that all members of a group must participate in the shared tasks and all actions should be visible to the group. No one should do all the work, nor should anyone do no work at all. This will be enforced in CIRCLE by means of a group status window, where the number of interactions each user has completed and when they completed it can be viewed by all members of the group.

Promotive interaction means that students actively communicate with one another in the group to achieve group goals. CIRCLE will include communication mediums so that students can discuss hypotheses, potential observations, and dichotomous key construction both synchronously and asynchronously.

Social skills are also required for positive group interactions. While not envisioned for the first iteration of CIRCLE, social skills could be prompted from students. For example, a student that is not participating could be encouraged to voice their opinion. Students could also be given a lesson on appropriate social skills or proper etiquette when discussing topics in an online setting. Soller [40] instructs users to use sentence "openers" rather than allowing students to type in a free form text box. Her system uses these sentence openers to guide users to more effective conversation skills.

Finally, group processing occurs when groups reflect on their progress towards group goals. Message boards with appropriate prompts provide an opportunity for students to state how they feel the group is progressing towards the creation of their classification structures, or make suggestions on how to improve the group process.

Once students have successfully co-created knowledge in their cooperative groups, they need a way to reinforce this understanding. This reinforcement occurs when a student's knowledge is assessed. This assessment can come at the end of a lesson in the form of summative assessments, or during the lesson in the form of formative assessments. Ongoing, formative assessment is the key to higher learning gains [41]. Studies in retrieval learning have shown that students learn best when they actively attempt to "retrieve" the knowledge from memory during self-assessment, as opposed to re-reading study materials [9].

Flashcards can be used effectively to retrieve knowledge from memory [1, 2]. Ideally, we hope to show that CIRCLE will provide a more interesting and potentially motivating method in the form of identification games. The final "game play" portion of the activity can be varied substantially. Students could be given an image or other multimedia content, a list of characteristics, or an example of where the object could be found. The number of images, and thus, the number of different available contexts, would only be limited by the number of images taken by the users. This combination of well-motivated learners, cooperative and collaborative co-construction of knowledge, and focused retrieval should provide an opportunity to help students learn identification and classification tasks in a more entertaining and effective way.

4 Discussion/Future Work

Implementation of CIRCLE is ongoing as a part of the primary author's Ph.D. dissertation. Upon completion of the described implementation, a series of experiments are planned to determine the usability and educational effectiveness of the proposed work.

A pilot study is planned to be held during May 2014. Approximately 20 STEM Education faculty and graduate students from North Dakota State University (NDSU) will be involved. Subjects will be divided into two groups: a software group and a manual group. Both groups will be given a bag of candy to identify and classify into a dichotomous key. The software group will use CIRCLE as described, making note of any difficulties they encounter. The manual group will use paper and pencil to perform the same task. The groups will be video recorded to determine similarities and differences in the identification and classification of objects in both a virtual and non-virtual setting. A secondary objective of the research is to determine any software errors and usability issues that exist in the initial prototype of CIRCLE. The Software Usability Scale [42] will be administered to the software group upon completion of their tasks. This will be a useful first step, as these users come from fields as diverse as biology, chemistry, and mathematics, and will provide excellent feedback.

After the completion of the pilot study, further experiments are planned for actual classroom implementation. Three separate courses at NDSU have been identified for the use of CIRCLE. These courses include introductory geology lab, weed identification, and ecology. In these classrooms, subjects in different course sections will either use the original method of teaching identification or CIRCLE. This will provide feedback on whether the software is educationally effective or not. Since CIRCLE is an online tool, data will also be collected on what particular tasks students do, when they do them, how long it takes them, and how they interact with other students. This collection of data can also be analyzed to characterize patterns of student use and how it compares to expert use of the system.

CIRCLE is available online at circle.cs.ndsu.nodak.edu.

References

1. Nist, L., Joseph, L.M.: Effectiveness and efficiency of flashcard drill instructional methods on Urban first-graders' word recognition, acquisition, maintenance, and generalization. Sch. Psychol. Rev. **37**(3), 294–308 (2008)

2. Kornell, N.: Optimising learning using flashcards: spacing is more effective than cramming. Appl. Cogn. Psychol. **23**(9), 1297–1317 (2009)
3. Game Fish Identification. http://appshopper.com/games/game-fish-identification
4. Engine Identification Game. http://www.americantorque.com/game/engine-id/
5. Geobirds. http://geobirds.com/play
6. Identify Rock Types Game. http://www.kidsgeo.com/geology-games/rocks-game.php
7. Letter Learning Game. http://kinderwebgames.com/a.html
8. Vygotsky, L.S.: Mind in Society: The Development of Higher Psychological Processes. (M. Cole, Trans.). Harvard University Press, Cambridge (1978)
9. Karpicke, J.D.: Retrieval-based learning: active retrieval promotes meaningful learning. Curr. Dir. Psychol. Sci. **21**(3), 157–163 (2012)
10. Montola, M.: Exploring the edge of the magic circle: defining pervasive games. In: Proceedings of DAC (2005)
11. Gaonkar, S., Li, J., Choudhury, R.R., Cox, L., Schmidt, A.: Micro-blog: sharing and querying content through mobile phones and social participation. In: Proceedings of the 6th International Conference on Mobile Systems, Applications, and Services. Breckenridge, CO, USA (2008)
12. Casey, S., Kirman, B., Rowland, D.: The gopher game: a social, mobile, locative game with user generated content and peer review. In: Proceedings of the International Conference on Advances in Computer Entertainment Technology. Salzburg, Austria (2007)
13. Lee, C.S., Goh, D. H.-L., Chua, A.Y.K., Ang, R.P.: Indagator: investigating perceived gratifications of an application that blends mobile content sharing with gameplay. J. Amer. Soc. Inf. Sci. Technol. **61**(6), 1244–1257 (2010)
14. Kukulska-Hulme, A., Traxler, J., Pettit, J.: Designed and user-generated activity in the mobile age. J. Learn. Des. **2**(1), 52–65 (2007)
15. Wijers, M., Jonker, V., Drijvers, P.: MobileMath: exploring mathematics outside the classroom. ZDM **42**(7), 789–799 (2010)
16. Grinter, R.E., Aoki, P.M., Szymanski, M.H., Thornton, J.D., Woodruff, A., Hurst, A.: Revisiting the visit: understanding how technology can shape the museum visit. In: Proceedings of the 2002 ACM Conference on CSCW. New Orleans, LA, USA (2002)
17. Schwabe, G., Göth, C.: Mobile learning with a mobile game: design and motivational effects. J. Comput. Assist. Learn. **21**(3), 204–216 (2005)
18. Perry, J., Rosenheck, L.: UbiqBio: a playful approach to learning biology with mobile games. In: 2012 Conference for the ISTE. San Diego, CA (2012)
19. Klopfer, E., Sheldon, J., Perry, J., Chen, V.H.H.: Ubiquitous games for learning (UbiqGames): Weatherlings, a worked example. J. Comput. Assist. Learn. **28**(5), 465–476 (2012)
20. Richardson, V.: Constructivist pedagogy. Teachers Coll. Rec. **105**(9), 1623–1640 (2003)
21. Palincsar, A.S.: Social constructivist perspectives on teaching and learning. Ann. Rev. Psychol. **49**(1), 345–375 (1998)
22. Deutsch, M.: A theory of co-operation and competition. Hum. Relat. **2**(2), 129–152 (1949)
23. Deutsch, M.: Cooperation and trust: some theoretical notes. In: Nebraska Symposium on Motivation, pp. 275–320. University of Nebraska Press, Oxford, England (1962)
24. Johnson, D.W.: Social psychology of education. Holt, Rinehart and Winston, New York (1970)
25. Johnson, D.W., Johnson, R.: Cooperation and Competition: Theory and Research. Interaction Book Company, Edina (1989)
26. Johnson, D.W., Johnson, R.T., Smith, K.: The state of cooperative learning in postsecondary and professional settings. Educ. Psychol. Rev. **19**(1), 15–29 (2007)

27. Norem-Hebeisen, A.A., Johnson, D.W.: The relationship between cooperative, competitive, and individualistic attitudes and differentiated aspects of self-esteem. J. Pers. **49**(4), 415–426 (1981)
28. Wang, X.H., Yang, B.: Why competition may discourage students from learning? Behav. Econ. Anal. Educ. Econ. **11**(2), 117–128 (2003)
29. Shindler, J.: Transformative classroom management: positive strategies to engage all students and promote a psychology of success. Jossey-Bass, San Francisco (2010)
30. Sharan, S., Sharan, Y.: Small-Group Teaching. Educational Technology Publications, Englewood Cliffs (1978)
31. Johnson, D.W., Johnson, R.T.: Living Together and Alone: Cooperative, Competitive, and Individualistic Learning. Prentice Hall, Englewood Cliffs (1991)
32. Kagan, S.: Cooperative Learning. Kagan Cooperative Learning, San Juan Capistrano (1994)
33. Slavin, R.E.: Cooperative Learning, 2nd edn. Allyn and Bacon, Boston (1995)
34. Brown, J.S., Collins, A., Duguid, P.: Situated cognition and the culture of learning. Educ. Res. **18**(1), 32–42 (1989)
35. Janis, I.L.: Victims of Groupthink. Houghton Mifflin Company, Boston (1972)
36. Koschmann, T., Kelson, A.C., Feltovich, P.J., Barrows, H.S.: Computer-supported problem based learning: a principled approach to the use of computers in collaborative learning. In: Koschmann, T. (ed.) CSCL: Theory and Practice of an Emerging Paradigm, p. 100. Lawrence Erlbaum Associates, Mahwah (1996)
37. Feltovich, P.J., Spiro, R.J., Coulson, R.L., Feltovich, J.: Collaboration within and among minds: mastering complexity, individually and in groups. In: Koschmann, T. (ed.) CSCL: Theory and Practice of an Emerging Paradigm, pp. 25–44. Lawrence Erlbaum Associates, Mahwah (1996)
38. Goldman, S.V.: Mediating microworlds: collaboration on high school science activities. In: Koschmann, T. (ed.) CSCL: Theory and Practice of an Emerging Paradigm, pp. 45–81. Lawrence Erlbaum Associates, Mahwah (1996)
39. Johnson, D.W., Johnson, R., Holubec, E.: Cooperation in the Classroom, 7th edn. Interaction Book Company, Edina (1998)
40. Soller, A.: Supporting social interaction in an intelligent collaborative learning system. IJAIED **12**, 40–62 (2001)
41. Wiliam, D.: What does Research say the Benefits of Formative Assessment are? Research Brief. National Council of Teachers of Mathematics, Reston (2007)
42. Brooke, J.: SUS: A Quick and Dirty Usability Scale. Usability Evaluation in Industry, pp. 189–194. Taylor & Francis, London (1996)

The PoSE Project: An Innovative Approach to Promote Healthy Postures in Schoolchildren

Ilaria Bortone[1](✉), Alberto Argentiero[1], Nadia Agnello[1],
Valentina Denetto[2], Cosimo Neglia[2], and Marco Benvenuto[2]

[1] KISS-Health Project (Knowledge Intensive Social Services for Health),
Mesagne, Italy
ilariabortone@gmail.com
http://kisshealth.it

[2] ISBEM, Euro Mediterranean Scientific Biomedical Institute, 72023 Mesagne, Italy

Abstract. Back pain in children and adolescents is quite common, so developing preventive strategies for back pain is highly desirable. This article describes a planned school-based postural education project (PoSE) to promote healthy behaviors among middle school students and their families and to moderate postural diseases. As first step, we evaluated which aspects of postural behaviors were integrated in children's lifestyle through a questionnaire. Then, the educational program consisted of interactive lessons on back posture and good principles both in class and at home. The strength of the participatory approach used in this study lies in the contribution to empowerment social change.

Keywords: Schoolchildren · Prevention · Posture · Back education · Engagement · Social · Empowerment

1 Introduction and Motivation

Recent epidemiological data showed that back pain starts early in life and prevalence rates increase rapidly during adolescence, reaching adult levels around the age of 18. Furthermore, back pain increases the risk of poor spinal health later in life, with all its well-known consequences, including very high societal costs [1]. Several authors considered long retained negative positions as a possible cause of postural diseases and they supposed their contribution in the development of pathological forms [2]. In this sense, early preventive interventions are desirable and during last decades back-care intervention studies in schoolchildren have been promoted supported by the European Guidelines regarding the prevention of back pain [3].

Considering the idea about three primary learning modalities (auditory, visual and kinesthetic), current interventions have focused on the first two showing positive evidences in terms of acquired knowledge and appropriate postural habits [4,5]. However, without sufficient student participation and engagement, classroom activities can not create proper pedagogical opportunities for student to

ⓒ Institute for Computer Sciences, Social Informatics and Telecommunications Engineering 2014
G. Vincenti et al. (Eds.): eLEOT 2014, LNICST 138, pp. 49–57, 2014.
DOI: 10.1007/978-3-319-13293-8_6

interact with content knowledge. The current state of art shows that the introduction of ICT resources to schools seems to have relatively little impact on the ways that teachers teach [6].

The objective of this study was to create a postural consciousness in young children and their families in order to moderate postural diseases by stimulating their bodily-kinesthetic intelligence. The school is the primary social environment of youth and no other institution has as much contact with children. In particular, middle school was selected as representing a strategic time and place in which to study interventions to influence postural behaviors on health. Children in the 1st to 3rd grades are generally 11–14 years old and in early adolescence and, as recent studies investigated, they are developmentally capable of increasing and assuming personal responsibility for behavior changes and choices [7].

The research team approached the Head of the Secondary School "Materdona Moro" in Mesagne, Italy, to introduce the KISS-Health Project (Knowledge Intensive Social Services for Health) and the opportunity to implement a school-based postural education program, called PoSE Project (Postural Education at School), to avoid the possible negative physical effects of retained bad postures. The KISS-Health has adopted recent developments in gesture-capture technologies, in particular the Microsoft Kinect® System, to recreate a Mobile Diagnostic Lab able to evaluate postural diseases [8,9]. Furthermore, the KISS-Health aims to introduce in the schools the idea of "Technological Learning", which is poised to become an even more important determinant of growth through its impact on innovation and the Kinect has the potential to facilitate the process.

The PoSE project provides principles that are based on working with people in environments, communities or settings in which they live and work: an Holistic process to evaluate and promote healthy postures in schoolchildren. Health promotion has moved beyond the provision of information and education to operate at many levels to empower people and communities to determine their needs for well-being. In this sense, the PoSE represents an Holistic Learning Model [10] with six defined key variables for learning: Attention, Motivation, Emotion, Memory, Physiology and Environment, with their individual determinants extruded. A lasting improvement in the safety and health of children and young people in school, or in other educational contexts, requires a preventive approach that considers: the physical, psychological and social factors; the school as a whole, as a relationship of organizational components, individual and environmental. A "holistic" approach aims to: (a) create or enhance the behaviors and perceptions of individuals in to health and safety in schools; (b) conceive the school as a workplace tailored to the needs of the students and teachers.

2   Materials and Methods

2.1   Subjects

We recruited pupils from the 1st, 2nd and 3rd grades (11–14 years of age) in the middle school of Mesagne, Italy. There were no exclusion criteria. Our aim was to include 813 participants for the intervention program and we enrolled 34

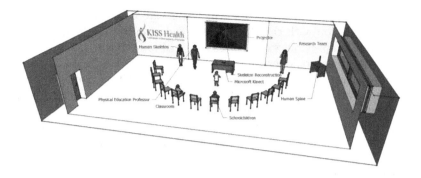

Fig. 1. Virtual reconstruction of the PoSE Scenario

classes in the project: 248 children for 1st grade, 283 children for 2nd grade and 282 children for 3rd grade classes. We also involved children's families in order to understand the social environment surrounding the young students.

2.2 Ethics and Data Collection

In order to deal with the problems set out above, where necessary, a request to guarantee the quality and the safety of the data will be send to the data Protection Commissioner entitled "Authorization to the processing of student and family data for scientific research", in observance to the Code for the protection of personal data (Provision of Guarantor No 2 of 16 June 2004, Official Gazette of August 14, 2004, No 190). Regarding ethical problems arising, we have achieved a positive opinion from Ethics Committees of the School. The data collection will be archived in KISS-Health data center to ensure the security in accordance with all applicable regulations. Students and their families were informed by the Head of the School about the preliminary process to assess the data. If necessary, we would recruit single groups of students and families to sign a written consent.

2.3 Design

The PoSE Project is a planned school-based postural education intervention to promote healthy behaviors and awareness among middle school students with the involvement of the class teachers during the school year. The project consists of three phases: Phase I, understanding the cultural level; Phase II, intervention program (Fig. 1); Phase III, evaluation for a socio-economic perspective.

Phase I: Understanding the cultural level. The PoSE Project expanded Physical Education (PE) from typical physical fitness and sports into the movements and postures associated with educational tasks. Previous experiences on similar approach can be found in [11]. The teachers were four Physical Education Professors from the pilot school, with several years of experience, and the KISS-Health team (a bioengineer, a biologist and a biotechnologist). At pre- and post-intervention, children completed a questionnaire at school with regard to their postural behaviors and social factors, which was elaborated by the KISS-Health group in collaboration with the PE teachers and a multidisciplinary team, taking in consideration previous experiences reported in literature [12]. To minimize socially desirable answers, questionnaires were signed with a code and they were informed about the anonymous data processing. In addition, guidelines on postural behaviors were provided for the class by teachers in order to optimize integration of the learned back posture principles.

Postural behaviors were questioned through 16 questions about: back posture principles during daily live (8 questions); postural behavior in class during lesson time (2 questions) and during studying at home (3 questions); postural aspects with regard to spinal loading during regularly sitting on a chair (3 questions). Socio-economic factors were investigated through 4 questions about: use of technological devices and internet applications (2 questions); lesson's contents (2 questions). A similar questionnaire with 22 questions was submitted to children's parents to be completed independently at home, but it was arranged to include other socio-economic factors, such as parental working activity (2 questions), educational level (2 questions) and their opinion about their children's education (3 questions).

Phase II: *Intervention Program.* The study was carried out over 8 days spread over a 2-week period in February and April 2014. The main issues of the educational program for school as taught in the middle school in Mesagne are summarized in Table 1.

The teaching methods involved more practical and interactive experiences with the use of various objects (human skeleton, human spine, ...), videos and games in order to install the relevant knowledge through different senses. We proposed a change in pedagogical practices by adopting educational technologies to contribute to successful teaching and learning.

Phase III: *Evaluation for a socio-economic perspective.* Traditionally economic evaluations involve the identifying, measuring and valuing both the inputs (costs) and outcomes (benefits) of alternative interventions [13]. The inputs and the outcomes included in this study depend on both the questions being addressed

Table 1. Content of the educational program for school.

Theme	Main Issues
The human body	The planes of motion
	The lower limbs - movement, pathologies
	The spine - structure, movement and posture
Sitting	Analysis of sitting position during the school day and at home
	The difference between comfortable sitting and correct sitting
	Sitting in front of the computer work-stations in school/home
Lifting/carrying	General aspects of lifting and carrying of different objects
	Lifting and carrying schoolbags

and the perspective of the study. For example, in our study, the education sector in a health promotion intervention (PoSE) may be compared to other uses, such as the teachers time for prevention, or the use of alternative equipment in terms of value for life-style. The main steps that will be developed through the project for a balanced socio-economic evaluation will be: (1) Life-style of students and families in the school life(input); (2) Digital divide of students and families (input); (3) Level of education (input). The focus of these results will be relevant in term of professional training, assessment of new technologies and adaptation of operational procedures for a health promotion intervention, like Postural Education at School.

2.4   Data Analysis

Statistical analysis was performed using SPSS®21.0. The pre-intervention data on children's and parents' postural behaviors during school time/work and daily activities were reported as prevalence and they were compared performing Fisher's exact Test. We considered as dichotomous variables the possible answers, assuming good postural behaviors as value 1 and incorrect behaviors as value 0.

3   Preliminary Results

Here we present the preliminary results of the PoSE Project related to Phase I. Table 2 presents group differences in personalized aspects of postural behavior conform a biomechanical favorable lifestyle between students and their parents. The non-responders' percentage (indicated as NR) was here reported, but it was not considered for the Fisher's exact Test. It should be considered that in the parents' test the question "When you make your work, do you stop your sitting activity?" was related to the question "Is your work sedentary?", which resulted positive for 31.4 % of all parents.

Significant differences were found for 10 of the 13 postural behaviors, while evaluation of the reports on some daily attitudes showed no differences between both groups. Further, the major part of the children reported that paying attention to the natural curve of their body, joining sport activity 3 times a week, carrying object as close as possible to their body and stopping their sitting activity were common habits (>60 % of all children). Similar results were reported by parents, except for joining sport activity and stopping their sitting activity (<42 %). A very limited percentage of children and their parents (<16 % of all) reported that they relax with lifted legs and place book on inclined surface. Finally, a large percentage of children and their parents reported they had included postural aspects preventing spinal loading during sitting activities (back rest use; arm support; feet on the floor).

Subsequently, we analyzed good postural attitudes between students grouped by class grade (1st, 2nd and 3rd grades). Only the results of significant differences are reported in Table 3. A large percentage of 1st grade students showed a better back posture awareness than the students of higher classes, while a higher

Table 2. Comparison of personalized good back posture principles between students and their parents (Fisher's exact Test).

Questions about postural behaviors	Students		Parents		p-value
	R(%)	NR(%)	R(%)	NR(%)	$* \leq 0.001$
					$** \leq 0.005$
Postural Behaviors					
Do you pay attention to the natural curve of your spine?	68.8	5.5	75.0	9.7	0.000*
Do you do sport 3 times a week?	63.8	5.2	35.8	10.3	0.000*
When you relax, how do you lie down?	14.0	7.3	15.7	11.2	0.176
When you lift an object, how do you do?	53.9	5.4	57.3	9.7	0.010*
Do you ask for help to lift a heavy object?	52.1	5.3	63.8	9.7	0.000*
Do you carry an object as close as possible to your body?	73.8	11.3	81.6	10.5	0.000*
Do you check the weight of schoolbag?	42.4	12.7	75.9	10.0	0.000*
When you read, how do you put books?	10.7	5.2	10.1	9.8	0.952
When you sit in classroom/at work, are you aware of your posture?	50.8	4.7	60.6	10.0	0.000*
When you make your homework/work, do you stop your sitting activity?	71.3	4.9	41.4	39.4	0.010*
When you sit on a chair with a backrest, do you use it?	76.1	4.9	67.6	10.8	0.049**
When you sit, how do you make that your arms are supported?	81.4	4.7	66.7	10.1	0.000*
When you sit, do you sustain your both feet to the ground?	73.3	4.7	69.2	11.7	0.485

percentage of 2nd and 3rd grade students reported changing their posture and interrupting their sitting activity as common habits.

4 Discussions

The main aim of the current study was to present an innovative approach to promote healthy postures in schoolchildren and to create a postural consciousness. The present total study sample consisted of 1516 subjects (only 9.2 % of parents and 4.3 % of students did not respond to the questionnaire). This sample size is relatively large compared to other intervention studies [11,12] and may suggest some general relevance. It is important to say that the children cooperated in an amazing way and they were excited about the initiative. We received also positive feedback from the families and the school management.

Table 3. Comparison of the number of students with good back posture principle grouped by class grades (Fisher's exact Test).

Postural behaviors	Students						p-value
	1st (%)		2nd (%)		3rd (%)		
	R(%)	NR(%)	R(%)	NR(%)	R(%)	NR(%)	*≤ 0.001
							**≤ 0.005
Do you pay attention to the natural curve of your spine?	77.8	4.0	64.0	5.3	65.6	7.1	0.001*
When you sit in classroom, are you aware of your posture?	61.7	2.4	47.7	4.9	44.3	6.4	0.001*
When you sit in classroom, do you change your posture?	63.3	3.6	72.1	4.2	77.7	6.7	< 0.001
When you make your homework, are you aware of your posture?	56.4	2.8	38.2	4.6	44.3	7.1	< 0.001
When you make your homework, do you stop your sitting activity?	66.1	2.8	76.0	4.2	74.5	6.4	0.003**

Comparable results to a previous study [12] can be found in the prevalence of children reporting that carrying an object as close as possible to the body, joining sport activities 3 times a week and preventing spinal loading were included postural aspects of their daily life. However, no previous studies have investigated the role of families and school in postural behaviors and awareness. A right knowledge of biomechanical favorable postural behavior is a necessary but not sufficient condition for the development of a conscious and healthy lifestyle with respect to good body mechanics. In this sense, the integration of good postural principles will be investigate with the results of the post-intervention questionnaire to explore more in depth the socio-economic perspectives (Phase III).

The Microsoft Kinect needs to be situated in combination with software and other hardware in order to create meaningful classroom interactions. In this preliminary phase, the sensor was introduced in the classroom environment as a support for teaching to impact on student participation, but subsequent works are required to exploit the potential of kinesthetic and gesture-based technologies in this context.

5   Perspectives and On-Going Work

The research team is currently working on the extension of the work by increasing the statistical sample both by number and by age group involving other schools in the pilot project. Furthermore, the temporal analysis will be extended in relation to the quantitative assessment of postural diseases that the KISS-Health Project will execute in the School with the Mobile Diagnostic Lab realized under this social innovation initiative [8,9]. To our knowledge, no previous studies have investigated the role of introducing educational technologies to vehicle preventive postural interventions. We are also exploring the possibility to submit a new questionnaire to both children and families with more specific questions about postural principles to avoid any possible confounding factors related to social desirable answers.

Acknowledgement. This work is partially supported by Italian Ministry for Education, University and Research (MIUR) in the framework of Smart Cities and Communities and Social Innovation in the framework of 2007–2013 National Operational Program for Research and Competitiveness (Grant PON04a3_00097).

References

1. Aartun, E., Degerfalk, A., Kentsdotter, L., Hestbaek, L.: Screening of the spine in adolescents: inter-and intra-rater reliability and measurement error of commonly used clinical tests. BMC Musculoskelet. Disord. **15**(1), 37 (2014)
2. Shalavina, A.S.: Qualitative and quantitative assessment of the state of the posture of junior school children. World Appl. Sci. J. **27**(7), 860–862 (2013)
3. COST B13: European guidelines for the management of low back pain. Eur. Spine. J. **15**(Suppl 2), S125S297 (2006)
4. Calvo-Muoz, I., Gmez-Conesa, A., Snchez-Meca, J.: Preventive physiotherapy interventions for back care in children and adolescents: a meta-analysis. BMC Musculoskelet. Disord. **13**(1), 152 (2012)
5. Kovacs, F., Oliver-Frontera, M., Plana, M. N., Royuela, A., Muriel, A., Gestoso, M.: Spanish back pain research network: improving schoolchildren's knowledge of methods for the prevention and management of low back pain: a cluster randomized controlled trial. Spine **36**(8), E505–E512 (2011)
6. Hsu, H.M.J.: The potential of kinect in education. Int. J. Inf. Educ. Tech. **1**(5), 365–370 (2011)
7. Venditti, E.M., Giles, C., Firrell, L.S., Zeveloff, A.D., Hirst, K., Marcus, M.D.: Interactive learning activities for the middle school classroom to promote healthy energy balance and decrease diabetes risk in the HEALTHY primary prevention trial. Health Promot. Pract. **15**(1), 55–62 (2014)
8. Bortone, I., Argentiero, A., Agnello, N., Sabato, S.S., Bucciero, A.: A two-stage approach to bring the postural assessment to masses: the KISS-Health Project. In: 2014 IEEE-EMBS International Conference on Biomedical and Health Informatics (BHI), pp. 371–374. IEEE, June 2014
9. Bucciero, A., Santo Sabato, S., Zappatore, M.: A biomechanical analysis system of posture. In: 8th International Conference on Pervasive Computing Technologies for Healthcare, Oldenburg (2014)

10. Riding, R., Rayner, S.: Cognitive Styles and Learning Strategies: Understanding Style Differences in Learning and Behavior. Routledge, London (2013)
11. Heyman, E., Dekel, H.: Ergonomics for children: an educational program for elementary school. Work J. Prev. Assess. Rehabil. **32**(3), 261–265 (2009)
12. Geldhof, E., Cardon, G., De Bourdeaudhuij, I., De Clercq, D.: Back posture education in elementary schoolchildren: a 2-year follow-up study. Eur. Spine J. **16**(6), 841–850 (2007)
13. Pommier, J., Guvel, M.R., Jourdan, D.: Evaluation of health promotion in schools: a realistic evaluation approach using mixed methods. BMC Public Health **10**(1), 43 (2010)

Experiential and Transformative Learning in an Informal Online Learning Environment: An Approach to Initiate Sustainable Changes

Efua Akoma[(✉)], Nichole Boutte-Heiniluoma, and Jacquelyn Petrovic

Ashford University, Clinton, USA
{efua.akoma,nichole.boutteheiniluoma}@ashford.edu,
petrojax@aol.com

Abstract. As the use of technology increased in educational settings, both availability and viability of online learning opportunities increased substantially. Research indicates that more and more institutions of higher learning are increasing online course offerings as a way to increase enrollment in formerly closed settings. Indeed, the use of online learning has paved the way for global connections in a once closed world. However, as a way of promoting the use of online technologies outside of the class environment, Ashford University has begun to promote sustainability efforts through their student Sociology Club. In this case, the use of a social networking site to connect faculty and students in an experiential learning environment was designed to help educate students while, at the same time, prompting community-based action no matter how geographic boundaries separated participants.

Keywords: Computer mediated communication · Computer supported collaborative learning · Experiential learning · LinkedIn · Sustainability · Transformative learning

1 Introduction

During its early years online education was ostracized in many areas in higher education. However, as time as passed, the stigma of participating in an online class or even obtaining a degree online has decreased. A recent study completed by The National Center for Education Statistics revealed 4.3 million undergraduate students, or 20 % of all undergraduates, took at least one distance education course in 2007–2008 [1]. This number climbed to 7.1 million undergraduates taking at least one online course in 2013 [2]. According to Allen and Seaman (2014), higher education institutions are acknowledging the extent to which online learning plays a role in their continued success with an increase from less than one half in 2002 to 66 % of institutions reporting online education is critical to their long term strategies in 2013.

Ashford University plays a critical role in the online learning programs and has a large online presence with over 58,100 students taking online class and 99 % (57, 235) of these pursuing their degree solely online [3]. Many of the students come into their online learning experience very familiar with technology while others become increasingly aware as they navigate their online classes. This familiarity, and in some

© Institute for Computer Sciences, Social Informatics and Telecommunications Engineering 2014
G. Vincenti et al. (Eds.): eLEOT 2014, LNICST 138, pp. 58–62, 2014.
DOI: 10.1007/978-3-319-13293-8_7

cases preference for, technology drives the creation of more learning arenas. The formal learning platform is essential in online learning platforms but informal learning experiences, particularly in collaborative modalities, are finding a home in the online learning experience as well. Investigating how this transpires and the best practices being implemented is an on-going process that continues to build upon this varied modality of knowledge acquisition. One element that deserves further investigation is group learning in the online learning environment.

2 Literature Review

Traditionally, students have presented pushback to group learning in the classroom [4] and because the online learning modality is one where individual interaction in the classroom is contingent on the individual's availability, group work can understandably be met with a lack luster response. After all, this kind of autonomy and ability to work on one's own time is a primary reason student's enroll in online programs. In the formal online learning environment, group projects also rely upon the participation of group members to produce a coherent and objective satisfying outcome to be submitted for evaluative purposes in a timely fashion. An informal computer supported collaborative learning (CSCL) approach alleviates many of these issues. This is primarily because students can log on and interact with the group in their own time while the group collectively adds to the body of data without reliance on each other in a time restricted way and the pressure of an evaluative grading process is alleviated. This method allows for autonomy while at the same time promoting group participation.

Using computer mediated communication (CMC) we are investigating how social media can be used informally for CSCL about sustainability initiatives for students in online learning programs as a transformative learning experience. The success of sustainability initiatives has been researched more widely in brick and mortar institutions, which give us insight into possible approaches for online learning platforms. Experiential and transformative learning in relation to sustainability is producing effective results in brick and mortar institutions through combining the hands-on elements with complimentary institutional philosophies and paradigms. Through experiencing, conceptualizing, analyzing and applying knowledge to real world issues [5], Texas University's "Common Experience" initiative connects experiences with knowledge about sustainability through activities that demonstrate practical purpose, and engage students in applying creativity, knowledge, and critical thinking to positively impact the campus, community and society in relation to sustainability. These efforts resulted in a shared vision and solution-discourse on sustainability [6]. Another example, the University of California, Davis uses "a personal 'Resource Consumption and Waste Audit'" [7] to engage students and involve them in sustainability practices beyond the theories. Both the 'Common Experience' and the 'Resource Consumption and Waste Audit' motivate their educational communities to change their behaviors in regards to sustainability.

Many institutions of higher education, in consideration of the United Nation's call for sustainability education [8], have implemented or expanded traditional, hybrid and distance curricula and programs in sustainability [9]. In *Many Roads Lead to Sustainability: a Process-oriented Analysis of Change in Higher Education*, Barth notes the results of a multi-case study analyzing the process of implementing sustainability, and concludes that the influencing factors are "student-led change from informal to formal learning, sustainability as a concern in campus operation; and sustainability as a unique selling-point" [10]. Reshaped through the processes of action, reflection, and knowledge, students emerging from traditional brick and mortar institutions, which implement experiential/transformative pedagogical practices, are empowered to affect social change. This research has shown that collaborative learner outcomes have been successful at transferring learning into social action beyond the classroom.

While effective in the traditional institutions of higher education, the online learning environment encounters unique challenges to enacting concrete change through experiential/transformative learning because it involves critical reflection on assumptions that result from critical-dialectical discourse to test the validity of the transformation [11]. To facilitate learners encountering the dilemma of sustainability in the distance education environment, there are issues that need to be examined and accounted for. Connecting to others who are exploring new roles, finding options in relation to sustainability, and planning a course of action that allows for building competencies and integrating new perspectives into life to affect social change, means that institutions employing online learning modalities must find avenues that permit the written word to transcend distance and generate co-learner experiences [12]. It is these avenues that have the ability to bridge the physical distance between like-minded students who are focused on sustainability.

Both experiential and transformative learning require reflection beyond the facts. However, opportunities for students to take initiative and engage with each other and society at large can pose challenges in the relative autonomous environment of the online classroom. Educators and institutions of online learning can cultivate the process of experiential and transformative learning in relation to issues of sustainability by employing interactive synchronous and asynchronous communication that gives impetus to the understanding of reality. Epistemology that accurately reflects the reality of the need for sustainability to transcend the knowledge realm, evolve into action, and prompts a shift in current assumptions can become the foundation for transferring knowledge into social action outside the classroom will be essential to online learning models on sustainability.

As higher education in online environments evolve, the importance of experiential and transformative learning's ability to generate social change in relation to sustainability issues hinges on how well it can work to create actions that inspire reflection about how humanity is collectively and individually embedded and interconnected in Earth's ecological systems. This demands that online learning arenas reach beyond the known limits of technology and work to employ experiences and transformative pedagogical strategies that inspire a shift to a systemic and collective action and thought in relation to sustainability in a globalized learning environment.

3 Current Study

Using the Time, Interaction and Performance (TIP) theory, we posit the collaborative social media entity LinkedIn can be used informally for CSCL about sustainability with students enrolled in online learning programs to cultivate a transformative learning experience. This theory proposes three things work simultaneously in group collaborations; (1) production function, which is the collaborative efforts towards task completion, (2) group wellbeing indicated by maintaining positive and consistent communication among the group members and, (3) supporting the members of the group as necessary [13]. Research suggests that individual and competitive efforts in CSCL are less effective than collaborative learning [14]. Johnson and Johnson (1996) also found CSCL promotes greater quantity and quality of daily achievement, greater mastery and application of factual information and greater success in problem solving. Because LinkedIn is a many-to-many interfaced modality, the potential to create collective intelligence or intelligence born of collaborative efforts is tenable. Our hypothesis is- Is an informal platform such as LinkedIn is a useful tool to facilitate transformative learning when used as an informal computer supported collaborative learning environment evidenced by 30 % or more of the membership participating in the sustainability challenge. Our research question- Is an informal online platform a useful tool to result in transformative learning?

Efforts to accomplish this initiative have included introducing tasks related to sustainable behaviors that help students understand not only why certain behaviors should be implemented but also details on how to implement them. The tasks vary in complexity but initial tasks require small changes with easy to follow instructions and increase in complexity as time passes and greater familiarity with sustainable practices is gained. Feedback is being required from participants on the results of their efforts, which serves to reinforce participation and provide support for continued interactions. There is an increased likelihood that students will engage in shared behavior if there is a sense of reciprocity in the sharing process. Recent research suggests "that using online social networks as educational platforms may support learners in forming social connections with others while they collaborate to share ideas, create products, construct identities, and receive timely feedback" [15]. For the purposes of this study, we are utilizing the Ashford University Sociology Club developed by the sociology program, which has been housed in LinkedIn for the past several months.

While a structured initiative such as the one we are currently conducting has not yet been tested for any other initiative in the sociology club, interactions among students in the club have been robust and consistent thus far. Interest has been expressed in understanding the interconnectedness of humanity as well as learning more and implementing behaviors that improve interactions between people locally and globally. This approach to initiate sustainable changes is the logical step in the evolution of the club as well as the first step in testing the grounds for working on sustainability initiatives in an informal learning environment using the many-to-many interface, LinkedIn.

References

1. Aud, S., Hussar, W., Kena, G.: The Condition of Education 2011. Institute of Education Sciences. National Center for Educational Statistics (2011). https://nces.ed.gov/pubsearch/pubsinfo.asp?pubid=2011033
2. Allen, I.E., Seaman, J.: Grade Change: Tracking Online Education in the United States, 2013 (2014). http://www.onlinelearningsurvey.com/reports/gradechange.pdf
3. Ashford University Institutional Research.: Behind the Numbers (2013). http://assessment.ashford.edu/behind-numbers/institutional-data
4. Dirkx, J., Smith, R.: Thinking out of a bowl of Spaghetti: learning to learn in online collaborative groups. In: Roberts, T.S. (ed.) Online Collaborative Learning: Theory and Practice. Information Science Publications, Hershey (2004)
5. O'Sullivan, E.V., Morrell, A., O'Connor, M.A.: Expanding the Boundaries of Transformative Learning. Palgrave, New York (2002)
6. Lopez, O.S.: Creating a sustainable university and community through a common experience. Int. J. Sustain. High. Educ. **14**(3), 291–309 (2013)
7. Savageau, A.E.: Let's get personal: Making sustainability tangible to students. Int. J. Sustain. High. Educ. **14**(1), 15–24 (2013)
8. UNESCO.: Education for sustainable development. United Nations Educational, Scientific, and Cultural Organization (2014). https://en.unesco.org/themes/education-sustainable-development
9. Owens, K.S., Remington, S.M.: Researching ocean acidification in general chemistry. Curriculum for the Bioregion (2009). http://serc.carleton.edu/bioregion/examples/59207.html
10. Barth, M.: Many Roads Lead to Sustainability: A Process-oriented Analysis of Change in Higher Education (2013)
11. Biesta, G.J.J., Miedema, S.: Instruction or pedagogy? The need for a transformative conception of education. Teach. Teacher Educ. **18**, 173–181 (2002)
12. Meyers, S.A.: Using transformative pedagogy when teaching online. Coll. Teach. **56**, 219–224 (2008)
13. McGrath, J.: Time, interaction and performance. Small Group Res. **22**(2), 147–174 (1991)
14. Johnson, D., Johnson, R.: Cooperation and the use of technology. In: Jonassen, D.H. (ed.) Handbook of Research for Educational Communications and Technology. Macmillan Library Reference, New York (1996)
15. Veletsianos, G., Navarrete, C.: Online social networks as formal learning environments: learner experiences and activities. Int. Rev. Res. Open Distance Learn. **13**(1), 144–166 (2012). http://www.irrodl.org/index.php/irrodl/article/view/1078/2077

Legal Risk Management: A Best Practice for e-Learning Legal Issues

Carlo Bucciero[✉]

University of Salento, Lecce, Italy
carlo.bucciero@libero.it,
bucciero.carlo@ordavvle.legalmail.it

Abstract. On-line education is a form of distance education" [8] and is usually defined as "An educational system in which the learner is autonomous and separated from his teacher by space and time, so that communication is by print, electronic, or other non-human medium" [12]. So - basic intent of e-learning is a moral good - making education available to those who have been deprived of it because location or expense or other circumstance is the main reason of on-line education. If ethical risks and vulnerabilities have to be acknowledged and to be addressed in the process, mainly eliminating the deepest reasons, legal issues have to be managed creating a best practice in order to protect both trainers and learners. In this way, legal risk management [16] is an innovative methodological approach aimed to integrated legal critical's management to prevent, or to minimize, the occurrence of legal risks associated with them.

Keywords: e-Learning · e-Education · Training on line · Legal risk management · Ethical risk · Legal risk · Data protection · Intellectual property · Best practice · Integrated management · Legal security

1 Introduction

This paper is based on the legal issues related to e-learning, e-education and training on-line and also suggests an integrated management of the related risks [14]. Legal risks can be defined as the negative consequences to enterprise arising from non-compliance of laws, directives and regulations. So, these negative consequences are always the result of decisions contrary to the law. Therefore, decision-makers have to know legal issues related to the use of e-learning services; they have to identify areas of critical issues and recognize relevant regulations; they have to avoid making choices contrary to the law that would lead to personal and corporate responsibility. For these purposes, legal risk management aims to be a best practice for e-learning companies, protecting both trainers and learners [10].

2 Research

This research is focused on management of legal risks. In the literature there isn't a real culture of integrated management about legal issues.

© Institute for Computer Sciences, Social Informatics and Telecommunications Engineering 2014
G. Vincenti et al. (Eds.): eLEOT 2014, LNICST 138, pp. 63–67, 2014.
DOI: 10.1007/978-3-319-13293-8_8

Similarly, literature reveals scant explicit concern in online education and e-Learning: e-Learning companies don't use their resources to create a system of integrated management and legal issues are usually managed individually; there isn't any process that can handle the connections between different risks.

To fill this methodological void is a new challenge for modern educational institutions and an important opportunity for the growth of e-learning and education on line [1]; research about e-learning must continue to investigate legal aspects, improve their integration, creating economies of scope through legal security of trainers and learners.

3 e-Learning: Ethic Values and Legal Issues

In a study of American Council on Education [6], R. A. Fass described early patterns of inappropriate behavior in e-Learning and identified the following categories of academic fraud in the e-Learning environment:

- *inappropriate assistance on examinations;*
- *misuse of sources on papers and projects;*
- *writing assistance and other inappropriate tutoring;*
- *misrepresentation in the collection and reporting of data;*
- *improper use of academic resources; disrespect for the work of others;*
- *lack of protection for human subjects in research;*
- *breaches of computer ethics;*
- *lack of adherence to copyright and copy-protection;*
- *inappropriate assistance to others;*
- *lack of adherence to academic regulations.*

The lack of ethic values is the real cause of academic fraud in e-learning, as is the case on campus, although dynamics are accentuated in the e-Learning environment by the phenomenon of psychological distance [5, 13]; e-Learning companies that have to manage ethical risks and their vulnerabilities [4], and also the legal issues [3], create the best practice in order to protect trainers and learners.

If ethic problems management is mainly linked to a rediscovery of lost values [7], in terms of efficiency and effectiveness a better management of legal issues is connected with an integrated approach. Main e-learning legal issues - identified in data protection, intellectual property [15], e-security, cybercrime, e-commerce - can be managed together, creating scope economies.

E-learning companies can achieve different goals with the same inputs (ex. same resources, same equipment, same know-how). By a complex process it is possible to manage different legal risks according to relatively fixed reports. To this end, a risk management of legal criticalities prevents the occurrence of connected risks or it minimizes negative impacts, representing a growth opportunity for the company [17].

4 Legal Risk Management: An Example of Best Practice

Legal risk management is an innovative methodological approach aimed at integrated managing of legal criticals and it is based on a series of activities designed to prevent the occurrence of legal risks associated with them, or at least, to minimize their negative impacts on the company.

A global vision of legal risks related to the activity brings benefits in terms of time, cost and company organization. An integrated management plan avoids litigations or minimizes the possibility of occurrence, saving economic resources; improves processes making them safer and reducing time; choose the most suitable human resources to the objectives to be pursued; improves quality of products and services.

To look at risk as opportunity is the challenge of legal risk management and it becomes a real key success factor for the company. In particular, ICT companies have to be able to manage risks and opportunities: technological innovation, fatally impacts legal issues [9]. These companies are confronted with a constantly changing reality, which forces them to manage law changing [11]. ICT products and services require a legal risk management activity, with a protection of competitive advantage intrinsically linked to their introduction and to their use.

In this way, e-Learning, e-education and training on-line type companies have to start a new challenge, realizing a best practice of integrated management of legal issues in order to protect trainers and learners. Deming cycle (plan-do-check-act) helps e-companies in building an integrated protection system to manage main legal risks in data protection [2], intellectual property, e-security, cybercrime, e-commerce [18]. Through legal risk identification, analysis, assessment and control, they can realize a real best practice, taking care the rights of trainers and learners.

As shown in Fig. 1, first step is legal risk identification: predict, detect and decline all the potential legal risks connected to specific e-learning services; second step is legal risk analysis of all the potential risks previously identified. Then, it's necessary to do a legal risk assessment to predict the potential loss and the probability of occurrence of legal risks connected to e-learning, ensuring also the company's ability to bear the risks identified. Last step consists in legal risk control: e-companies have to define technical and legal strategies to control risks through the elimination or reduction of all the critical issues within the physiological limits.

Fig. 1. Legal Risk Management process

5 Conclusions

E-Learning, e-education and training on-line inevitably have impact on ethical and legal issues [13]. Ethic issues find an appropriate solution in the rediscovery of lost moral values; otherwise, legal risks have to be managed through an integrated process, in order to protect trainers and learners.

The Legal risk management is an integrated approach aimed to prevent the occurrence of legal risks or to minimize their negative impacts; through the Deming cycle (plan-do-check-act), legal risk management is able to control legal risks, improving legal security of processes. In this way, e-companies can achieve different goals with the same inputs (same resources, same equipment, same know-how...), creating economies of scope through legal security of trainers and learners.

So, legal risk management is a real best practice, able to combine technological innovation and web 2.0 security in legal matters, and able to protect the competitive advantage related to e-learning services.

Acknowledgments. Unione Europea (UE) - Ministero dell'Istruzione, dell'Università e della Ricerca (MIUR) - Ministero dello Sviluppo Economico (MISE) - Regione Puglia - Università del Salento - Universus CSEI Consorzio Interuniversitario per la Formazione e l'Innovazione - Isbem Istituto Scientifico Biomedico Euro Mediterraneo - HSEPGEST "Health, Safety and Environmental Protection Manager & Consultant" - National Operational Programme "Research and Competitiveness 2007–2013" Convergence Regions AXIS I - Support to structural change - Operational Objective: Scientific-technological areas generating processes of transformation of the production system and creating new sectors Action: Interventions in support of industrial research Decree directorial of 18 January 2010 no. 01/Ric.

References

1. Babbie, E.: The Practice of Social Research. Wadsworth Publishing Company, Belmont (1992)
2. Bolognini, L., Fulco, D., Paganini, P.: Next privacy. Il futuro dei nostri dati nell'era digitale, Etas (2010)
3. Bravo, F.: Responsabilità delle società da reato ex d.lgs. 231/2001. Il controllo sociale della criminalità economica e i reati informatici. Clueb (2010)
4. Brown, T.: Ethics in eLearning. In: Workshop for Net Business Ethics. Honolulu, United States (2008)
5. Carsten Stahl, B.: Ethical Issues in E-teaching - a Theoretical Framework (2002)
6. Fass, R.A.: Cheating and plagiarism. In: May, W.W. (ed.) Ethics and Higher Education, pp. 170–184. Macmillan Publishing Company and American Council on Education, New York (1990)
7. Johnson, D.G.: Computer Ethics, 3rd edn. Prentice Hall, Upper Saddle River (2001)
8. Ko, S., Rosen, S.: Teaching Online: A Practical Guide. Houghton Mifflin Company, Boston (2001)
9. Langford, D.: Beyond human control - some implications of today's internet. In: Pourciau, L.J. (ed.) Ethics and Electronic Information in the 21st Century, pp. 65–75. Purdue University press, West Lafayette (1999)

10. Lee. S.: Background Issues to Online Teaching: Tools & Projects. In: Lee, Stuart et al. (eds.) Online Teaching: Tools & Projects (2001). http://info.ox.ac.uk//jtap/reports/teaching/. Accessed 23 Oct 2001
11. Mason, R.O., Mason, F., Culnan, M.: Ethics of Information Management. SAGE, Thousand Oaks (1995)
12. Moore, M.G., cited in Matshazi, M.J.: In Search for a Distance Education Model: A Look at Practices and Experiences in the Scandinavian Countries. Centre for International Development Studies, University of Oslo, Oslo (1988)
13. Mpofu, S.: University of Namibia: Ethics and legal issues in online teaching. www.col.org/pcf2/papers%5Cmpofu.pdf
14. Pellerino, G., Bucciero, C.: Rischi e opportunità di natura giuridica connessi alla creazione di una piattaforma di condivisione dati per i knowledge workers. Aica, Mondo Digitale, Torino (2011)
15. Rice, C.: Copyright and Fair Use. Stanford University Libraries (1998). http://fairuse.stanford.edu/rice.html
16. Trzaskowski, J.: Legal Risk Management - Some Reflections. Article, DJØF Publishing, Copenhagen (2005)
17. Trzaskowski, J.: Legal risk management in electronic commerce -managing the risk of cross-border law enforcement Book. Ph.D. Thesis, Ex Tuto Publishing (2005)
18. Trzaskowski, J.: Legal risk management in a global, Electronic marketplace. A Proactive Approach. Scand. Stud. Law **49**, 319–337 (2006)

From Planning to Launching MOOCs: Guidelines and Tips from GeorgetownX

Dedra Demaree$^{(\boxtimes)}$, Anna Kruse, Susan Pennestri, Janet Russell,
Theresa Schlafly, and Yianna Vovides

Center for New Designs in Learning and Scholarship, Georgetown University,
3520 Prospect St. NW #314, Washington DC 20057, USA
{dd817,alk34,sqp,jsr49,tbs27,yvll}@georgetown.edu

Abstract. This paper presents guidelines and tips from the Massive Open Online Course (MOOC) creation process at Georgetown University's Center for New Designs in Learning and Scholarship (CNDLS). Topics address the initial planning phase; core elements for MOOC design; the overall instructional design process; the video planning and production process; documentation; copyright; and quality assurance. This paper is meant to provide general guidelines and points to consider but is not intended as a complete guide for MOOC creation.

Keywords: Guideline · Instructional design · MOOC · Online course

1 Introduction

In December 2012, Georgetown University (GU) established ITEL (the Initiative for Technology-Enhanced Learning), an internal grant program administered through the Center for New Designs in Learning and Scholarship (CNDLS). ITEL projects explore new approaches to interactive learning, including the redesign of large introductory courses, cross-disciplinary learning environments, and the development of massive open online courses (MOOCs [1]) in partnership with edX. MOOCs are free and open to anyone and intended for a general audience. CNDLS administers the MOOCs using a team-based approach in conjunction with the GU faculty and other campus partners such as the library. The CNDLS MOOC team includes specialists in project management, videography, graphic design, and instructional design.

As of April 2014, GU has launched two MOOCs (Globalization's Winners and Losers: Challenges for Developed and Developing Countries in the fall of 2013, and Introduction to Bioethics in the spring of 2014), has a third MOOC (Genomic Medicine gets Personal) ready to launch in June 2014, and two more launching in the fall of 2014 (The Divine Comedy: Dante's Journey to Freedom, and Terrorism and Counterterrorism). The GU MOOCs are hosted on edX and are referred to as GeorgetownX courses.

Since the initial planning of the first GeorgetownX course, CNDLS has maintained an effort to document our MOOC creation process, develop instructional design templates, streamline workflow, and conduct research on the efficacy of our design process (the details of the research plan are beyond the scope of this paper). This paper provides

© Institute for Computer Sciences, Social Informatics and Telecommunications Engineering 2014
G. Vincenti et al. (Eds.): eLEOT 2014, LNICST 138, pp. 68–75, 2014.
DOI: 10.1007/978-3-319-13293-8_9

some general guidelines and points to consider while planning a MOOC. This paper is intended to give a sense of the overall course planning and production process, and is not to be taken as a complete guide.

2 Initial Planning

Before MOOC content is created, there are several pre-planning steps that are critical for informing the process. These planning steps were adopted from a homework assignment in an ELI (Educause Learning Initiative) short course on Designing and Delivering a Quality MOOC [2] and the checklist the course utilized was adapted from Ray Schroeder [3].

- It is critical to identify the purpose of the course and the target audience, and be familiar with the open education philosophy [4] of a MOOC.
- A timeline should be created with detailed tasks (see section four of this paper).
- Plan should be made for communications such as marketing the course to potential enrollees, managing regular emails to enrolled students, and using social networking (not addressed in this paper).
- The objectives for offering the course should be identified, including determining the optimum time frame for the course, and conceptualizing a course design (such as open, structured, or non-linear – the GeorgetownX courses are all in a structured format meaning students are encouraged to progress linearly through the course on a specific timeline) and release format (for examples releasing all the content at launch or releasing it on a week-by-week basis).
- Broad learning outcomes should be specified along with how they will be assessed and what level of achievement will be considered acceptable for receiving a course completion certificate.
- An assessment should be made of needed and available resources including technologies, general staffing and specialized human resources needs, space needs (such as for filming), what kind of assessments and feedback will be desired for students during the course, and how the course materials will be archived and/or repackaged after the initial deployment of the course (for example, GU is repackaging some MOOC content on DigitalGeorgetown which includes a GU Institutional Repository).
- Plans should be put in place for both faculty and staff development and handling potential needs of enrolled students, including plans for dealing with disruptions or challenges.

3 Common Core Elements for GeorgetownX MOOCs

Following best practices for online course design, CNDLS created a list of common core elements for our GeorgetownX courses. With these elements forming a common base for learning design and assessment, course design teams and faculty are better able to focus their time on experimentation within the MOOC space, ultimately enabling evidence-based learning design decisions for deeper learning. (Note this list does not include the communications plan, including managing emails, Facebook, and Twitter.)

Elements for the overall course:

- Use GeorgetownX Syllabus Template (including a course description with key learning outcomes, descriptions of faculty, a detailed course content outline, expectations for participation, certification, and faculty communication, netiquette guidelines, and academic integrity)
- Pre- and post-course surveys which include demographics, reasons for enrolling in the course and desired outcomes, and the Communities of Inquiry survey [5] for assessing the course design (along with the course analytics)
- Asynchronous engagement using frequent prompts for students to post on the Discussion Board and polling questions throughout the course
- Self-assessment questions where students compare their answer against an instructor-written response and grade themselves based on a provided rubric
- Objective questions such as multiple choice, multiple mark, numerical input, and dropdown for both formative and summative assessment
- Orienting banners for the course and for each sub-section
- Navigation instructions on every course page

Elements to include on the course Landing Page:

- Welcome text and video from lead faculty
- Links to course surveys
- Guidance on how to get started as a student in the course
- Handouts section including syllabus and learning checklist

A Course Overview as the first section to orient students including: What is the course about? What does the course include? What will I learn in the course? How do I use the course features?

Recommended section-level course structure includes:

- Introduction including learning outcomes, and video lead-in
- Transcribed video content with learning objectives stated, a placeholder for student notes (CNDLS uses the edX discussion boards), and faculty-provided notes
- Aligned formative assessment questions for each video
- Conclusion and Looking Ahead section including what to expect next, and a placeholder for student questions to be posted via the discussion boards including instructions on how to up-vote questions
- Summative quiz or exam questions for the section and/or homework assignments
- A placeholder for faculty and/or teaching assistants to respond to the most highly up-voted questions from students on the discussion boards.

4 Creating a Timeline

Several factors contribute to the substantial amount of time needed to complete preparations for a MOOC. Faculty and course team members should be prepared to dedicate a significant amount of time to planning, filming, reviewing footage, creating assessments, etc. Substantial time is required to create video content, including adding graphics and transcripts to the videos. The instructional design process is lengthy and involves coordination with many other aspects including scripting and filming. Time also needs to be devoted to training a team of people to build out the course including creating, testing, and proofreading assessments within edX.

In order to maintain instructional alignment, scripts for video production and other courseware projects (assessment design, site architecture) need to be based on a detailed course alignment document to ensure that individual teams are able to work relatively independently and stay on track with the timeline.

Once the overall course outline and syllabus has been created, edX recommends putting together a single representative week of the course within edX (including text, video and assessments). This Mock Week is an excellent way to test the workflow and estimate timing for producing the remainder of the course.

All content should be ready by at least 2 weeks before the course launch date to allow time for testing, quality assurance, and so forth. Table 1 below shows a sample, fairly fast-paced, 6 months timeline for creating a high-impact MOOC.

5   Instructional Design Process

CNDLS adheres to instructional design principles and a design-based research [6] approach in the development of the curriculum for each GeorgetownX course. This is conducted with the intention of increasing learner engagement and therefore retention and achievement of the desired learning outcomes. The instructional designers at CNDLS identified access, retention, and achievement as factors that influence learner activity in MOOCs. The key factors influencing a learner's own desired learning outcomes are learners' academic goals, confidence, and feeling of connectedness to the learning environment [7].

Another critical step in the instructional design process focuses on mapping learner engagement within edX to key concepts which are themselves aligned with the learning outcomes and individual assessment questions, including discussion threads. Even though it is time-consuming to achieve this level of mapping, the level of documentation is a required part of the instructional design process for all GeorgetownX courses as part of quality assurance.

The Community of Inquiry (CoI) model is used to provide consistency across the different GeorgetownX courses. The CoI model, proposed by Garrison and Archer [5], has been used to support design of and assessment in online learning environments. At Georgetown, CoI is being used to enable the researchers to create a learning analytics model that addresses different types of online presences in relation to engagement, retention, and learning outcomes to allow for more precise course design modifications in future iterations of the courses (detailed in a separate publication).

Early on in the design process, the course design team should begin thinking about and deciding on the major topics of the course and learning objectives for the course. The Instructional Design team from CNDLS works with the course team to complete a chart for aligning the content as it becomes more specific and detailed. Then, once the

Table 1. Sample course construction timeline, # indicates week of the course, sample table is for a 10 weeks course, so for example (#3, #4) means weeks 3 and 4 of the course.

Months until launch	First half of the month	Second half of the month
6	Confirm sequence of topics, begin instructional design work with faculty (#1, #2), confirm filming locations	Schedule filming dates, begin scripting, continue instructional design work on alignment with learning objectives, draft detailed course overview document, begin copyright permissions work including preliminary reading list for entire course
5	Continue scripting, begin filming, continue instructional design work	Finish filming, begin editing, discussing graphics, continue individual instructional design work, schedule filming dates/locations with faculty (#3, #4)
4	Complete filming, editing, graphics, continue individual instructional design work (#3, #4)	Mock week completed? Continue copyright permissions work, begin scripting, filming, editing (#3, #4), continue work on assessments with faculty (#3, #4), begin instructional design work (#5, #6)
3	Continue filming, editing (faculty #3, #4), continue individual instructional design work (#5, #6) begin scripting, filming, editing (faculty #5, #6)	Complete filming, editing, graphics (#3, #4, #5, #6), begin instructional design work with remaining faculty (#7–#10)
2	Begin scripting, filming, editing (#7–#10), continue work on assessments, readings	Reading list completed for entire course, copyright approval finalized, finalize syllabus (certificate requirements, etc.), all filming completed, X # of weeks drafted in edX Studio
1	Assessments completed, final edits to course sequencing, etc.: all weeks up in Studio	QA; Testing; Transcript review
0	Launch	Launch

topics and objectives are solidified (along with who will be providing instruction for each section), they work on identifying subtopics, planning content delivery and readings for those subtopics, activities that will not be assessed (discussion board, etc.), and assessments that will demonstrate accomplishment of the objectives for those subtopics (formative assessment questions, quizzes, exams and homework).

Table 2 provides a checklist for the instructional design and development tasks for GeorgetownX development.

Table 2. Checklist for instructional design and development tasks

Task
☐ Course-level learning goals confirmed
☐ Learning objectives for each class session in relation to the course-level goals confirmed
☐ Course content outline aligned with learning objectives
☐ Course material selected
☐ Course management confirmed (outputs go into syllabus)
☐ Course structure (section, sub-section, units) confirmed
☐ Learner engagement techniques (such as activities, discussion board prompts, and polling questions) determined
☐ Course components confirmed based on learner engagement plan
☐ Course syllabus and calendar of activities completed
☐ Course development within edX completed
☐ edX course environment evaluation and pre-launch testing completed

6 Video Scripting, Filming, and Editing

Prior to filming actual content, CNDLS conducts a "test filming" session to test out different locations, setups, and lecture delivery styles. Once this footage has been reviewed and an approach has been decided on, actual filming will begin.

Faculty should plan their notes such that video content is divided into short segments of approximately 5–7 min each. Script outlines and any notes or slides are acquired several days prior to filming. These do not need to be word-for-word scripts, but rather detailed enough outlines to allow someone who is not familiar with the content to follow along. This is critical for several reasons, such as:

- Ensuring that all needed topics have been covered;
- Keeping track of timing during the filming process;
- Confirming consistency and accuracy of terminology, numerical examples, etc.; and
- Providing a common reference point for videographers, video editors, instructional designers, teaching assistants, and others.

These scripts are also used for initial alignment of video segments to learning objectives, and to brainstorm possible assessments for each segment.

As a very general rule of thumb, a 2 h session should be sufficient to cover approximately 30 min worth of edited content. During the shoot, segments are filmed multiple times, and content may need to be filmed in multiple locations. Later retakes may also be necessary. The content should be filmed in short segments and will undergo substantial editing, so faculty need not feel pressured to deliver long sections in single takes. Because filming is very tiring, multiple sessions with the same faculty member should not be planned in a single day. Instead, CNDLS uses time following a shoot for footage review and planning.

During the filming, it is essential to have someone present who can act as a content expert, such as a TA or other course team member. This person will follow along with the outline and try to catch any omissions or mistakes, helping to avoid later retakes.

Someone else should also be present to take notes that will later aid the video team in editing the raw footage. With the video script outlines and notes, the video team can create rough edits of the footage for faculty review.

7 Documenting Course Progress

In order to coordinate the various course elements, CNDLS organizes its documents and processes using Google Drive. Folders are populated for budget, graphics, instructional design documents, meeting notes, progress reports, timelines, video, and working documents. The working documents folder includes a sub-folder for copyright materials, assessments, polling questions and discussion board prompts, scripts and notes for each week of the course, and the course syllabus.

One document CNDLS finds particularly useful for coordination is our Google spreadsheet for categorized assessments and videos. This spreadsheet contains a tab for assessments grouped by week/topic, where problems are aligned with the learning objectives, and includes the question, question type, key, provided explanation, and type of learning this assessment supports (using Bloom's taxonomy [8]). A second tab is for video links and includes the video titles, the status (i.e. needs graphics, content approved by...), and the link for viewing the video. Other tabs include progress tracking and transcription details. This document serves multiple needs: it provides a backup for all information that ends up in edX, it allows for the video team and learning design team to do development simultaneously and stay coordinated, and it provides a simple way to send content to course faculty for approval.

8 Readings and Copyright

At GU it is the responsibility of the course team to obtain copyright clearance for any readings, images, and video clips in consultation with university librarians. This process should begin as soon as possible as it can be quite time-consuming. Until clearance has been obtained, direct references to specific materials should be avoided in video content (or alternate versions should be filmed).

9 Quality Assurances

There are several different types of quality assurance that need to happen while building a MOOC.

- While filming, the course team will watch for accidental mistakes so that reshooting can happen immediately. In reviewing footage, they will check again for inaccuracies and inconsistencies. The edited video is then sent for transcription and a course team member(s) conducts a quality check of the transcript.
- With assessments, it is important to double-check the veracity of the answers to questions with determined answers (e.g. multiple choice, dropdown).

- With course resource pages and other content, a team member will need to check that all author names, readings, etc. are accurately represented.
- There will also need to be quality assurance and testing of the completed course in the edX platform. This will include running through a trial version of the course to check for any misplacements of content, functionality of all interactions, functionality of all links, and integrity of grammar/spelling.

10 Efficacy of the GeorgetownX Process

The process of developing a MOOC is a substantial time commitment. The GeorgetownX process has been carefully vetted by CNDLS for the purpose of delivering a MOOC that has strong instructional design leading to the potential for higher-than-average student retention rates and evidence of design efficacy (to be reported in a separate publication). Although the MOOC development process outlined in this paper is complex, it has the potential to lead to a high-impact student experience, achieved desired learning outcomes from their perspective, and learning objectives generated by the faculty team.

References

1. MOOCs Directory. http://www.moocs.co/
2. Educause Learning Initiative Short Course: Designing and Delivering a Quality MOOC webpage. http://www.educause.edu/eli/events/eli-short-course-designing-and-delivering-quality-mooc
3. Adapted from Ray Schroeder, Center for Online Learning, Research and Service, University of Illinois Springfield. https://sites.google.com/site/makingmooc
4. Deimann, M., Sloep, P.: How does open education work? In: Meiszner, A., Squires, L. (eds.) Openness and Education, vol. 1, pp. 1–23. Emerald Group Publishing Limited, Bingley (2013). Advances in Digital Education and Lifelong Learning
5. Garrison, D., Archer, W.A.: Community of inquiry framework for online learning. In: Moore, M. (ed.) Handbook of Distance Education. Erlbaum, New York (2003)
6. Reimann, P.: Design-based research. In: Markauskaite, L., Freebody, P., Irwin, J. (eds.) Methodological Choice and Design, Methodos Series, vol. 9, pp. 37–50. Springer, New York (2011)
7. Lotkowski, V., Robbins, S., Noeth, R.: The role of academic and non-academic factors in improving college retention. In: ACT Policy Report (2004)
8. Bloom, B., Engelhart, M., Furst, E., Hill, W., Krathwohl, D.: Taxonomy of Educational Objectives: The Classification of Educational Goals. Handbook I: Cognitive Domain. David McKay Company, New York (1956)

Computer Animation for Learning Building Construction Management: A Comparative Study of First Person Versus Third Person View

Hazar N. Dib[1][(⊠)], Nicoletta Adamo-Villani[2], and Jun Yu[2]

[1] Department of Building Construction Management, Purdue University,
401 N. Grant St, West Lafayette, IN 47907, USA
hdib@purdue.edu
[2] Department of Computer Graphics Technology, Purdue University,
401 N. Grant St, West Lafayette, IN 47907, USA
{nadamovi,yuj}@purdue.edu

Abstract. The paper reports a study that investigated the effect of egocentric versus exocentric view in an educational animation whose goal was to teach undergraduate students the various tasks that a construction manager performs in the field. Specifically, the study aimed to determine the effect of perspective view on students' subject learning and preference. Findings show that while students have a preference on perspective view, the perspective view does not have a significant effect on students' learning outcomes.

Keywords: Educational animation · Egocentric view · Exocentric view

1 Introduction

Several studies found in the literature suggest that 3D computer animation can be an effective educational approach [1–4]. In most 3D animations, scenarios are presented in either first- or third-person view. *"A view of a 3D world is the 2D projection of the world presented to the user. It is entirely defined by the camera's location, angle, and field of view (FoV). A first-person view places the camera where the user's eyes would be in the virtual environment. A third-person view moves the camera away from the object of control, and often increases the angle of the camera to reduce occlusion"* [5]. In animations where a character performs a sequence of tasks, either view can be used. In the first-person view, the camera is placed in front of the character's eyes and the animation is rendered as seen by the character; in the third-person view the camera is placed beside the character and the animation is rendered as if a third person is observing what the character is doing.

While several studies can be found in the literature on the effect of perspective view on user performance/preference in interactive games and simulations, to our knowledge, no study exists on the effect of perspective view in educational animations. The work reported in the paper aims to fill this gap; it investigated the effect of egocentric versus exocentric view in an educational animation whose goal was to teach undergraduate

© Institute for Computer Sciences, Social Informatics and Telecommunications Engineering 2014
G. Vincenti et al. (Eds.): eLEOT 2014, LNICST 138, pp. 76–84, 2014.
DOI: 10.1007/978-3-319-13293-8_10

students the various tasks that a construction manager performs in the field. Specifically, the study aimed to determine the effect of perspective view on students' subject learning and students' preference.

2   Existing Studies on the Effects of Different Perspective Views

Researchers have studied the effect of different perspective views in games and interactive simulations. A change in perspective view in a game/interactive simulation usually involves a change in the position and rotation of the center of the camera. In addition to visibility changes, a different perspective view provides the viewer with a different type of experience (e.g. more or less immersive) [6].

A study by Bateman et al. [5], shows that while there was no significant effect of perspective view on player's driving performance in a car racing game, there was an effect on player's preference. In Bateman's test, participants preferred the first-person view and predicted that they could perform better with such view. This may be because first a-person view provides a better sense of player immersion [6].

Salamin et al. [7] examined whether it is beneficial for users to have the choice to switch from first-person to third-person perspective in virtual and augmented reality environments. They asked participants to perform various tasks in both views including: walking through a gallery with obstacles, putting a ball into a cup of coffee, receiving and sending a rolling ball with the feet and with the hands. Results showed that while some actions, such as looking down or hand manipulations (catching a close object) are performed better in first-person perspective, others, such as interaction with moving objects, require a third-person perspective. This is due to the fact that a third person view offers a larger field of view, and therefore provides the user with more cues to evaluate the distances and anticipate or extrapolate the trajectory of mobile objects.

Salamin et al. [8] also conducted a study whose goal was to quantify the differences between the effects induced by training participants to the third-person and first-person perspectives in a ball catching task in virtual reality. Results of the experiment showed that for a certain trajectory of the ball, the performance of the participants after training to the third person perspective was similar to their performance after baseline perspective training. Performance after first person training varied significantly from both third person and baseline perspectives. The researchers concluded that usage of the third person perspective in training and learning methods might prove to be more effective as it facilitates performances and leads to quicker adaptation of distance evaluation in the extra personal space.

Anquetil and Jeannerod [9] conducted a study in which subjects simulated a grasping action with two levels of difficulty. In one condition, they simulated the movement from their own, first person perspective, while in the other condition they simulated the same movement made by a person facing them (third person perspective). The time to complete the movement was found to be almost the same in the two conditions and a similar difference in time between easy and difficult grasps was retained in the two conditions. These results show that a self-generated and an observed action share the same representation and this representation can be used from different perspectives.

Pazuchanics [10] investigated two methods to increase UGV (uninhabited ground vehicles) operators' performance. Typically, UGV cameras provide their operators with a very narrow, field of view (FOV) and a first-person camera perspective. His study investigated two methods for providing an operator with additional contextual information: widening the FOV and capturing a third-person perspective of the vehicle in its environment. Findings show that the additional information provided by either method can increase navigation performance. Of the two methods, widening the FOV produced the greatest performance benefit, however capturing a third-person perspective may also facilitate certain aspects of navigation. The benefits associated with each method were found to be cumulative and therefore ideal video displays may incorporate both methods.

3   Description of Study

The objective of this study was to investigate the effect of different perspective views, in educational 3D animations, on students' learning of building construction management tasks, and students' preference. The study compared two types of computer animations: one rendered using an egocentric perspective view, and one rendered using an exocentric perspective view. The animations presented to the participants were designed for an undergraduate course in building construction management. The content was identical and focused on the tasks that a building construction manager needs to perform on a construction site. The first person view animation can be accessed at:

http://www.youtube.com/watch?v=g4gAlqJv9F4&feature=youtu.be

The third person view animation can be accessed at:

http://www.youtube.com/watch?v=kW7SAZllumo&feature=youtu.be

Figure 1 shows frames extracted from both animations.

The study used a quantitative approach and tested the hypotheses listed below.

In instructional 3D animations for building construction management education:

H01:   There is no difference in the learning effect between first-person perspective view and third-person perspective view
Ha1:   There is a difference in the learning effectiveness between first-person and third-person perspective view
H02:   There is no correlation between the learning effectiveness of a specific perspective view and concept/task being presented
Ha2:   There is a correlation between the learning effectiveness of a specific perspective view and concept/task being presented
H03:   Users do not have preference on perspective view
Ha3:   Users have preference on perspective view
H04:   The student preference of perspective view does not change based on the concepts/tasks being presented
Ha4:   The student preference of perspective view changes based on the concepts/ tasks being presented.

In addition, the study also tested the following hypotheses to determine whether watching the animation, either first or third person view, had an effect on students' learning:

Ha5:   There is a difference in subject learning between students who watched the educational animation (first or third person view) and those who did not watch the animation and used the textbook

H05:   There is no difference in subject learning between students who watched the educational animation (first or third person view) and those who did not watch the animation and used the textbook

For hypotheses 1, 2 and 5, the learning objective considered by the study was the student's ability to demonstrate knowledge and understanding of the tasks that a building construction manager performs on a construction site (these tasks are listed in the left column of Table 1). We measured this learning objective using pre and post educational intervention competency testing. The study included three independent variables: the first-person view animation, the third-person view animation, and the traditional textbook. The subjects were divided in three groups: control group (1)–exposed to text book, experimental group (2)–exposed to first-person view animation, and experimental group (3)–exposed to third-person view animation. The dependent variables were the mean scores of the test in the three groups after the experiment.

To test hypotheses 4 and 5, a survey including questions about the subjects' experience was administered to the students.

The experiment included two phases. In phase 1 the study collected data on students' preference and formative feedback on the animation. In phase 2 the study collected summative data on students' learning outcomes.

3.1   Phase 1

The objective of phase 1 was to test hypotheses 3 and 4 and collect formative feedback.

Subjects: 34 undergraduate students enrolled in a Building Construction Management program. All subjects had prior knowledge of the educational content presented in the animation.

Testing instrument: An online survey comprised of 19 multiple-choice questions and 1 open-ended question. The first question asked the students whether the animation could have helped them learn the content more efficiently. The second question asked about their overall perspective view preference. The following 16 questions asked about perspective view preference (and prediction of learning more efficiently from this view) for each individual task simulated in the animation. The open-ended question prompted students for comments and suggestions for improvements.

Procedure: Each subject sat in front of a monitor displaying the two animations side by side (as shown is Fig. 1). Subjects had the option to play the animations as many times as they wanted. After watching the animations, the subjects completed the online survey and submitted their answers.

Findings and discussion: Findings show that 67 % of the subjects thought the animations are effective tools for learning the content. Results also show that participants have a preference on perspective view in computer animation. The distribution of the response for general preference shows that 20 % of the participants prefer the first-person view, 73 % of the participants prefer the third-person view, and 7 % do not have a preference. Findings demonstrate that subjects' preference on perspective view changes based on the type of task being simulated. For example, participants strongly preferred the first-person view when the task depicted in the animation is about checking the footing size and the location of anchor bolts. Whereas users indicated stronger preference for the third-person view when the task focuses on verifying the top of beam elevations, checking the elevation at both ends of sloped beams, checking the vertical alignment of the wall after building CMU blocks and coordinating the anchor bolt layout with concrete pour schedule.

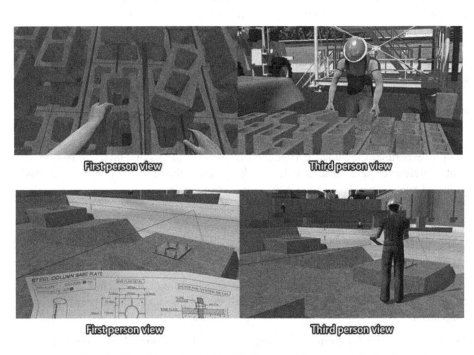

Fig. 1. Example screen shot of first person view and third view.

In general, users preferred the first-person view when the environment is not relevant and the simulated task requires focusing on a small object/detail. In contrast, the third-person view is preferred for tasks that require understanding of the environment or of a larger system/area. One participant commented that the third person view is very helpful to students who are inexperienced as it provides an *"effective overview of the construction site and puts the various activities into context."* A summary of results is included in Table 1.

Table 1. Findings from the survey on perspective view preference

Question	Yes	No	Not Sure
Watching the animations would have helped me learn the content	67 %	10 %	23 %
	1.First person view %	2.Third person view %	3.No preference %
Overall preference of perspective view	20	73	7
1. Coordinate the anchor bolt layout with concrete pour schedule	30	67	3
2. Check footing size and location of anchor bolts	73	24	3
3. Check footing size	70	20	10
4. Establish anchor bolt survey requirements and verify elevation of anchor bolt	33	60	7
5. Check the typical details (in the floor slab or steel supports beneath the opening) for additional reinforcing for opening	30	60	10
6. Verify top of beam elevations and check elevation at both ends of sloped beams	13	74	13
7. Materials must be properly handled stored and prepared	30	53	17
8. Units must be laid with full head and bed joints, joints must be tooled properly	27	56	17
9. CMU alignment, CMU color inspect units and the mortar, texture of the units, check pattern by the type of bond and the unit	40	50	10
10. Materials must be properly handled stored and prepared, check walls' layout and openings location	50	37	13
11. If steel is to be fireproofed, inspect thickness of fireproofing material	23	63	14
12. Check location of expansion joints and make sure they are properly caulked	23	60	17
13. Check joints are tooled and finished properly. Example showing Concave joints	37	33	30
14. Check joints are tooled and finished properly. Example showing weathered joints	47	33	20
15. Checking joints are tooled and finished properly. Example showing V shape joints	37	53	10
16. Checking the vertical alignment of the wall after building CMU blocks	23	77	0

3.2   Phase 2

The objective of phase 2 was to test hypotheses 1, 2 and 5.

Subjects: 66 students enrolled in a Building Construction Management undergraduate course.

Testing instruments: a 7-question test including 6 short essay questions and 1 true/false question. The test focused on the "STEEL" part of the animation, e.g. tasks 1- 6 and 11 listed in the left column of Table 1.

Procedure: all subjects were given a pre-test to assess their basic knowledge of the educational content. After the pre-test, a randomized complete block design was used to divide the subjects into three groups with similar pre-knowledge: control group (1) – traditional textbook; experimental group (2) – first person view animation, and experimental group (3) – third person view animation. One week after the pre-test all students were given a 45-min lecture on the content. One week after the lecture, group 2 interacted with the first person view animation for 30 min in the lab; group 3 interacted with the third person view animation for 30 min in the lab; and group 1 reviewed the content using the textbook for 30 min. Two weeks later, all participants were administered a post-test which was identical to the pre-test.

Findings: Two One-way ANOVA were performed to compare the differences in pre-test and post-test scores for each group. Ten students missed the post-test (eight of them from Group 1), so their data was discarded.

Results show that attending the lecture and watching the animation (1st or 3rd person) led to an increase in subject content learning by 4.28 % and 4.27 % respectively, compared to the control group. Group 1 (control)'s post-test score increased by

Table 2. Summary of findings

		N	Mean	Std. deviation	Std. error	95 % Confidence Interval for mean		Minimum	Maximum
						Lower Bound	Upper Bound		
PreTest	1	22	0.1682	0.07487	0.01596	0.1350	0.2014	0.05	0.30
	2	22	0.1659	0.09308	0.01984	0.1246	0.2072	0.00	0.40
	3	22	0.1682	0.07799	0.01663	0.1336	0.2028	0.00	0.30
	Total	66	0.1674	0.08109	0.00998	0.1475	0.1874	0.00	0.40
PostTest	1	14	0.3429	0.10535	0.02816	0.2820	0.4037	0.15	0.50
	2	21	0.3833	0.08266	0.01804	0.3457	0.4210	0.20	0.55
	3	21	0.3857	0.10385	0.02266	0.3384	0.4330	0.20	0.60
	Total	56	0.3741	0.09676	0.01293	0.3482	0.4000	0.15	0.60

ANOVA

		Sum of Squares	Df	Mean Square	F	Sig
PreTest	Between groups	0.000	2	0.000	0.006	0.994
	Within groups	0.427	63	0.007		
	Total	0.427	65			
PostTest	Between groups	0.018	2	0.009	0.976	0.384
	Within groups	0.497	53	0.009		
	Total	0.515	55			

17.47 % from pre-test. Experimental group 2 (1st person) post-test score increased by 21.74 %, while for group 3 (third person), the increase was of 21.75 %. Results show that the difference in learning gains between the two experimental groups is not statistically significant. They also show that the difference in total learning gains between the control and the experimental groups is not statistically significant (F (2, 53) = 0.976, p > 0.05; M (Group 1) = 0.3429 SD (Group 1) = 0.10535; M (Group 2) = 0.3833; SD (Group 2) = 0.08266; M (Group 3) = 0.3857; SD (Group 3) = 0.10385;). Table 2 shows a summary of results.

In summary, perspective view did not have an effect on students' learning outcomes, although students had expressed a preference for third-person view and had predicted to learn more from this view for 5 out of the 7 tasks relevant to the test.

4 Discussion and Conclusion

In this paper, we have explored the effect of perspective view in educational animations on students' learning of building construction management tasks, and on students' preference. Results show that students have a preference on perspective view, however perspective view does not influence learning outcomes. The study also investigated the efficacy of animation as a teaching/learning tool. Findings show that animation led to higher learning gains than traditional teaching/learning methods, although the difference in learning was not statistically significant in this study. This finding adds to the body of research that suggests that animation can be an effective educational approach.

Our study had one main limitation: a relatively small sample size. Because of the limited number of participants, we cannot generalize the results and we can only suggest that perspective view does not have an influence on students' learning in educational animations. In order to build stronger evidence, additional studies with larger pools of participants, in different subject domains and in different settings will need to be conducted.

References

1. Rias, R.M., Zaman, H.B.: Can different types of animation enhance recall and transfer of knowledge? A case study on a computer science subject. Asian J. Teach. Learn. High. Educ. **4**(1), 32-43 (2012)
2. Khalil, M., Johnson, T., Lamar, C.: Comparison of computer based and paper based imagery strategies in learning anatomy. Clin. Anat. **18**, 457–464 (2005)
3. Tversky, B., Morrison, J.B., Betrancourt, M.: Animation: can it facilitate? Intl. J. Hum. Comput. Stud. **57**(4), 247–262 (2002)
4. Taylor, M.J., Pountney, D.C., Baskett, M.: Using animation to support the teaching of computer game development techniques. Comput. Educ. **50**(4), 1258–1268 (2008)
5. Bateman, S., Doucette, A., Xiao, R., Gutwin, C., Mandryk, R.L., Cockburn, A.: Effects of view, input device, and track width on video game driving. In: Proceedings of Graphics Interface 2011, Canadian Human-Computer Communications Society, pp. 207–214 (2011)
6. Rouse III, R.: What's your perspective? ACM SIGGRAPH. Comput. Graph. **33**(3), 9–12 (1999). ACM New York, USA

7. Salamin, P., Thalmann, D., Vexo, F.: The benefits of third-person perspective in virtual and augmented reality? In: Proceedings of the ACM Symposium on Virtual Reality Software and Technology, pp. 27–30. ACM, New York (2006)
8. Salamin, P., Tadi, T., Blanke, O., Vexo, F., Thalmann, D.: Quantifying effects of exposure to the third and first-person perspectives in virtual-reality-based training. IEEE. Trans. Learn. Technol. **3**(3), 272–276 (2010). IEEE Computer Society
9. Anquetil, T., Jeannerod, M.: Simulated actions in the first and in the third person perspectives share common representations. Brain Res. **1130**, 125–129 (2007)
10. Pazuchanics, S.L.: The effects of camera perspective and field of view on performance in teleoperated navigation. In: Proceedings of the Human Factors and Ergonomics Society Annual Meeting, vol. 50(16), pp. 1528–1532. SAGE Publications (2006)

A Qualitative Exploration of the EU Digital Competence (DIGCOMP) Framework: A Case Study Within Healthcare Education

George Evangelinos$^{(\boxtimes)}$ and Debbie Holley

Anglia Ruskin University, Faculty of Health Social Care and Education,
East Road, Cambridge CB1 1PT, UK
{george.evangelinos,Debbie.Holley}@anglia.ac.uk

Abstract. A case study on qualitative exploration of the EU Digital Competence framework within Healthcare Education; it investigates one of the eight lifelong learning key-competences required for managers, doctors, nurses and other health-related professionals. The research was conducted in a Higher Education Institutional setting through semi-structured interviews according to the hermeneutic methodologies allowing for a dialectic approach; it aims at gaining a better understanding of the digital skills which are considered as the most generic and transferable skills, and the training needs of healthcare professionals. The results, defined by 22 themes, express the participants' experiences, knowledge and level of comprehension of the subject. The research reveals that the DIGICOMP framework is applicable as a generic framework for professional practice. The interview data indicate highly individualised digital competence characteristics and behaviours of the participants.

Keywords: Digital competence · Digital literacy · EU DIGCOMP digital competence framework · Competence analytics

1   Introduction

Digital competence is considered as the most transferable competence [1] among eight key-competences for continuous, life-long learning [2]. In 2011 the European Union Directorate-General for Education and Culture commissioned the Digital Competence (DIGCOMP) project. The project documented the current state of knowledge among experts in research, education, training and work. It utilised an iterative Delphi-type survey that recorded the views of the experts, validated, refined and shared the results among the expert group, and collected feedback from peer review by engaging a significant number of 95 experts [3]. Work on a review of the literature [4] and the analysis and synthesis of existing digital competence frameworks [5] preceded this study and established a baseline of the prevailing digital competence and digital literacy theories.

In the Health Sector digital competences are a requirement for managers, doctors, nurses and other health-related professionals; digital technologies are increasingly used for office administration as well as for medical diagnostics and interventions. The pervasiveness of digital technology and the resulting demand for digitally-competent

© Institute for Computer Sciences, Social Informatics and Telecommunications Engineering 2014
G. Vincenti et al. (Eds.): eLEOT 2014, LNICST 138, pp. 85–92, 2014.
DOI: 10.1007/978-3-319-13293-8_11

users can threaten traditional jobs; people who lack the required digital skills may see their positions worsening and progressively marginalised in the labour market [6–8]. Thus it can be argued that healthcare trainers have a duty to modernise their curricula and ensure that digital skills become a graduate attribute.

This paper documents a qualitative exploration of the DIGCOMP framework within a higher educational institution in the United Kingdom in an attempt to assess its applicability as a theoretical framework for a wider research project aiming at embedding digital competences into curriculum development and delivery. This project is a partial fulfilment of the requirements of the main author's professional Doctorate in Education and has been carried out in the third year of a five year doctoral programme.

2   Methodology

Participants completed a bespoke online digital competence self-assessment questionnaire prior to the interviews commencing. The Evangelinos and Holley questionnaire toolkit [9] comprised of groups of five statements that described in detail each of the competence areas summarised in the table below that emerged from the initial results of the DIGCOMP framework [3] (Table 1).

Table 1. DIGCOMP framework competence areas

DIGCOMP Framework Digital Competence Areas	
<ul><li>General knowledge and functional skills</li><li>Use in everyday life</li><li>Specialized and advanced skills for work and creative expression</li><li>Technology mediated communication and collaboration</li><li>Information processing and management</li><li>Privacy and security</li></ul>	<ul><li>Legal and ethical aspects</li><li>Balanced attitude towards technology</li><li>Understanding and awareness of the role of ICT in society</li><li>Learning about and with digital technologies</li><li>Informed decisions on appropriate digital technologies</li><li>Seamless use demonstrating self-efficacy</li></ul>

Interviews were conducted according to the hermeneutic methodology [10] utilising a dialectic approach with eleven participants who volunteered from a pool of healthcare trainees and academic professionals within the institution. Informed consent was obtained in writing according to the research protocol governed by the university's ethical procedures. To investigate the interviewees views, assess their experiences and gain an insight into perceptions on their digital competences they were asked to describe, comment and expand on their choices in the questionnaire. Barker and Johnson [11], Walford [12] and Kvale and Brinkmann [13] all claim that this type of enquiry allows for a higher degree of variability of experiences, knowledge and level of comprehension of the subject matter among the research participants.

Five academics, three students and three admin professionals self-selected for interview and established the participant group. The inclusion of participants from all stakeholder groups of healthcare education was deliberate as the suitability of the framework had to be investigated from all perspectives and incorporate a variety of experiences and views. The audio recordings ranged from 90 to 120 minutes for each interview and produced a transcribed corpus of approximately 193,000 words. The interviews were recorded, transcribed and analysed through the use of the QSR NVivo software. The analysis was conducted by coding the interview corpora into emerging themes following the recommendations from Miles and Huberman [14] and Guest et al. [15]. The theme patterns were formed by counting the frequency of occurrence of the digital competence references mentioned by the participants and the number of individuals reporting on a theme to indicate its relative 'power'. The themes were then mapped onto the appropriate DIGCOMP framework area to investigate its suitability.

3 Results

Overall twenty-two themes emerged; twelve of them were mentioned by most of the participants. The first number in the parenthesis next to each theme indicates the number of individuals that mentioned a theme and the second number accounts for the total number of references (Table 2).

Table 2. Interview themes mapped onto the DIGCOMP framework areas

Dominant Competence Areas	Secondary Competence Areas
Use in everyday life (11/205) - *Technology use* (11/116)* - *Technology-use barriers* (9/47)* - Digital devices (10/28) - Online banking (8/14) **Specialized and advanced skills (11/119)** - *Technology use in education* (9/86)* - Content authoring and remixing (11/22) - Specialist digital skills (9/11) **Learning about/with technologies (11/97)** - *Learning skills and support* (11/85)* - Learning about new technologies (6/12) **Communication and collaboration (11/89)** - Communication/collaboration (10/43) - Social networks and media (11/37) - Communities of practice (5/9) **Balanced attitude (10/76)** - *Balanced use of technology* (10/76)* **Privacy and security (11/55)** - Security and privacy (11/55) **Information management (11/54)** - Information management (11/54)	**General knowledge and functional skills (7/38)** - Manuals and instructions (7/16) - General knowledge (5/9) - Hardware and software (7/9) - Operating systems (4/4) **Legal and ethical aspects (9/33)** - *Legal and ethical aspects* (9/33)* **Understanding and awareness of the role of ICT in society (8/20)** - Social issues (4/11) - Technology and the environment (4/9) **Informed decisions on appropriate digital technologies (0/0)** - N/A **Seamless use demonstrating self-efficacy (0/0)** - N/A

An analysis of selected (*) themes follows.

3.1 Analysis

'Technology use' emerged as the most significant theme and a fairly broad category that included a variety of user experiences. This was a direct result of an extensive range of the interviewees' experiences, and the non-prescriptive nature of the questionnaire toolkit used. This theme includes everything that can be interpreted as belonging to the sphere of technology use and does not fit within any of the other themes. Examples of common attitudes include the various types of e-commerce, the use of e-Government services (online taxation, driving licensing and passport renewals), the listening of music, reading e-books, watching movies and TV programmes, the use of mapping services, photography, auctioning, accessing information and news, word processing, video editing and job hunting. The use of technology specific to health included the online or over the phone booking of medical appointments, getting the results from clinics as a text message, digital vital sign monitoring and tele-care.

'Technology use in education' was equally important mainly due to the characteristics of the group of participants (academic professionals and students). Naturally, interviewees were expressing their lived experiences, and were drawing examples from their day-to-day engagement with the institution. Their examples can be split into technology-use in and outside the classroom. In-classroom technologies included the better utilisation of interactive boards, the use of digital assets such as hand-outs, visual aids and mind maps. The use of dynamic visualisation software, lecture capture/ recording and the structured use of multimedia such as video and audio to enhance the lecture with activities and make the delivery more interesting, interactive and engaging. Other uses of technology in education include: technology for assessment in the form of e-submission and e-assessment, video conference and other types of communication (including social and new media networks) to facilitate learning at a distance and experimenting with creative use of video logs and blogs for teaching.

The *'Learning skills and support'* theme included the preferences on how interview-participants best acquire technological skills and the kind of support they prefer. All traditional ways of learning (formal, classroom-based, self-directed, peer-learning and on-the-job) have been mentioned. All of the participants indicated that they preferred to learn through examples relevant to their jobs and they would like to be given opportunities to try things out themselves (hands-on the job); they said they learn best what to do through example and demonstration, rather than through the narrative process. They would also like to engage with technology from an early stage and to be informed in what ways this engagement could be beneficial to them. Continuous support and the availability of help were also their concerns; some of them admitted that without support and help they feel helpless and they panic at times. The majority of the participants seek support and help from friends or family and only the confident ones search for answers online. Help sheets and/or online e-learning should be made available in addition to other forms of learning. All interviewees commented that they learn best if up-to-date software and other equipment are owned, since ownership provides them with opportunities to engage with technology in an informal way.

The *'Balanced, safe and efficient use of technology'* theme included comments on how people feel with (and without) technology and how technology should be used in a safe and healthy way. To some extent, all the participants mentioned the importance of technology in their lives, and all but one reported negative consequences of lack of technology at their fingertips. However, one interviewee makes a conscious effort not to be dependent on technology and actively avoids using it when not necessary. Comments such as '*I could survive but it will be hard*', '*iPad and phone are never off*' and '*... there are very close to my heart but I could survive without them*' indicate dependence on the use of technology. This view is strengthened by the fact that in certain cases technology is so embedded/merged in the participant's daily life that they are not aware they are using it and at times they are multi-tasking with two kinds of technology (for example, they are using a phone/tablet while watching TV). The health and safety aspects of using technology safely include posture, positioning, size of screen, keyboard layout, foot rest, use of light, document holder and hearing protection, just to name a few. The participants have often felt that the relentless use of technology induces a type of techno-stress that arises from endless information overflow that often acts sub-consciously.

'*Technology-use barriers*' were also expressed by the participants. Academics highlighted the fact that even relatively simple tasks such as referencing can be challenging to some students. This may be due to a more generic trend of lax student engagement with particular technologies, not due to lack of engagement with technology in general, or lack of skills. This fact was attributed to a generic trend of '*lack of student motive*', which means that the students are not in charge of their learning and they have not become independent learners. Academics also mentioned that students still see learning as '*parts of knowledge related to assessment*' and not as a continuous, life-long process for self-improvement. The merging of their personal and professional identities and transferability of skills are not always apparent. One of the academics, when she tried to enhance her teaching with technology, noticed that digital devices (especially phones) are considered as private devices for fun, not as tools for work and learning by students. This view was reinforced by the fact that when they were asked to use a different device (a laptop or tablet) their mind-set often shifted and they became more open in using it for work or study. Another barrier highlighted by academics is that of some students' digital competence and engagement with technology. As one participant put it, '*Some students I could email from now until eternity and they may never read any of the emails that I send*'. This could be due to lack of skills and/or interest; however, this is the group of students we target to engaging, as they will benefit the most. Other students, although technologically capable and engaged, use only specific platforms and technology (e.g. mobile phones and social networks).

'*Legal and ethical implications of technology use*' also formulated a theme. Participants collectively expressed an awareness of copyright legalities, and academic attribution ethical requirements. Illustration of this understanding could be seen in responses that included the downloading of music, videos, films and software, just to name a few. The right of an individual to privacy and personal space was also discussed. Participants defended the right to privacy and respect of the individual's rights even in a public space. It was also acknowledged that since the development of modern technology and the advent of social networks the right to privacy is being increasingly diminished. The need for establishing appropriate, informal codes of conduct (sort of behavioural etiquette) for online digital communications (including social networks) was a consistent theme.

4 Discussion and Conclusion

The aggregate numbers of individuals and of mentions of the themes are ranked in the figure below per each competence area. Arrangement of the data according to the DIGCOMP competence areas reveals that two significant areas, 'Informed decisions on appropriate digital technologies' and 'Seamless use demonstrating self-efficacy', were not discussed/mentioned by any of the participants; therefore, they are not appropriate as participants cannot identify with them. The structure of the framework with its 12 competence areas is very accommodating and flexible and can be used to categorise the experiences of the participants (Fig. 1).

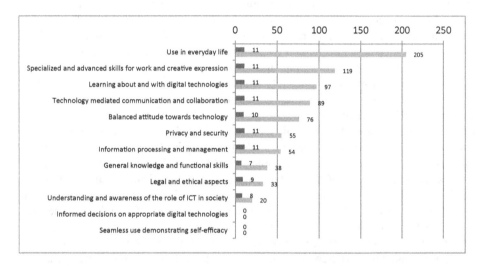

Fig. 1. Mapping of themes onto the DIGCOMP areas

Students were mainly preoccupied with the use of technology for academic study and in their personal lives. Examples of engagement with digital information through the library, the use of the World Wide Web, the Virtual Learning Environment and the creative use of technology to compile assignments and presentations were pervasive. In their personal lives they used technology mostly to communicate with their friends and family via a mixture of phone calls, messaging services and social networks. Most seemed to be aware of the 'dangers' of technology use and in particular of the Internet but did not always know how to protect themselves. Students seemed to be techno-logically fairly capable and engaged but this was primarily with a relatively small set of specific platforms and technology (e.g. mobile phones and social networks). This type of user is difficult to engage as their experiences (and consequently their skills) are limited and narrow and they often do not recognise their lack of necessary digital skills; on the contrary, they consider themselves as reasonably (and sometimes very) tech-nologically competent. A student was using a Kindle E-Book reader to store a large collection of PDFs and books that practically could not be stored in student accom-modation premises if they were in printed editions; otherwise the student would enjoy reading the printed books and other material.

Most academics stated that they are engaging with technology on a regular basis as they use it for work and leisure. They were particularly concerned with the continuous influx of work-related information on their private devices (such as smart phones or tablets). They felt that digital technologies offering enhanced access encourage the culture of considering a person as 'always on' and 'always available'. This has increased their stress levels and the feeling of restlessness [16]. They also felt that although technology-use in education can enhance the student experience, device ownership is not universal and some students do not own smart technologies; some students are completely disengaged from technologies and involving them in the use of technology may prove really difficult. One academic reported that when experimenting with interactive whiteboards and tablet technologies to deliver group work in the classroom, it was discovered that some students were less likely to engage with technologies; however, exposure to technology was beneficial and allocating a device to a small group of students rather than to each individual student spurred their motive for engagement.

Administrative professionals seemed to be using technologies as a matter of routine in their day-to-day lives, to carry out their work and for personal use. Reported experiences were similar to those of the academics and to some extent to those reported by the students that had shared use of a number of institutional systems. Their attitudes towards technology were positive as confidence was being increased and eventually they started carrying out complicated technology tasks as part of their workload. They welcomed the policy and protocol for technological system processes and they perceived these as advantageous; exactly the opposite assumption was reported by the academics who described the same processes as restrictive and bureaucratic. A senior administrator argued that advanced technological skills, such as drawing in specialist design software, could be gained 'on the job' and on-demand as these were required by the business workflow.

Given that digital technologies are increasingly used in healthcare provision [17] further work is required to define the digital competence characteristics pertinent to the healthcare profession. The DIGCOMP framework areas can be used as a generic guide to characterise the digital competence profiles of groups and individuals [9].

The interviews have identified significant themes that can be explored in more detail to further define the skills, views, practices and attitudes of the participants. Profiling of the digital competences and skills of groups and individuals can be used to baseline the digital competence characteristics of groups and individuals. The research data indicate that the characteristics of digital competence tend to be highly personalised and depend upon the individual's experiences. Specifying healthcare-specific digital competence characteristics may not be possible as, quite often, technology is used pervasively and interchangeably across education, work and leisure.

References

1. European Commission: transferability of skills across economic sectors: Role and importance for employment at European level. Report, European Commission (2011)
2. European Commission: key competences for lifelong learning. European Commission (2006)

3. Janssen, J., Stoyanov, S.: Online consultation on experts' views on digital competence. Technical Report, European Commission Joint Research Centre Institute for Prospective Technological Studies (2012)
4. Ala-Mutka, K.: Mapping digital competence: towards a conceptual understanding. Technical notes, European Commission Joint Research Centre Institute for Prospective Technological Studies (2011)
5. Ferrari, A.: Digital competence in practice: an analysis of frameworks. Technical report, European Commission Joint Research Centre Institute for Prospective Technological Studies (2012)
6. Didero, M., Husing, T., Korte, W.: Monitoring E-skills Supply and Demand in Europe, Synthesis report: The evolution of supply and demand E-skills in Europe. Report, Empirica GmbH (2009)
7. The Economist. http://www.economist.com/news/briefing/21594264-previous-technological-innovation-has-always-delivered-more-long-run-employment-not-less
8. The Huffington Post. http://www.huffingtonpost.co.uk/chris-e-jones/robots-versus-humans_b_4659577.html
9. Evangelinos, G. Holley, D.: Developing a digital competence self-assessment toolkit for Nursing Students. In: From Education to Employment and Meaningful Work with ICT E-learning at Work and the Workplace. Book of Abstracts and Electronic Proceedings of the EDEN 2014 Annual Conference, pp. 206–212. European Distance and Elearning Network, Zagreb, Croatia (2014)
10. Denzin, N., Lincoln, Y.: The Sage Handbook of Qualitative Research. Sage., Thousand Oaks (2011)
11. Baker, C., Johnson, G.: Interview talk as professional practice. J. Lang. Educ. **12**(4), 229–242 (1998)
12. Walford, G.: Doing Qualitative Educational Research: A Personal Guide to the Research Process. Continuum, London (2001)
13. Kvale, S., Brinkmann, S.: Interviews, 2nd edn. Sage Publications., Thousand Oaks (2009)
14. Miles, M., Huberman, M.: Qualitative Data Analysis, 2nd edn. Sage, Beverley Hills (1994)
15. Guest, G., Namey, E., Queen, E.: Applied Thematic Analysis. Sage Publications., Thousand Oaks (2012)
16. The Mercury News. http://www.mercurynews.com/ci_24243534/tech-stressbuilds-proliferation-digital-devices
17. National Institute for Health and Care Excellence. http://www.nice.org.uk/usingguidance/healthtechnologiesadoptionprogramme/HealthTechnologiesAdoptionProgramme.jsp

An Innovative Educational Format Based on a Mixed Reality Environment: A Case Study and Benefit Evaluation

Alessandro Fiore$^{(\boxtimes)}$, Luca Mainetti, and Roberto Vergallo

Department of Innovation Engineering, University of Salento,
Via Monteroni, 73100 Lecce, Italy
{alessandro.fiore,luca.mainetti,
roberto.vergallo}@unisalento.it

Abstract. We are in the midst of an information revolution, in which emerging technologies are creating new products and services that are redefining many aspects of our lives. The introduction of Information and Communication Technologies (ICT) in the educational context has allowed leading researchers and practitioners to find new ways of performing learning processes. It is evident that students are naturally attracted by activities that incorporate technology. In this work we propose an innovative competition-based educational format, known as "TIWE Linguistico," that exploits a Mixed Reality (MR) environment in order to encourage the learning of English as a foreign language. The "TIWE Linguistico" has been used experimentally in an Italian high school and the benefits obtained have been validated by exploiting the FEE (Features Extractions) method.

Keywords: Mixed reality · Collaborative Virtual Environment · M-learning · Features Extraction · QR-Codes

1 Introduction

Over the past decade, we have witnessed the invasion of a number of innovative ICT applications into many different spheres of our lives. Disruptive technologies such as smartphones, tablets, social networks and game stations have dramatically changed the way we interact with each other and with the environment. Many people no longer go out for a walk without their smartphone, and social networks have become the main site for sharing real time media and thoughts.

Young people today grow up surrounded by digital media and hardware and thus are dubbed 'digital natives.' Handheld video game players, music players and smart devices are at kids' fingertips. Unsurprisingly, parents worry about the content being delivered and the amount of time spent on digital devices, and thus often see such tools as an encroachment on the education of their children.

Having innovative content and relevant services for children is even more important at school. It has been shown that adopting ICT-based pedagogical approaches to delivering educational content and co-ordinating learning activities can lead to significant benefits [1] such as best subject comprehension, acquirement of new skills,

© Institute for Computer Sciences, Social Informatics and Telecommunications Engineering 2014
G. Vincenti et al. (Eds.): eLEOT 2014, LNICST 138, pp. 93–100, 2014.
DOI: 10.1007/978-3-319-13293-8_12

inclusion benefits and best class cohesion. Also, both central and local governments have realized that the virtual augmentation of classrooms is worth investing in, so considerable economic efforts have been made so that schools can catch up with and exploit students' computer skills more effectively.

Nevertheless, traditional teachers and principals often dislike technologies they cannot control, therefore many schools remain behind the curve in this ICT revolution. Another problem with this ICT revolution at school is that educational experts are often left alone to configure their innovative educational formats, resulting in the adoption of poor or inappropriate technology or in technical problems during the delivery of the educational experience delivery.

In this paper we evaluate the experiences we had designing, experimenting and evaluating with innovative educational formats based on Mixed Reality (MR). The aim of this educational format, known as "TIWE Linguistico," is to encourage students to learn English as a foreign language by exploiting two technologies that pupils love: Android smartphones and 3D virtual worlds. The MR game consists of a crime novel based on an adventure of Sherlock Holmes by Sir Arthur Conan Doyle ("The Hound of the Baskervilles"). The content (texts and questions) and the learning objectives were prepared and arranged accordingly by the teachers. Two interviews with the teachers – before and after the delivery – were carried out, and the most relevant features of the experience were extracted according to the FEature Extraction (FEE) method, in order to assess the teachers' expectations and the results obtained.

The rest of the paper is organized as follows: In Sect. 2 we report on the main related works in the field of MR formats at school. Section 3 presents the TIWE Linguistico educational format. Section 4 reports on the test bed made in an Italian school and the experimental results. Finally, in Sect. 5 we summarize the lessons learned as well as future research.

2   Related Work

Several research works have explored the benefits and issues that emerge when teachers use multi-user 3D Virtual Learning Environments (VLE) in order to augment their educational activities [2, 3]. Moreover, a remarkable number of experiments have been carried out in order to introduce these technologies in an educational context.

For example, in [4] a Virtual Interactive Storytelling is created. This makes real-time story generation possible, as well as user intervention in a storyline. User involvement can take different forms: a user can participate in the story, play the role of an actor, or intervene in the course of action from a spectator's perspective.

In [5], an experiment that ends up in a survey about a global distance-learning course attended by 68 students is performed. The survey was conducted to identify factors that may have an influence on the effectiveness of VLEs. The results included a set of features such as students' characteristics, their attitudes towards VLE, technology reliability, media richness and virtual team support related to the effectiveness of virtual learning.

An important element of the work which is related to the use of MR environments in the education scenario is MiRTLE (Mixed Reality Teaching & Learning Environment)

[6] which allows teachers and pupils to take part in real-time mixed and online classes, interacting with avatar representations of the other participants. In MiRTLE, the teachers in the physical classroom can deliver traditional lectures, but in addition they have a presentation station, consisting of a large display mounted in the classroom, showing the remote students' avatars. MiRTLE uses the full potential offered by the Shanghai e-Learning Platform [7].

Other works bringing to the attention the more frequent use of auto-identification technologies exist in the learning context. In [8], mobile phones are used as QR-code readers to conduct surveys during classes, in order to provide feedback to the teacher in the middle of a long class (i.e. of 90 min).

3 The "TIWE Linguistico"

The related works examined show that different pieces of technology can be used together in order to improve the outcomes of learning processes. However, existing MR environments for education are not free to download and not easy to set up [9]. MiRTLE appears to be the best MR environment for the educational context, but MiRTLE learning experiences have not been rigorously classified or shared. Therefore we felt it necessary to build up our own MR-based format, experiment with it in an Italian school and identify its main experiential features by exploiting a rigorous methodology.

Before introducing the "TIWE Linguistico," it is necessary to define what we mean by an "educational format". From our point of view, an educational format is a didactic project characterized by certain levels of abstraction and decontextualization (compared to its applicability/experimentation). Thanks to such features, such a format is potentially transferable to any educational level and has three dimensions:

1. The pedagogical and didactic dimension, referring to the educational models that can be implemented by the format itself.
2. The tools dimension, referring to the "technologies" that can support both the learning processes and the evaluation of the educational format.
3. The organizational dimension, which interacts with the educational models and the tools that are adopted.

The "TIWE Linguistico" is a competition-based educational format whose purpose is to encourage the learning of English as a foreign language. The format is based on the novel "The Hound of the Baskervilles" by Sir Arthur Conan Doyle and implements a treasure hunt carried out in a MR environment where two teams compete in order to solve a crime. Each team is composed of two groups:

- 3D Group: the players in the virtual world, who guess the crime's perpetrator and the weapon used by interacting with some 3D objects in four different virtual environments (game levels);
- Sherlock Group: the players in the real world, who have to answer a set of questions using a smartphone for reading objects labeled with QR-Codes in 4 real classrooms (QR-Rooms).

To access the next levels of the game, each member of the 3D Group has to wait for the corresponding Sherlock Group to communicate relevant clues to them. A particular clue can be obtained by answering a specific question correctly in the real world. Pupils in the Sherlock Group can show and answer the question by reading the associated QR-Code tag, using a smartphone with the "TIWEApp" installed. If the given answer is correct, the 3D players can receive help to find some secret 3D objects (the clue). By clicking on such objects, the 3D Group can show and answer a new question, which allows them to gain access to new crime information and then go on to the next level of the game. The number of game levels (environments) is four, i.e. there are four real classrooms and four game levels. The winner is the team whose 3D Group guesses the right culprit and weapon the fastest. In Fig. 1 the interaction between the virtual world and real world is shown.

The "TIWE Linguistico" involves three main technologies:

- **WebTalk04** (WT04) [8] is a Collaborative Virtual Environment (CVE) which is able to deliver three-dimensional multimedia learning experiences in real-time. WT04 provides a runtime 3D rendering engine which is fully configurable through XML in order to easily modify virtual world settings as well as collaborative interaction rules, thus allowing geometries, forms of behavior and content to be controlled independently. In the "TIWE Linguistico," the WT04 platform is used for proposing educational activities through navigation in the virtual world and interaction with blackboards that show contents or propose more complex questions. The WT04 client (see Fig. 2) runs on a regular web browser. This feature makes it easier to deliver 3D experiences at school – for example in the computer room – avoiding difficult and time-consuming setup procedures like installation and updating. WT04 uses a central server to retain a shared state among objects and for propagating a user's state changes (such as chat, movements or interactions).
- **TiweApp** (see Fig. 2) is a mobile learning system (m-learning), which allows the delivery of multiple choice quizzes by reading objects labeled with QR-Code tags. Thanks to the simplified interface, students are not distracted by the difficulties of interacting with the device. TiweApp contents can be configured by editing an XML file. It also provides a scoring mechanism. The latest version is available for Android [10]. All the contents required for the interaction are stored on a memory card, hence it is not necessary to connect the device to the network. A log file

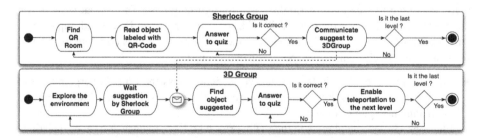

Fig. 1. The interaction between Sherlock Group and 3D Group. To access the next environment, 3D Group must wait the correspondent Sherlock Group to communicate them the clue to find.

containing data on correct/wrong answers, attempts, and time spent is generated so it can be used later in a debriefing phase.

- **Moodle** is a free, open-source PHP web application for producing modular Internet-based courses that support a modern social constructionist pedagogy. Students can find out about documents, tutorials and multimedia materials, which allow them to have out rich educational experiences.

4   Test Bed and Experimental Results

The "TIWE Linguistico" has been used experimentally at the "Luigi Scarambone", an Italian vocational high school located in Lecce, during the 2012–2013 school year. This involved two English teachers and 24 pupils selected from the most talented of the school's third and fourth classes. In this case, the experience was tailored to strengthening the English level for the best performing pupils rather than a recovery tool for the less well performing ones. The learning experience lasted 10 days and was structured as follows:

- **Preliminary Phase.** In this phase we held two meetings with the students and teachers, in order to increase their familiarity with WT04 and the TiweApp. During the last meeting, the story of "The Hound of the Baskerville" was presented to the pupils by playing a video that included clips from one of the movies of the story. In addition, we created and assigned the Moodle login credentials for each student so that they could refer to the documentation available at any time. During the same phase, the two English teachers worked on the contents of the format in order to adapt them to the level of knowledge of the students.
- **Experience delivery.** During the experience day, the pupils were split into two teams of twelve students. Each team was then divided into a Sherlock Group (6 students) and a 3D Group (6 students). The school provided 4 classrooms to be used as QR-Rooms, and one computer laboratory for hosting both the 3D Groups. Each Sherlock Group was equipped with one smartphone on which was installed the TiweApp, and one netbook for communicating with the 3D Group by using WT04 chat.

The experience lasted 2 h, in which the pupils co-operated to solve a crime before the opposing team did so. In order to obtain a qualitative analysis of our experiment, we adopted the FEature Extraction (FEE) method [11]. This consists of carrying out two interviews with the teachers (before and after the experience), and then "extracting" the relevant features. The FEE method aims to highlight the benefits achieved by the educational format. The expectations interview has been taken before the "Tiwe Linguistico" was implemented and reflects what the teachers expected from the format. The results interview was carried out after the implementation of the learning experience and reflects the actual outcomes. We transcribed the interviews with the teachers, then extracted the relevant features in order to create a synthesis of all the interesting aspects of the educational experience. We filled out four different FEE forms: an expectation FEE, a result FEE, a comparison FEE and an experience FEE form. Figure 3 shows an extract from the transcription of the results of the interviews.

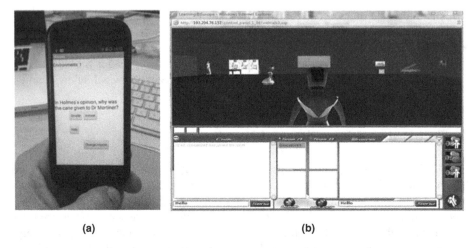

(a)   (b)

Fig. 2. The main technologies used in the "Tiwe Linguistico": Webtalk04 on the left and TIWEApp on the right. Firstly, in (a) the Sherlock student has shot a QR code placed in a real classroom and a question shows up. Giving the right answer makes it possible for him to access the next real classroom. The real student also gives the clue to the 3D students via the WT04 chat (in this case, he asks him to search for something like a 'cane' in the 3D world).

By conducting FEE method analysis we deduced that the MR experience had helped achieve a number of significant benefits. From the point of view of integration, the students had improved their ability to work in teams thanks to the purely co-operative characteristics of the learning format. Furthermore, they had explored several semantic-linguistic aspects, which allowed them to understand the text more easily and answer the questions more quickly. The students used technologies autonomously without any external support, proving that the innovative tools involved were easy to

I: What kind of benefits do you think your students have achieved during the experience?

T: *A little bit of everything, because the students have had the possibility of using technologies that they know very well, so they have started to improve their English [...] Students have deepened several concepts and worked in group with a certain autonomy without the help of the teacher, whose contribution was limited to finding relevant content before the experience of implementation.*

I: In your opinion, what were the crucial features of your experience that made these achievements possible?

T: *It was crucial to have the same level of language and technological skills.*

I: Did you notice unexpected benefits?

T: *Sure! The team that was apparently weaker (because of the patchy composition of race and social condition) did exploit a cooperation method that was effective for winning the game.*

Fig. 3. Transcription of the interview

use and encouraged learning. The teachers highlighted how the school had become a place where the ludic experiences make studying more interesting than traditional frontal lectures. The one major problem was related to the school's network infrastructure, whose network speed did not match up to the requirements of the tools.

5 Conclusions and Future Work

In this paper we have presented an innovative educational format based on Mixed Reality (MR) environments. The format uses two technologies beloved by pupils – Android smartphones and 3D virtual worlds – in order to encourage the learning of English as a foreign language while fostering a sense of community among the players. The format is structured as a competition between two teams. Such teams can be two schools or two classrooms in the same school. The object of the game is to detect the culprit and the weapon in a crime novel, based on the stories of Sherlock Holmes.

In order to prove the validity and effectiveness of the system, we experimented with the "TIWE Linguistico" in the Luigi Scarambone high school, with the collaboration of two English teachers. The contents delivered (texts and questions) and the learning objectives have been prepared and arranged accordingly by the teachers during the preparational phase. Two interviews with the teachers – before and after the experience delivery – were carried out in order to assess the teachers' expectations and the results obtained. This kind of evaluation was structured according to the FEature Extraction (FEE) schema.

The educational format we delivered at the Luigi Scarambone high school has proved that this kind of technology can be used at school without any particular effort by the pupils, and that the use of such innovative tools can significantly encourage pupils during the learning process.

This experience confirmed that an educational renewal in the school is still required and cannot be postponed any longer. A strict collaboration between those who develop the technology and those who create the learning objects will be absolutely necessary to get the best from an innovative educational format. Unfortunately, many schools still struggle to catch up and exploit the pupils' computer skills. Also, a set of problems was identified during the process of experience delivery. Firstly, the IT assets of the school were not always reliable. For example, the WiFi network signal strength was not always sufficient. Secondly, a number of learning professionals did not appear to approve the changes, probably because they require a considerable effort on their part.

In the future we plan to move into two important research areas. From the technical perspective, we are intending to enrich the "TIWE Linguistico" with more and more engaging technologies such as Near Field Communication (NFC), indoors localization, and interaction with social networks (Facebook, Twitter, and Google+). From an educational perspective, we hope that teachers will get even closer to the technology, in order to try to minimize the mental block that too many teachers still have about it.

Acknowledgment. The work is partially funded by the Italian Ministry of Education, University and Research (MIUR) under the PON04a2_B EDOC@WORK3.0 (EDucation On Cloud) national research project.

References

1. Youssef, A.B., Dahmani, M.: The impact of ICT on student performance in higher education: direct effects, indirect effects and organizational change. Revista de Universidad y Sociedad del Conocimiento **5**(1), 35–44 (2008)
2. Warburton, S.: Second life in higher education: assessing the potential for and the barriers to deploying virtual worlds in learning and teaching. Br. J. Educ. Tech. **40**(3), 414–426 (2009)
3. Cavazza, M., Charles, F., Mead, S.J.: Developing re-usable interactive storytelling technologies. In: Jacquart, R. (ed.) Building the Information Society. IFIP, vol. 156, pp. 39–44. Springer, Heidelberg (2004)
4. Tang, N., Yan, S.: Study of the effectiveness of virtual learning. Psychol. Sci. **27**(2), 462–465 (2004)
5. Callaghan, V., Gardner, M., Horan, B., Scott, J., Shen, L., Wang, M.: A mixed reality teaching and learning environment. In: Fong, J., Kwan, R., Wang, F.L. (eds.) ICHL 2008. LNCS, vol. 5169, pp. 54–65. Springer, Heidelberg (2008)
6. Shen, L., Wang, M., Shen, R.: Affective e-learning: using emotional data to improve learning in pervasive learning environment. Educ. Tech. Soc. **12**(2), 176–189 (2009)
7. Susono, H., Shimomura, T.: Using mobile phones and QR codes for formative class assessment. Curr. Dev. Tech. Assist. Educ. **2**, 1006–1010 (2006)
8. Barchetti, U., Bucciero, A., Mainetti, L.: Collaborative learning through flexible web CVE: the experience of webtalk. In: Vincenti, G., Braman, J. (eds.) Teaching Through Multi-User Virtual Environments: Applying Dynamic Elements to the Modern Classroom, pp. 471–490. IGI Global Publications, Hershey (2011)
9. Vergallo, R.: Classroom 3.0: the real world meets virtuality through ambient sensing in education. In: Proceedings of the 12th IEEE International Conference on Advanced Learning Technologies (ICALT) 2012, Rome, Italy, pp. 722–723, 3–6 July 2012. doi:10.1109/ICALT.2012.76
10. Google Android. www.android.com
11. Paolini, P., Di Blas, N., Guerra, L, Falcinelli, F., Mainetti, L., Costabile, M.F., et al.: Assessing and sharing (technology-based) educational experiences. In: Proceedings of World Conference on Educational Multimedia, Hypermedia and Telecommunications (EdMedia 2011), pp. 3150–3157. AACE Press (2011). ISBN 1-880094-35-X

Virtual, Immersive, Translational, Applied Learning: The VITAL Project

Charles S. Layne[1(✉)], Lisa Alastuey[1], Amber M. Chelette[1],
Anne Ogborn[1], Tracey A. Ledoux[1], Prashant Mutgekar[1],
Rebecca E. Lee[2], and Brian K. McFarlin[3]

[1] Department of Health and Human Performance, University of Houston,
3855 Holman Street, Houston, TX, USA
clayne2@uh.edu
[2] College of Nursing and Health Innovation, Arizona State University,
Phoenix, USA
[3] Department of Kinesiology, Health Promotion, and Recreation,
University of North Texas, Denton, USA

Abstract. The VITAL Project is an interdisciplinary project that uses teams of students from multiple courses in a single semester to investigate a health-related topic, propose programs or therapies to ameliorate the health issue and deliver a presentation at a virtual three-day health conference held in Second Life. The purpose of VITAL is to provide opportunities for the students to gain a better understanding of the multifactorial nature of many public and individual health issues, as well as exposing them to technologies that enable them to virtually collaborate. The teams are composed of students from each of the four courses participating in VITAL in a given semester so that the content area of each course is represented on a given team. All team activities, such as meetings and presentation practice, are conducted on the department's island in Second Life.

Keywords: Health · Virtual worlds · Second Life · Education · Collaboration

1 Introduction

The department of Health and Human Performance at the University of Houston is devoted to the understanding, development, and promotion of a healthy lifestyle. As such, the department offers a number of graduate and undergraduate degree programs that can be considered health-oriented, including degrees in exercise science, motor behavior and nutrition. Given the multifactorial nature of many public health issues, the department has adopted an integrated curriculum that includes required courses in the scientific disciplines mentioned above. The multidisciplinary approach provides the students with the optimal preparation for both understanding the nature and consequences of many health issues as well as preparing them for entry into their professional life.

Paralleling the tremendous gains in computing power in the last 20 years, the development of virtual worlds has increased exponentially. Corresponding with the

© Institute for Computer Sciences, Social Informatics and Telecommunications Engineering 2014
G. Vincenti et al. (Eds.): eLEOT 2014, LNICST 138, pp. 101–115, 2014.
DOI: 10.1007/978-3-319-13293-8_13

gains in computing power, the use of virtual worlds for employee [1], medical training [2, 3], education, [4, 5], rehabilitation [6], and business functions [7, 8] has expanded. The instructors involved in the VITAL project believe that exposure to virtual worlds is an essential component of the preparation necessary to be successful in the current marketplace, regardless of a student's particular academic discipline. Providing the opportunity to work in a virtual world in a structured and collaborative manner to complete an academically relevant project enables our students to experience success beyond the boundaries of the environment that typically operate in.

2   Departmental Environment

In addition to the interdisciplinary nature of the curriculum, students in the program also experience multiple opportunities to interact with educational technology. Many courses are delivered exclusively online while others utilize the hybrid model with content being delivered on online with class time being used for demonstrations, explanations and content reinforcement. Several instructors require their students to complete video projects that are shared with their classmates while others make use of Second Life to provide virtual demonstrations and 'hands on' learning experiences. A well-equipped computer lounge provides students who lack the required technology to access the required educational technologies. The department was also the first at the University of Houston to offer a fully online degree when it launched an online Masters of Physical Education in 2003.

Today's students, the so-called "net generation," [9] use a variety of technology in their everyday lives and can be disenchanted by traditional face-to-face classrooms and even 'traditional' online learning environments that fail to engage them as a result of offering only one way content delivery. Outside of the classroom, students play games in virtual worlds, spend hours following the activities of friends and classmates on Facebook, and use text and Instagram messaging as an alternate to telephone calls. The department's faculty embrace these aspects of students' lives and incorporate a variety of learning technologies to meet the unique needs to today's college students. For many years, the faculty have been utilizing 'clickers' in the face-to-face classrooms as well as a variety of digital 'game-like' quizzes and activities that promote student engagement and content reinforcement. Currently, departmental faculty are developing massive open online courses (MOOCs) some of which will be taken by the department's degree seeking students. It is in this educational technology-rich environment that the VITAL project was developed as the instructors felt confident the students' varied experiences have adequately prepared them for educational technology and the innovative use of a virtual world.

During the exploration and implementation of various educational technologies, it has been found that regularly collecting feedback from the students is an important form of engagement. Additionally, student feedback provides insight to make needed changes in course content and delivery methods. Having found that mandatory end of term course evaluations do not provide sufficient information to evaluate the effectiveness of the introduction of new technologies into learning environment, instructors increasingly rely upon Survey Monkey and anonymous Blackboard discussion boards to solicit feedback regarding what students like most and least about their courses and new technologies. Much of what has been learned over the past several years from student responses is incorporated into the VITAL project.

3 Rationale Underlying VITAL

As mentioned, the various degrees offered by the department are all multidisciplinary in curricular approach. The VITAL project builds upon the idea that many health-related issues are multidimensional and therefore requires a multidisciplinary approach to their understanding, treatment and possible prevention. Health issues that impact millions of individuals, such as obesity or depression, are often consequences of complex interactions between lifestyle, genetics, public policy, laws and environmental factors [10]. Delivering a compartmentalized education to students, that oversimplifies health problems by dividing them into distinct scientific or curricular areas, compromises student success as future investigators, clinicians and health-industry employees [11]. An educational approach to an issue that is comprehensive and translational produces graduates with a broader foundation of health knowledge, advanced critical thinking abilities, and creative problem solving skills [12]. The VITAL project bridges the gap across distinct courses to foster students' understanding of the comprehensive nature of any public or personal health issue. The innovative use of educational technology provides the opportunity to integrate multiple courses into a collective project with students from various health-related classes bringing their unique perspective to address the health issue in question. By doing so, students' knowledge about a particular health problem is improved by promoting a multidisciplinary approach to learning. Today's graduates will work in environments that require them to interact with a variety of professionals who have received formal training in many different health-related fields. It is therefore important to develop a comprehensive curricular network approach to learning such that graduates are well positioned to excel in the workplace.

Given that departmental degree plans are already integrated with courses from multiple disciplines included within the plans, VITAL has been conceived to implement curricular integration at the individual course level. The within course integration enables students in different courses to work together on a health-related issue in a way that students from each individual course contribute a unique set of knowledge about a given health issue to the project. In this way, students from multiple classes begin to understand the multidimensional challenges associated with a health issue and develop a multidisciplinary solution.

4 Health and Human Performance's Island in Second Life

In 2007, the department rented an 'island' in the virtual world of Second Life (SL). Although the use of an avatar within SL is free to both students and university personnel, the ability to control and develop the department's own site was critical to realizing the vision a virtual world presented to the faculty. Early development activities included branding the island with both University of Houston and Health and

Human Performance (HHP) department signage and flags, separate buildings associated with each degree program, a common green space pond and park, an alumni, a research and advising center, and an SL orientation building. The orientation building provided directions and opportunities to practice controlling an avatar. The intent was to create an environment the students were familiar with in the hopes they would become comfortable exploring our island and then branch out into the wider world of SL. In parallel with this effort, several faculty worked with a SL designer to develop demonstration activities specific to their courses. These activities were located in the levels above the island itself, essentially in the 'sky' and could be reached through activation of labeled teleporter poles. Several faculty members involved in the VITAL project have previously published articles concerning innovative uses of virtual worlds to promote healthy behaviors [13] and student persistence [14]. Once the VITAL project was conceived, it was necessary to remodel the HHP island to create more favorable spaces for team activities. The remodeling of the island included building multiple gazebos that can be reserved using the VITAL Services system, an avatar tracking system, and an orientation 'path' around the island. This orientation path contained 20 different activities or skills that are essential for reasonable avatar functioning within SL. Generally the path's activities are arranged from most critical, for instance, controlling avatar movement to more sophisticated skills such as simple building principles. This path is a tremendous improvement over the original orientation building and allows the island to accommodate many students at one time all while developing avatar skills early in the semester. Map stands are placed throughout the island to aid in navigation around the island. An outdoor coliseum structure in which the virtual health conference is held has also been also built (Fig. 1).

A critical feature of the coliseum is the presentation stage that allows avatars on the stage to navigate their presentations on the coliseum's projection screen. Only avatars on stage have access to the virtual technology that controls the presentations, a critical feature that prevents unnecessary distractions by audience members. After the initial semester in which the VITAL project was conducted, a gazebo containing exemplar VITAL presentations and practice stage was built. The technology on the practice stage was identical to that used during the students' actual presentations at the virtual health conference. This enabled the students to become familiar with how the microphone and navigation features of the presentations worked, as well as practice their presentations in front of a small audience or their teammates.

5   Operationalization of VITAL

The basic approach used to operationalize the vision underlying VITAL is to form teams of students from four different classes, have them chose either a public health issue or personal disease, for example, Parkinson's disease, explore the features of the issue and ultimately present their findings and recommendations in a virtual health conference within SL. Although different courses are included in the project in different semesters, VITAL teams always consist of students from four different classes that allow multidisciplinary exploration of the health issue (Fig. 2). For instance, one semester students from the Motor Learning and Control, Physiology of Human

Fig. 1. Aerial view of the VITAL island. The coliseum is the round structure in the middle of the island at the top portion of the figure. The white circular structures are the meeting gazebos. The orientation path can be seen in the bottom left hand corner.

Performance, Seminar in Nutrition Research, and the Urban Fitness Programming course participated in VITAL. Other semesters a psychology of sport and exercise, design and evaluation of physical activity programs, or a nutrition seminar course may substitute for one of the above courses (Fig. 3).

The grouping of courses results in team members from the various disciplines encompassed within the course they are enrolled in to focus on exploring and submitting material to the team that is directly related to that particular course. For example, a student enrolled in Motor Learning exploring Parkinson's disease submits information about the etiology of the disease and related movement characteristics, students enrolled in the Designing and Evaluating Physical Activity Programs course may submit information about physical activity programs that can be implemented with individuals with Parkinson's disease. Likewise, students on a team addressing adult obesity and enrolled in the Exercise Physiology course may submit material about the physiological impact of obesity while those students enrolled in a Public Health course are responsible for providing information about the prevalence and the annual cost of obesity to the economy.

Fig. 2. An example of one of the gazebos that students used for virtual VITAL meetings.

All instructors participating in VITAL within a given semester provide identical information about the project in their syllabi. This information includes a description of VITAL's purpose, a template of what aspects of the health-issue need to be addressed, for example, incidence rate and diagnosis, milestones to be met during the development of their final presentation, use of Second Life, peer evaluation form, and a grading template. All instructors equally weight the value of VITAL project towards the students' final grade in their course. Most semesters, the value of the VITAL project is approximately 25 % of the final grade. In addition to the information in the syllabus and in-class discussion, three face-to-face orientation sessions are held in the student computer lounge. The orientation sessions include information about VITAL as a process, including the expectation of a first class virtual presentation as the final outcome of the process and information and hands on experiences with SL. Although these orientation sessions are optional, they are generally well attended.

Once students download SL and created their avatar, printed and online class material directs them to the HHP island in SL. Once they teleport to the island, a large billboard directs them to enroll in the VITAL tracking system. This system requires that they provide their actual name and their avatar name. The tracking system allows the instructors to monitor the overall avatar usage on the island and determine which areas of the island, for example, the orientation path, receive the most traffic during different times of the day.

Each semester the students from two of the four VITAL courses are assigned the role of Team Leads with the students from the other two courses being assigned the role of Team Members. For logistical ease, the students in the courses with the smaller number of enrolled students are assigned as the Team Leads. The number of students in

Fig. 3. The VITAL coliseum during a presentation.

these courses determines the number of VITAL teams that are formed. If the smallest classes still have a large number of students, two students from those classes are assigned a co-Team Lead role. All team leads have at least one student from the other two courses. Each team ranges between four and six students, depending upon the enrollment of the courses participating in VITAL in a semester. Depending upon the size of the other courses contributing team members to a project, a particular team can have up to three students from a particular class, although this is rare. The team leads or co-team leads are responsible for choosing the VITAL team's health-related topic from a list provided by the instructors.

To this point in the process, communication about the VITAL process and development occurs through email using the university's course management system (Blackboard) or in class announcements, depending upon whether the class was fully online, hybrid or face-to-face. Once the teams are formed, each team member is placed within a separate course shell within Blackboard. This important step allows the team to communicate exclusively with each other using Blackboard's email, discussion board, and document upload features. The next step is the team lead contacts his or her team members to schedule a virtual meeting on the HHP island and use the VITAL

Services reservation system. The use of the reservation system ensures a particular gazebo is available to conduct the team meeting. Each team leader is required to virtually meet five times across the semester and each team member is required to attend at least three of the five meetings. The team lead is responsible for tracking the attendance of each team member and reporting it to the instructor as part of a team meeting summary report. To allow the instructor to determine the overall quality of the meetings and make sure each team is on track towards the development of a final presentation, both the team leads and team members copy the chat log from within SL and submits it as a text document as part of their meeting summary report. The chat log contains a record of when and where the meeting took place, each team member's avatar's name, and contribution to the meeting, including what was discussed. The chat log provides important documentation of attendance and level of team member participation should any disputes concerning these two issues arise.

As the semester progresses, the team is required to accomplish milestones designed to ensure continued progress toward the development of their final presentation. A brief description of each milestone is presented in Table 1.

The culmination of the VITAL experience is a three-day virtual health conference held in the coliseum on the HHP island. Each team lead provides a 15 min presentation while on the virtual stage using the SL microphone feature. This feature allows the audience to hear the presentation through their computers while viewing the presentation on the virtual screen contained in the coliseum. Five minutes are allowed for audience members to ask questions of the presenters. Students enrolled in the courses participating in VITAL within a given semester are required to attend at least five presentations and provide a written summary report of each presentation. In their summary report, the students are to answer what they found interesting about the presentation, at least one new fact they learned, what areas of the presentation they would improve, and any suggestions for additions to the presentation. Each semester the virtual health conference is promoted using hallway posters, the department's Facebook and web page, and in the student newspaper. Anyone with a SL avatar is invited to attend the conference regardless of if they are currently enrolled or not in the VITAL courses. It is not uncommon for avatars with no affiliation with the university but interested in health-related issues, to attend the conference. The number of presentations at the conference range from 35 to 55 depending upon enrollment and the number of teams within a given semester. Although the presenter can physically be anywhere there is access to the internet, as a convenience, the department provides an isolated room with internet access and a large screen monitor that the team leads can use to make their presentations. Instructors are also present to monitor the room during the presentations and support staff assisted with any technological problems.

6   Lessons Learned and Development of VITAL Support Methodologies

As the VITAL methodology developed it became increasingly clear that to realize the full potential embedded within the VITAL experience, we needed to provide the students with a great amount of specific information. Given that only a small percentage of

Table 1. Listing and description of VITAL activities required to be completed by the participating students.

Activity	Purpose
Face-to-face Second Life Orientation (optional)	Introduce VITAL project and SL to students
Second Life Quiz (Blackboard)	Learning tool to determine that students have begun using SL
Enroll in Vital Services (SL)	Provides avatar tracking & meeting reservations privileges
Introduction of assignment (Blackboard)	Students provide introductory information to their teammates (names, class, one interesting fact about themselves)
Virtual team meetings (SL)	Working team meetings required for the development of final presentation. Each of the 5 meetings must be completed by an instructor provided deadline
Submit meeting chat logs (Blackboard)	Provides instructor with information about attendance & relative contribution of each team member to meeting
Submit reference articles (Blackboard)	Each team member submits two pdf articles relevant to the presentation topic. Articles contain information about aspects of the topic based upon the course they are enrolled in. Example – students enrolled in nutrition courses submit articles about nutritional aspects of the presentation topic, those enrolled in the physiology course submit information about physiological aspects of the topic
Submit sample presentation slide (Blackboard)	Each team member submits a slide with summarized information from the submitted articles for inclusion in final presentation
Upload final presentation (SL)	Required only of team leads; provides instructors a culminating record of the teams' assignment
Deliver virtual presentation (SL)	Required only of team leads; provides instructor an opportunity to evaluate presentation skills of team lead
Virtually attend 5 VITAL health conference presentations (SL)	Submit a written summary of each presentation attended using an instructor provided template, provides student accountability
Submit peer evaluation of each team member (Blackboard)	Provides instructor information and reinforces team member accountability through the VITAL process
Complete VITAL follow up survey (SurveyMonkey)	Provides instructors information about the overall VITAL process and strength and weakness of the process

our students had done anything other than play games within a virtual environment, it quickly became apparent they were having a difficult time grasping the concept of working collaboratively and ultimately presenting material in SL. This finding is consistent with the report that even students who are relatively sophisticated users of technology are slow to embrace new uses for educational technology [15]. As mentioned above, after the first semester in which VITAL was employed, examples of high quality presentations were provided to the students. This enables them to gain a sense of what their final presentations are to look like. Feedback indicated that the ability to 'see' examples of the final presentations early in the semester provided a level of comfort and confidence that they also could be successful in the virtual world.

The first semester that VITAL was employed, the instructors focused on the VITAL process and the difficulties our students were having using the unfamiliar technology. What we failed to realize early on was that many of our students were lacking in organizational skills and the 'soft' skills often required for assembling and directing a team. This oversight was revealed to us as we, in the form of our avatars, virtually attended a number of team meetings. Almost none of the team leads had prepared any sort of meeting agenda or had a clear goal for what they hoped to accomplish in the meeting. The first meetings of the semester tended to quickly veer off into complaints about why they had to participate in the group project, let alone a virtual group project. We intervened at this point with each instructor speaking to their class about how to conduct meetings and established some assignments with due dates. This helped to provide some structure for the students and ultimately led to more successful experiences.

To ameliorate some of the difficulties the students were having in conducting productive meetings, example scripts were developed. These scripts were transcripts of well run, productive meetings conducted by the instructors with other instructors and VITAL staff serving in the roles of team lead and teammates. Scripts of poorly run meetings were also developed and provided to the students. Both the 'well run' and 'poorly run' meetings were filmed in SL, uploaded and the students were provided a link so they could watch the meetings.

Another early oversight was the assumptions that the team leads would choose a spot on the department's island to serve as meeting place for his or her team. For example, 'meet by the duck pond at 6:00 pm on Thursday'. Instead, all of the teams tried to conduct their meetings very close to the island's landing pad. Students would teleport to the island, wander around to a group of avatars, and listen to the conversation trying to determine if they were in the correct team meeting. This was a concrete example of our student's inability to properly organize a meeting. This problem was solved by building five gazebos designed as team meeting spaces, each with a unique name. Using the VITAL Services system, team leads were able to reserve a particular gazebo at a particular time. This reservation system completely solved the problem of students wandering the island in search of their team.

During the first implementation of VITAL, we also learned that not having standardized assignments with common due dates across the different courses was an invitation to chaos. Teammates from different classes would inform other team members of assignments and due dates that were not relevant to those students' particular classes, leading to difficult class management issues for the VITAL instructors. To resolve this issue, the instructors developed standardized assignments and due dates and made sure they were emphasized within the class syllabus for each of the classes participating in VITAL that semester.

Another lesson learned was that many of the students were unable to assemble a high quality presentation or present it in a professional manner. As mentioned above, this issue was addressed by providing examples of good presentations from previous semesters and providing the students a template of what elements need to be addressed in their presentation. For example, a particular disease's characteristics, incidence rate, etiology, nutritional factors that may exacerbate or assist in the management of the condition, physiological functioning and therapeutic protocols and technologies are examples of items that are required for inclusion in a presentation concerning a particular disease condition. Public health issues, such as childhood obesity or teen depression, have their own template of required elements. Eventually, VITAL manuals for team leads and team member were developed that contain all of the information necessary to participate in a successful VITAL experience. These manuals are available for download and contain text, pictures and valuable links to online material that served as an effective student resource. A VITAL manual was also developed for faculty that enables relatively smooth incorporation of new faculty into the VITAL project.

We learned that the relative value in terms of a student's course grade must be very similar across classes. It is important that each team member has the same relative externally provided incentive to contribute to the group project. During the inaugural use of VITAL, different instructors gave the project a different relative weight of the student's final grade. In retrospect it was not surprising to discover those who efforts would more strongly influence their final class grade contributed more than those whose efforts counted less. Eventually, the instructor team decided that VITAL counts approximately 25 % towards a student's final grade regardless of which class they are enrolled in. This seems to be a reasonable number that indicates to the students that the instructors view VITAL as an important component of their particular course while at the same time, not overwhelming the other assignments in the course.

Finally, acceptance of VITAL became greater as those that were teammates in their sophomore and junior level courses eventually enrolled in senior level courses where they served as team leads. Having previously gone through the VITAL experience prepared them to take leadership roles that led to successful final presentations.

7   Student Feedback

The feedback provided by the students indicates general acceptance of the VITAL process with some students thinking that it was an innovative and exciting use of technology while a small number are unhappy being forced to participate in a team project that requires them to learn a new technology. As technology improved, particularly the video cards used in laptops, the students experienced fewer technological problems with the use of SL. Early on, complaints about SL itself were quite prevalent. These types of complaints abated over the years.

The other area that initially drew of criticism was that of collaborations with teammates. These generally took the form of teammates complaining that 'my team lead ignores my input regarding when the team meetings should be and he or she is disorganized'. Conversely, team leads complained that their teammates did not show up for the virtual meetings, provide the requested information and were generally nonresponsive to the team lead's requests. These issues were dealt with through the development of formal, graded assignments with common deadlines across class and the development of extensive VITAL manuals. Additionally, a team member and team leader peer evaluation form was developed. The team lead(s) complete a survey rating their team members and team members complete two surveys, one rating their team leads(s) and the other rating their fellow team members. There is also a self-evaluation section on the form. The results of these surveys are factored in to the student's course grade. The peer survey provides an increased level of accountability across the students and has resulted in fewer complaints about unequal effort across the student teams.

Finally, acceptance of VITAL became greater as those that were teammates in their sophomore and junior level courses eventually enrolled in senior level courses where they served as team leads. Having previously gone through the VITAL experience prepared them to take leadership roles that led to successful final projects.

In the most recent VITAL survey, 60 % of the students rated the VITAL experience at either 'excellent' or 'good'. A strong majority of the students indicated that VITAL should continue to be incorporated into the curriculum. The examples below are representative of the type of feedback that is received on the surveys administered after the completion of the VITAL project.

In response to the question 'What did you like MOST about VITAL?' comments included the following representative statements.

'My VITAL experience truly showed how people from different curriculum areas could be integrated within the unique environment of Second Life to develop a high quality presentation. Until VITAL I had never experienced such a unique learning experience.'

'The interactive nature of the group project and its 'global' perspective. You work with students from many other classes, which is quite amazing in fact.'

'It taught me how to lead better.'

'The opportunity to attend class mates presentations (my course was online).'

'Participating in something entirely new, presenting a presentation virtually, and witnessing presentations virtually.'

'The array of projects and ideas that were presented. Some of the projects were well thought out and seemed very professional like they could be carried out as they were, I was very impressed by level of projects.'

'The outside of my comfort zone experience.'

'The assignments that students in each class had to complete that uniquely contributed to the final project. That made me feel that I was still learning the information that I needed to learn in 'home' class but was also contributing information to a larger project without any of the team members duplicating effort.'

In response to the question 'What did you like LEAST about VITAL?' comments included the following representative statements.

'Technical difficulties are inevitable but it is definitely a big issue.'

'Giving the presentation through Second Life. I had a lot of technical problems even on the computer at campus.'

'There are too many glitches and technical issues associated with the program.'
'A few team members did not attend meetings or did not provide any feedback.'
'A project like VITAL requires a lot of communication.'

In response to the question 'What would you recommend to improve the VITAL project?' comments included the following representative statements.

'Have more tutorials for Second Life with an instructor present to help students in person.'

'Meet once in person before the project begins.'

'Instructors involved with the VITAL Projects should hold introductory meetings in Second Life.'

'Maybe a tutorial of how to use the program.'

'Set clear guidelines of what is expected of each student.'

Finally, the next two student quotes provide extended commentary about two interrelated issues concerning 'soft' skills and leadership skill development that were inherently imbedded within the VITAL experience. These quotes are representative examples of students who clearly gained knowledge beyond just that of health-related content.

'As a team lead, I initially was only concerned with the content of the presentation I was scheduled to present. However, I very soon realized that I was being presented with learning opportunities embedded with the VITAL project that I hadn't previously considered. For instance, I quickly learned that there is a skill involved arranging and conducting productive meetings, how to effectively manage team members who don't fulfill their assignments and how to develop informative presentations. I quickly learned that these are all skills that require practice and VITAL provided those opportunities to learn those professional skills. I am sure these 'extra' skills will be valuable in my future professional life.'

'The next semester, I was in Dr. Layne's motor learning class and served as a team lead. Up to that point at UH I had not been asked to serve in a leadership role for my classmates. I quickly learned that I would need to improve my organizational skills if I was going to lead a successful project. Having been a team member previously gave me a much needed perspective on how to be a more effective team lead. Serving as the team lead made me realize that one of the strengths of the VITAL project was that because it involves multiple classes, the students in the department would eventually serve in both the team lead and team member roles and in that way gain a larger perspective about how teams work to complete a project. Those types of lessons extended beyond the basic content I learned about the topic.'

8   Expansion of the VITAL Methodology

In its essence, VITAL is a learning management system that can be utilized by any combination of courses whose content can be logically integrated. The methodology, with its seamless integration between Blackboard (or any learning management system) and SL (or any virtual world), has evolved to the point that the full potential of a virtual world can now be utilized. For instance, professors from various academic departments can use the VITAL methodology to develop a class that demonstrates relationships between various disciplines that at first blush might seem unrelated. For example, VITAL can be used to link a motor learning class, a dance class, and an art class that featured paintings of human physical actions. The VITAL methodology can also be used with students in classes from civil, mechanical and electrical engineering to develop a simulated building within a virtual world. Essentially, any group of instructors, located anywhere in the world, can implement the VITAL methodology to provide their students a unique and engaging learning experience that emphasizes the integrated nature of our world.

9 Potential Barriers to the Use of VITAL

Two barriers that may prevent widespread adoption of VITAL include cost and associated staff resources. The cost of renting an island in SL can be prohibitive for many institutions. However, as open SIM technologies become more prevalent, the cost of maintaining a site on which to conduct virtual activities will decrease. The development of a functional virtual world can also be quite expensive, as most institutions currently do not have staff members capable of building relatively sophisticated virtual structures. Generally, more elaborate SL construction needs to be subcontracted out to professional designers whose compensation rates can vary. The development of the VITAL Services reservation and tracking system revealed itself to be essential to conducting VITAL and such a system required relatively high level programming. The current VITAL methodology involves a number of assignments that require some level of 'grading'. Most of the grading is relatively cursory in that it primarily involves confirming the teammates have completed the required assignment by the due date. For example, graders determine if the team members submit their required articles on time. However, the grading of some activities requires a significant time commitment, for instance, scanning the chat logs to determine who was actively participating in a team meeting or assessing the final presentation. At the University of Houston, we are fortunate in that teaching assistants are available to assist the instructors with the lower level assignments thereby freeing up the instructors to grade the more involved assignments. Our instructor teams also benefitted from competitive university-level programs that provided modest levels of funding to support the development of VITAL materials and SL island improvements. Finally, for VITAL to be an optimal learning experience, a team of like-minded instructors who believe in the value of integrated, cross disciplinary learning utilizing non-traditional approaches, is needed. As students complained about VITAL, particularly in its development stage, it was important to present a unified and consistent message to the students as to why we believed VITAL was an important part of their education.

10 Conclusions

To date, over 1000 students have participated in VITAL, over 22,000 h have been spent in VITAL activities on the department's SL island and over 250 health-related virtual presentations have been made. These metrics provide a snapshot of the reach of the VITAL project into our study body. The high quality of many of the presentations combined with much of the feedback we receive indicates the goals of fostering a positive, collaborative experience in a virtual world are being accomplished through the VITAL project. We feel confident that the VITAL experience has provided our students with a level of curiosity and confidence to further explore virtual worlds and other innovative technologies as they embark upon their professional careers.

References

1. Mujber, T.S., Szecsi, T., Hashmi, M.S.J.: Virtual reality applications in manufacturing process simulation. J. Mater. Process. Technol. **155–156**, 1834–1838 (2004)
2. Walsh, C.M., Sherlock, M.E., Ling, S.C., Carnahan, H.: Virtual reality simulation training for health professions trainees in gastrointestinal endoscopy. Cochrane Database Syst. Rev. CD008237 (2012). doi:10.1002/14651858.CD008237.pub2
3. Cohen, D.C., Sevdalis, N., Patel, V., Taylor, D., Batrick, N., Darzi, A.W.: Major incident preparation for acute hospitals: current state-of-the-art, training needs analysis, and the role of novel virtual worlds simulation technologies. J. Emerg. Med. **43**, 1029–1037 (2012)
4. Eschenbrenner, B., Nah, F.F., Siau, K.: 3-D virtual worlds in education: applications, benefits, issues, and opportunities. JDM **19**, 91–110 (2008)
5. Sims, E.M.: Reusable, lifelike virtual humans for mentoring and role-playing. Comput. Educ. **49**, 75–92 (2007)
6. Fluet, G.G., Deutsch, J.E.: Virtual reality for sensorimotor rehabilitation Post-Stroke: the promise and current state of the field. Curr. Phys. Med. Rehabil. Rep. **1**, 9–20 (2013)
7. Shen, J., Eder, L.B.: Exploring intentions to use virtual worlds for business. JECR **10**, 94–103 (2009)
8. Vijayan, P., Perumal, V., Shanmugam, B.: Multimedia banking and technology acceptance theories. JIBC **10**, 10 (2005)
9. McNeely, B.: Using technology as a learning tool, not just the cool new thing. In: Oblinger, D.G., Oblinger, J.L. (eds.) Educating the Net Generation. EDUCAUSE, Washington (2005)
10. McGinnis, J.M., Williams-Russo, P., Knickman, J.R.: The case for more active policy attention to health promotion. Health Aff. **21**, 78–83 (2002)
11. Patel, V.L., Yoskowitz, N.A., Arocha, J.F., Shortliffe, E.H.: Cognitive and learning sciences in biomedical and health instructional design: a review with lessons for biomedical informatics education. J. Biomed. Inform. **42**, 176–197 (2009)
12. Rubio, D.M., Schoenbaum, E.E., Lee, L.S., Schteingart, D.E., Marantz, P.R., Anderson, K.E., Platt, L.D., Baez, A., Esposito, K.: Defining translational research: implications for training. Acad. Med. **85**, 470–475 (2010)
13. Lee, R.E., Layne, C.S., McFarlin, B.K., O'Connor, D., Siddiqi, S.: Obesity prevention in Second Life: the international health challenge. In: Russell, D. (ed.) Cases on Collaboration in Virtual Learning: Processes and Interactions, pp. 110–119. IGI Global, Hershey (2009)
14. Layne, C.S., Lee, R.E., O'Connor, D.P., Horn, C.L., McFarlin, B.K.: Using digital communities to enhance student persistence and retention. In: Russell, D. (ed.) Cases on Collaboration in Virtual Learning: Processes and Interactions, pp. 140–153. IGI Global, Hershey (2009)
15. Littlejohn, M.A., Vojt, G.: Are digital natives a myth or a reality? university student's use of digital technologies. Comput. Educ. **56**, 429–440 (2011)

Guess the Score, Fostering Collective Intelligence in the Class

Josep M. Monguet and Jaime Meza[(✉)]

Universitat Politècnica de Catalunya, Barcelona, Spain
jm.monguet@gmail.com, jaime.meza@estudiant.upc.edu

Abstract. This paper proposes the use of serious games as a tool to enhance collective intelligence of undergraduate and graduate students. The use of games in teaching, at different levels of education, has been widely discussed by researchers [1]. The development of social skills of individuals in a group is related to the performance of the collective intelligence of the group manifested through the shared and collaborative development of intellectual tasks [2]. Guess the Score GS, is a serious game implemented by means of an online tool, created to foster the development, interaction, collaboration and engagement of students with the educational activity. The game has been designed with the intention of facilitating the development of individual's social skills in a group in order to promote education of collective intelligence. The first part of this article is devoted to the presentation of the fields of knowledge which may be involved in collective intelligence education. The second part presents GS game in the context of a model-based learning to promote collective intelligence. In the final part the results of the implementation are discussed. This paper concludes that the design of learning activities using serious games as a support tool in education, increased social skills and improves student performance groups, therefore the development collective intelligence.

Keywords: Collective intelligence education · Serious games · Learning · ICT tools · Patterns

1 Introduction

Education is a field with continual challenges and educational institutions are constantly searching new models to improve the results of their students. Besides the development of individual competencies and attitudes, are necessary new models and strategies for the development of social and collective capabilities. Furthermore, the use of serious games in education has been explored since the 90's, in order to exploit its various advantages [3]. Under these two assumptions, this paper investigates the design of learning activities based on the application of serious gaming.

A simple analysis of the available literature in the field of education of collective intelligence, its relevance to the innovation and implementation of serious gaming as a means of interaction, shows that academic effort in this area is still scarce [4].

The focus of this work has involved the design, development and operation of "Guess the Score" (GS), an online game developed using services oriented architecture SOA. GS promotes the development of social skills among students through interaction

© Institute for Computer Sciences, Social Informatics and Telecommunications Engineering 2014
G. Vincenti et al. (Eds.): eLEOT 2014, LNICST 138, pp. 116–122, 2014.
DOI: 10.1007/978-3-319-13293-8_14

and engagement with members of your group and the class in general. GS is a tool that enables each student individually and as a group see in real time, their results on the detailed monitoring of the activities of the class. The instructional design of the class sessions is such that interventions when students exhibit their practical exercises are used as an input of the game to assess how the students understand the content being studied. In each iteration the system, both the individual and the work group displayed its position on the class, the dispersion of the scores, and can make an immediate self-assessment, to proceed with the next iteration to improve its performance.

The set of iterations executed by students, generate data that allow finding patterns of behaviors of both individuals and the group in the development of the assigned tasks.

2   Collective Intelligence Education

Collective intelligence has always existed between human beings. From the most primitive tribes to the large modern corporations generate collective intelligence [5], so, P. Lévy defines collective intelligence as "recognition and mutual enrichment of people" [6]. Today with the development of ICT [7], exchange information quickly and agile which has generated that to the collective intelligence concept increasing. Diverse studies confirm that the development of collective intelligence with the support of ICT is an important issue. Malone established as a basic question in the collective intelligence center at MIT "How can people and computers be connected so that—collectively—they act more intelligently than any person, group, or computer has ever done before?" [8], furthermore, I. Lykourentzou et al. 2009, define collective intelligence: "an emerging research field which aims at combining human and machine intelligence, to improve community processes usually performed by large groups" [9]. This guidance promotes, among others, the need to educate the collective intelligence. GS was developed considering various strands of thought in the field of social intelligence, design and task management in learning processes and the impact of serious gaming in education.

3   Fostering Collective Intelligence

With the general idea of foresting collective intelligence in educational environment, a prototype of learning model has been designed, developed and tested and it's formally presented in this section and synthetically drawn in Fig. 1. The model allows teacher, students and groups, gradually improve the outcomes obtained from learning activities. So the system facilitates the interaction and engagement of students and groups, along with cyclical improvement of activities design. GS is part of the model, as a facilitator of engagement of participants.

The central hypothesis of this model is that if a group of students learn in a collective intelligence awareness environment, it increases both the outcomes of the groups and the learning level of individual students. Furthermore it increases also the social intelligence of individuals.

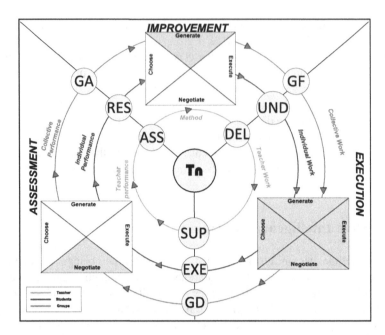

Fig. 1. General view and components of a learning model to promote collective intelligence

The model considers incremental and iterative design in order to improve the activities. This model is based in Deming circle and the Task Circumplex framework of McGrath (Fig. 2). GS into the model responds to the objective of facilitating a way of measuring collective intelligence of the group, together with the assessment of individual students. The data obtained from interaction of students during the realization of activities will use to find patterns of behaviors of groups.

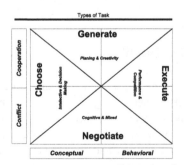

Fig. 2. Task types for learning, adapting from McGrath (1984).

As shown in Fig. 1, the model follows three domains (sectors), circuits (circles) and matrixes which are: execution, assessment and improvement; teacher, students and groups and types for learning respectively. All circuits are concentric with the core task, it is supported by a serious gaming through a list of milestones summarized in the Table 1.

Table 1. Components of model

Milestone	Description
Delivery (DEL)	Definition of the list of task according to quadrants of Circumplex Model and the challenge of activity. Serious game proposal according to the nature of challenge
Support (SUP)	Support given to students during the development of individual and groups task
Assessment (ASS)	Adjustment of the activity for the next application, using information from massive data
Understanding (UND)	Understanding of contents and strategies for the development of the task. Evaluation of self-benefit of the activity
Execution (EXE)	Interaction with the task development: choose, decision making, creativity, bargaining, and so on
Result (RES)	Real time access to scores, self-assessment and new goals
Formation (GF)	Formation of groups of work. The S.P.A.C.E formula [10], to determine profile for each student
Dynamic (GD)	Visualization of group dynamics, considering individual social skill as well as group behaviors
Assessment (GA)	Real time access to scores, self-assessment and new goals for the groups

4 Generation and Application of Massive Data in Class

GS has been applied in two groups of students of pre and postgraduate (eighty students), in this section have been summarized its application by each milestone.

DL: The learning activity was Capital Innovation IC, and was aimed at facilitating the understanding of concepts and tools for the identification and protection of intellectual assets produced through innovation activities. The learning activities tasks involved: intellective, decision making, generation of ideas and executing performance task of the Circumplex Model. GS was specifically designed to foster participation of students in the assessment of all activities realized during the class. The gaming consisted on trying to guess the value that the teacher will score at works presented in class by students. The students had to qualify the groups presenting their works, according to the parameters of the activity: Inventory of value protection, Threats and risk analysis, cost-benefit of protection and Intellectual capital SWOT. The criteria for the score were: (1) very loose, (2) Pretty lazy, (3) Normal, (4) Good, (5) Pretty good, (6) Very good. The rubrics for the score are: exactly to the teacher plus 1 point, deviation in value of "n" points: Subtract "n−1".

SUP: During the execution of activities the teacher explained to the class the content of the activity, and helped to specific groups to solve details of the different task. In the public presentation of works of groups the teacher discussed about the correctness and mistakes of the tasks. All students of the class where able to follow discussion and participate.

ASS: The data generated by the participation of students in the "guess the score" gaming, during a two hour class were in a rank of between 10 and 20. This data correspond to the assessments made by each student about the level of performance of tasks, presented by any other students, and expressed before the teacher made public his particular assessments. With all this data it was possible: At the individual level measure the deviation between the score of the teacher and each particular student. In each consecutive task assessed, the student was able to improve his or her capacity to apply the concepts related to intellectual capital. At the group level: measure the deviation between the median of score of the group against the teacher and against the other groups. The groups were able to improve its dynamics analyzing their performance as a groups and individually.

UND: Participants had to attend to the session to understand the activity and the tasks for each activity.

EXE: The students working in groups had to solve the list of task of activities.

RES: The students are able to visualize the scores and its ranking individually, as well as in group. Rankings presented included: individual position in relation to the class and group, the student behavior along practices, and position of group in relation to the class (Fig. 3).

GF: The groups were formed freely according to the preferences and affinity of the students.

GD: The group according with the result obtained in each cycle established the goals for the next cycle.

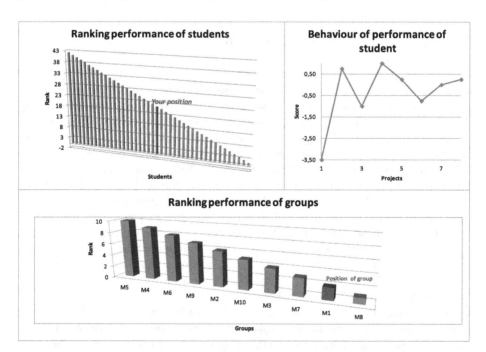

Fig. 3. Rankings of: individual position in relation to the class and group, the student behaviour along practices and position of group in relation to the class.

GA: With the information of each practitioner, the groups, they analyzed their results and how they could improve it in future activities, the resources available are: the S.P.A.C.E formula [10] of group, the average of deviation respect to the experimenter, rate from the minimal to maximal score of groups and so on.

The findings of the test with the first GS prototype are useful to align the next step of research: Some of the results are: As shown in Fig. 4 the gaming strategy is a key element to succeed in student engagement; the process of collecting data from the participation of students has demonstrated efficient and works appropriately; and the S.P.A.C.E [10] application has a limited utility to validate the student social profile.

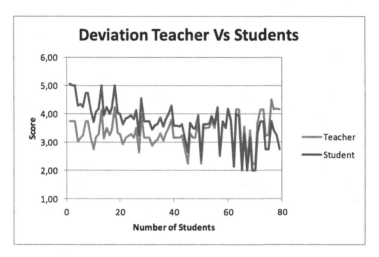

Fig. 4. Deviation between of teacher and students in the application of "guessthescore" game

5   Conclusions

The objective of the work presented here is to share the advances in a research program which intention is to provide a model, strategies, tools and resources to help improve the collective intelligence education. The GS and its theoretical framework is very wide and open and it's necessary much more research to find a consensus about which are the relevant theoretical elements.

The use of GS in the class has allowed obtaining some evidence about student's engagement, the increase of attention during the class and the increasing level of outcomes of exercises and practices. The model proposed, and the corresponding tool, had been the result of a creative combination of theoretical, practical and applied perspectives. From this point, with a consistent model, it will be possible to continue with the development of new functionalities oriented to make recommendations in the improvement continue the knowledge of collective intelligence education.

References

1. Connolly, T.M., Boyle, E.A., MacArthur, E., Hainey, T., Boyle, J.M.: A systematic literature review of empirical evidence on computer games and serious games. Comput. Educ. **59**(2), 661–686 (2012)
2. Woolley, A.W., Chabris, C.F., Pentland, A., Hashmi, N., Malone, T.W.: Evidence for a collective intelligence factor in the performance of human groups. Science **330**(6004), 686–688 (2010)
3. Susi, T., Johannesson, M., Backlund, P.: Serious games – an overview (2007)
4. Ilon, L.: How collective intelligence redefines education. In: Altmann, J., Baumöl, U., Krämer, B.J. (eds.) Advances in Collective Intelligence 2011. AISC, vol. 113, pp. 91–104. Springer, Heidelberg (2012)
5. MIT Center For Collective Intelligence: Handbook of Collective Intelligence. http://scripts. mit.edu/~cci/HCI/index.php?title=Main_Page#Why_study_collective_intelligence_now.3F
6. Lévy, P.: Inteligencia colectiva por una antropología del ciberespacio. Panamericana de la Salud (Unidad de Promoción y Desarrollo de la Investigación y el Centro Latinoamericano y del Caribe de Información en Ciencias de la Salud), Washington, DC, p. 141. (2004)
7. Lévy, P.: Toward a self-referential collective intelligence some philosophical background of the IEML research program. In: Nguyen, N.T., Kowalczyk, R., Chen, S.-M. (eds.) ICCCI 2009. LNCS, vol. 5796, pp. 22–35. Springer, Heidelberg (2009)
8. MIT Center For Collective Intelligence: MIT Center for Collective Intelligence. http://cci. mit.edu/
9. Lykourentzou, I., Vergados, D.J., Loumos, V.: Collective intelligence system engineering. In: Proceedings of the International Conference on Management of Emergent Digital EcoSystems - MEDES '09, p. 134 (2009)
10. Albrecht, K.: Theory of Social Intelligence. https://www.karlalbrecht.com/siprofile/siprofiletheory.htm

A Way of Supporting Non-Arabic Speakers in Identifying Arabic Letters and Reading Arabic Script in an E-Learning System

Ahmed Mosa[1,2(✉)] and Kakehi Katsuhiko[1]

[1] Computer Science Department,
3-4-1 Okubo, Shinjuku, Tokyo 169-8555, Japan
Ahmed_mosa_egypt@yahoo.com,
Ahmed_mosa_egypt@fuji.waseda.jp, kakehi@waseda.jp
[2] Educational Technology Department, Boutros St., Tanta, Egypt

Abstract. This paper reports how a new e-learning system for Arabic language supports the beginners of non-Arabic speakers in identifying each Arabic letter in a word and reading/pronouncing Arabic script. In Arabic, letters forming a word are connected to each other. Each Arabic letter has three different figures according to its position in a word (beginning, middle or end). Users' studies were conducted with 77 examinees in Japan to find which one is preferable for identifying letters of two alternatives: coloring letters or separating letters with spaces. Results showed that colored alternative is preferable. We are developing an e-learning system that incorporates the coloring way and our right-to-left phonetic to support learners in identifying and reading/pronouncing Arabic script by themselves.

Keywords: E-Learning · Arabic learning · Multimedia · Roman phonetics · Mirrored form

1 Introduction

Arabic specific features may be obstacles for non-Arabic people to learn Arabic. Arabic script runs from right to left, as opposed to the other languages. There are 29 letters which are connected in a word, not only in hand writing but also in printed materials. Letters change their figures in the script depending on their position in a word: at the beginning, in the middle, or at the end, as exemplified in Table 1, as for the letter "ب", which represents the consonant "B".

Table 1. Example of the three figures for the letter " ب "

Position			The letter
End	Middle	Beginning	
ـب	ـبـ	بـ	ب

Each Arabic letter represents its specific consonant. A word consisting of only letters does not show its pronunciation Usually letters appeared in Arabic script are attached with one of 10 diacritics to show how that letter be pronounced with/without

© Institute for Computer Sciences, Social Informatics and Telecommunications Engineering 2014
G. Vincenti et al. (Eds.): eLEOT 2014, LNICST 138, pp. 123–129, 2014.
DOI: 10.1007/978-3-319-13293-8_15

one of three Arabic vowels, as exemplified in Table 2. Thus, once one can identify each letter appearing in a word as it is, one can easily read/pronounce the word.

Table 2. Arabic script with diacritics

Pronunciation	Arabic script
BaBiBu	بَـبِـبُ
BuBiBa	بُـبِـبَ
BiBaB	بِـبَـبْ

Children may start reading in traditional way of repeated drilling on Arabic script as it is. Grown-ups find difficulty in reading/pronouncing Arabic script, especially in identifying each letter and recalling its pronunciation, since they do not endure simply repeating drilling. Learning materials, especially of e-learning ones, should provide support for learners to get used to right-to-left reading, and identify letters of a word to recall their pronunciation when intended learners may include grown-ups.

2   How to Identify Letters in a Word

2.1   Two Ways to Identify Every Letter

There are two existing alternatives or ways, found in our surveying of Arabic teaching materials [1–3, 10], to show every letter in a word for readers; first one is coloring each letter alternating two colors, and second one is inserting spaces between each two letters, as shown in Fig. 1. E-learning system should be designed and developed depending on effective multimedia to support the learning and its activities [4]. So in our developing e-learning system, one of the alternatives of identification should be used according to the learner request as a multimedia support.

Fig. 1. Two ways of identifying letters in a word

2.2   Investigation of Users' Preference

To find out possible users' preference, a user study was conducted in Japan with 77 non-Arabic examinees in Arabic classes, culture exchange meetings and laboratory activities. Examinees were Arabic students in the Islamic center, volunteers from Muslims with different nationalities and from students of the computer Science department at

Waseda University. They were of 7 nationalities and had difference in their speaking ability (only one language, two or three languages). They were 44 male and 33 female. Among 77 examinees, 66 were interested in Arabic learning and 49 have experience in Arabic language. Examinees are covering wide range of personal prosperities, profiles and ages. Some of them are university students and others are graduated.

Examinees were taught about Arabic letters and their changing figures depending on their positioning in a word. Then examinees were shown a card, like Fig. 2, exemplifying two ways of helping identification of letters in a word, and asked which one they prefer: (A) by coloring each letter one after another with alternating colors, or (B) by putting a space between adjacent letters.

Arabic script	بِسْمِ ٱللَّهِ ٱلرَّحْمَنِ ٱلرَّحِيمِ	Arabic script	بِسْمِ ٱللَّهِ ٱلرَّحْمَنِ ٱلرَّحِيمِ
Form A	بِسْمِ ٱللَّهِ ٱلرَّحْمَنِ ٱلرَّحِيمِ	Form B	بِسۡمِ ٱلۡلَّهِ ٱلۡرَّحۡمَنِ ٱلۡرَّحِيمِ

Fig. 2. A card showing two ways of letter identification

2.3   Results of the Questionnaire on Users' Preference

Among 77 examinees, 60 preferred the coloring more than separating. Namely a great percentage (78 %) of the examinees in all prefer coloring to spacing, as seen in Fig. 3.

As the examinees are categorized on their gender, interest in Arabic and experience in Arabic, statistics by those attributes are shown in Tables 3, 4, and 5. There are no significant differences, in any of those three categories, between preference percentages of coloring on the two attribute values: male 75 % vs. female 82 %, interested 78 % vs. not interested 72 %, and experienced 84 % vs. not experienced 68 %.

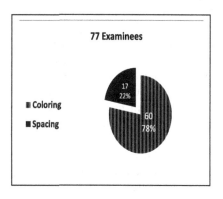

Fig. 3. Preferences of identification way

Table 3. Gender

	Male	Female	Total
Coloring	33	27	60
Spacing	11	6	17
Total	44	33	77

Table 4. Interest in Arabic

	Interested	Not interested	Total
Coloring	52	8	60
Spacing	14	3	17
Total	66	11	77

Table 5. Experience in Arabic

	Experienced	Not experienced	Total
Coloring	41	19	60
Spacing	8	9	17
Total	49	28	77

3   Designing an Interactive Support

3.1   Mirrored Roman Phonetics Representation

Arabic letters are unfamiliar to the novices, and Arabic letters with diacritics represent the pronunciation. There are lots of combinations, and some consonants have quite different sound comparing to sounds in other languages. It is important to have phonetics shown time to time for novices. Arabic is written right-to-left. It is also hard for the novices to get used to the right-to-left reading. Phonetics are written left-to-right in available and common transliterations systems [12]; those phonetics themselves are easy to read, but may obstruct the novices to get used to right-to-left reading. Phonetics for Arabic shall be also right-to-left. If we use Roman letters as phonetics arranged right-to-left, the novices may read them left-to-right since Roman letters are usually read left-to-right.

We decided to use Roman letters in mirrored form right-to-left along with the direction of Arabic script. Roman upper-case letters are for Arabic letter and Roman lower-case letters are for diacritics [6, 7]. Phonetics will be displayed under Arabic script, and as far as possible phonetics are in the same length to the Arabic script, as far as possible, in order to help learners to see easily and to feel correspondence between Arabic letters and their phonetics [8, 9], as shows in Fig. 4.

Fig. 4. Roman phonetics along with Arabic script

3.2   Support on Demand

We decided to provide supports discussed above for users in our e-learning system for Arabic learning: letter identification in a word and mirrored Roman phonetics [11]. Our philosophy for providing supports is: any support shall be provided on a user's demand, and be provided only while a user is demanding in action: [5]. When a system provides some support for users automatically or unconditionally, users get used to the environment and might become lazy enough and could not live in the actual world without the support by the system.

First support on demand is displaying Arabic letters in two colors as long as the learner is pressing down the button for letter identification help. Once he/she releases the button, the script turns back to all the black, in order to let him/her identify the letters of the script. The system, then asks the learner to submit his/her writing (hand writing/keyboard writing), as shown in Fig. 5, to receive instructor feedback/judgment.

Second support on demand is displaying the mirrored Roman phonetics (right-to-left) corresponding to the Arabic script [7, 8], as long as the learner is pressing down the read/pronounce button, according to his/her need. Once he/she releases the button, mirrored Roman phonetics disappear, in order to let him/her to read/pronounce the script, and then the system asks the learner to submit his/her recorded reading/pronouncing (Audio/video), as shown in Fig. 6, to receive instructor feedback/judgment.

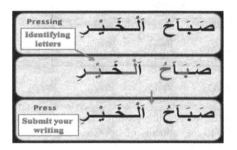

Fig. 5. Identifying Arabic letters by coloring

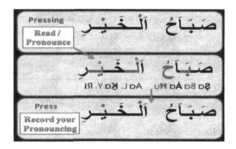

Fig. 6. Reading/pronouncing Arabic letters using colored mirrored phonetics

4   Discussions

We are developing an e-learning system for Arabic learning called ETaJWa, with user supports on demand described above. A course is designed on this system for novices, to learn daily life conversation, such as common Arabic greetings, introduction of themselves and talking about their families [11].

In the main window of this system, the learner can explore the lessons menu, choose a lesson to study and ask for support and explanation, as well as he/she can press button to study Arabic alphabet. Moreover, he/she can press the button for services on demand to obtain feedback from the instructor to guide him/her in improving his/her skills and can press a button for online and/or offline contact.

Every lesson is displayed in a window of the same format, as seen in Fig. 7. A learner can see, on the top line, Arabic sentences/expressions that shall be studied in that lesson. A learner can press a button to tell the system if he/she already knows it, and then a learner should practice the required activities. A learner can press a button for support on demand to know the meaning and the usage of the sentence/expression. Moreover, a learner can press a button of reading to identify and/or read/pronounce Arabic letters. Also, a learner can press a button of pronouncing in order to show the right-to-left mirrored phonetics helps. A learner can ask for a support for listening to the correct pronunciation. As well as a learner can ask for a support for practicing writing using his/her handwriting and/or keyboard and submitting his/her writings to the instructor. A learner can practice skills and activities which enable him/her in reading/pronouncing and submitting his/her recorded voices as audio/video file. Also, learner can press a button for communication with the instructor and/or the other learners as synchronous/asynchronous learning by skype, chatting and emails.

Assessment and/or evaluation of usability, effectiveness, et al., of our supporting methods and ETaJWa as a whole system will be conducted to assess how those features promote learning of Arabic.

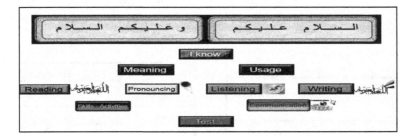

Fig. 7. Facilities of ETaJWa for every lesson

Acknowledgments. This research has been supported by Egyptian government in a form of a scholarship to one of the authors. We are grateful to the students of the Computer Science Department at WASEDA University, the students of YUAI School, the Islamic community and ISLAMIC CENTER in Japan.

References

1. Abdulla, A.: Yomeru Kakeru, Arabia Moji Renshuu Printo Read and Write Arabic Characters, Print Practice (in Japanese). Shogakukan Inc, Japan (2006)
2. Badawi, E., Carteroch, M.G., Gully, A.: Modern Written Arabic: A Comprehensive Grammar. Routledge, London (2004)
3. Hassan, H.: NHK terebi teksto: gogaku shiries terebi de arabiago NHK television text: language series 4.5; Arabic language in the TV (in Japanese). Japan Broadcasting Corporation. NHK Publishing, Japan (2012)
4. Ismail, J.: The design of an e-learning system: beyond the hype. Inter. Higher Educ. **4**(3), 329–336 (2001) (Elsevier Science Inc)

5. Mosa, A., Kakehi, K.: Towards a multimedia based e-learning system for effective acquisition of Arabic language. IPSJ SIG Technical Report (CLE), 2012-CLE-7(3), 1–3 (2012)

6. Mosa, A., Kakehi, K.: Searching for a suitable way to transliterate Arabic into roman letters as for a device in Arabic e-learning systems. In: International Conference: e_Society 2013: IADIAS, pp. 448–452. Lisbon, Portugal, 13–16 March 2013

7. Mosa, A., Kakehi, K.: Through the looking-glass: roman letters in phonics for Arabic as a part of multimedia support. In: 9th WSEAS International Conference on Educational Technologies (EDUTE '13), pp. 120–125. Kuala Lumpur, Malaysia, 2–4 April 2013

8. Mosa, A., Kakehi, K.: Designing a new transliteration system for Arabic language into Roman letters as for a device in Arabic e-learning systems. In: 2013 Hanyang-Waseda IT Workshop. Hanyang University, Seoul, Korea (2013)

9. Mosa, A., Kakehi, K.: Letting Non-Arabic speakers read and pronounce Arabic sounds using roman phonetic codes in the mirrored form -a feature of ETaJWa, an Arabic e-learning system. Int. J. Inf. Technol. Comput. Sci. (IJITCS), 2091-1610 (2014)

10. Nagato, Y.: Nyuexpres Ejipto Arabiago New Express Egypt Arabic Language (in Japanese). Hakusui Publishing, Japan (2011)

11. ETaJWa, an Arabic e_Learning system. http://mash.kake.info.waseda.ac.jp/moodle/course/view.php?id=15

12. In Wikipedia, Standard Arabic Technical Transliteration System. http://en.wikipedia.org/wiki/SATTS

Social Collaborative e-Learning in Higher Education: Exploring the Role of Informal Learning

Francis Otto[(✉)] and Shirley Williams

School of Systems Engineering, University of Reading, Reading, UK
F.Otto@pgr.reading.ac.uk, Shirley.williams
@reading.ac.uk

Abstract. This position paper presents work in progress (within the first year) of the doctoral research into adoption of social collaborative e-learning in higher education. The research coins three concepts which intersect to form the fourth, *social collaborative e-learning*. These concepts are: informal learning, social networking and learning management. This paper explores the conceptual and theoretical role of informal learning practices in building social collaborative e-learning environment. Specifically the paper will:

1. Explain the role of informal learning in formal educational setting
2. Introduce informal learning strategies that can be adopted within formal educational programmes to scaffold e-learning
3. Discuss the implications of involving educators and learners in informal interactions as a scaffold to formal education.

The paper concentrates on how strategies can be used to promote social collaborative e-learning within a higher education context. The desk-based research method was used in this research leading to the development of a framework for informal learning proposed in this paper.

Keywords: Social e-learning · Collaborative e-learning · Informal learning · Formal learning · Informal learning strategies · Higher education

1 Introduction

Learning is the process whereby new knowledge, skill, value, belief, attitude or behaviour is acquired. It may occur as a formal process, following institutional ladder that goes from preschool to graduate studies [1] or a non-formal process, when learners opt to acquire knowledge or skill by studying voluntarily with teachers who assist their self-determined interests, by using an organized curriculum, as is the case in many adult education courses and workshops [2, 3] or sometimes unconsciously through informal social interactions with others. It can therefore be argued that informal social communications and interactions especially using social networking platforms promote learning (Fig. 1).

© Institute for Computer Sciences, Social Informatics and Telecommunications Engineering 2014
G. Vincenti et al. (Eds.): eLEOT 2014, LNICST 138, pp. 130–137, 2014.
DOI: 10.1007/978-3-319-13293-8_16

Informal learning results from daily life activities related to work, family or leisure. It is not structured (in terms of learning objectives, learning time or learning support) and typically does not lead to certification. Informal learning may be intentional but in most cases it is non-intentional or "incidental" [4]. Considering the fact that the use and influence of social networking platforms is evolving significantly, higher education institutions stand to benefit from the learning opportunities provided by this emerging and evolving technology. In this paper the following three questions are explored:

1. What is the role of informal learning in formal educational setting?
2. What informal learning strategies can be adopted within formal educational programmes to scaffold e-learning?
3. What are the implications of involving educators and learners in planned informal interactions as a scaffold to formal education?

The paper starts by differentiating the concepts of formal and informal learning before explaining the various dimensions of informal learning and the resulting learning strategies. These strategies are discussed from theoretical perspectives based on the review of empirical evidence in literature. The informal learning strategies within formal educational programme are presented as basis on which the concept of informal learning environment is built. The on-going research will establish among other things, the effectiveness of the informal learning environment in two universities in Uganda. Finally, the role of educators in promoting informal learning is discussed. The on-going study will evaluate this role by examining the perception of educators and learners in adopting these strategies in light of increased use of social networking platforms in higher education.

2   Formal Learning vs. Informal Learning

Historically formal and informal learning have been at the centre of debate especially about the inherent superiority of one or the other. Scribner and Cole [5] argued that much of the research and theorizing about learning in advanced industrial societies focused primarily on formal learning. Therefore more efforts, science and enlightenment-based rationality were applied to formal learning with the assumption that when effectively provided, it had clear advantages over informal learning.

Furthermore this kind of assumption put the knowledge gained from formal learning to be more generalizable in the sense that it could be used or applied in a wide range of contexts and circumstances as opposed to the informal learning which was seen to be context-specific. For example, it is asserted that formal learning of Mathematics can be used in any context where numerical values are relevant while learning to play darts only equips a person to use numbers in that very restricted setting.

Another author whose work added to this debate was Bernstein [6] whose argument made it clear that formal learning opened up high status knowledge. These arguments resulted to a belief that formal learning and informal learning were two mode of learning that served different purposes and suited in different settings in which case, formal learning was preferred. Formal learning was therefore equated with education in schools and universities; non-institutional or informal learning was overlooked or dismissed and known to be in outside 'school' setting.

Several researchers, however, have come out clearly to oppose this debate on supremacy. Billett [7] does not believe that there is such thing as informal learning. He argues that norms, values and practices shape and sustain activities and interactions within workplaces, as in other social practices, such as homes or educational institutions are structures that constitute performance.

This paper argues that formal and informal learning are both significant in higher education and therefore they should be viewed as complementary modes. With the increased use of social networking services, online informal interaction can be integrated in the learning process to support e-learning. The research, which is exploring adoption of social collaborative e-learning in higher education institutions, is intended to among other things; determine the perception and practices of students and lecturers in two Ugandan universities on the use of informal learning strategies to scaffold formal educational goals. With the advancement of social networking technology enhanced learning, the two modes need to be embraced as complementary. The increased use of social networking technology in educational institutions has meant that there is greater role that informal learning in education as students and lecturers are spending a great deal of time engaging in online social interactions.

The focus of this position paper is therefore on the role of informal learning as a scaffold for formal education with the view that informal strategies can be planned within the design of formal educational programme in higher education (Fig. 1). Basing on this, the current learning management platforms can be integrated with the social networking features to make e-learning more captivating. There are few, if any, learning situations where either informal or formal elements are completely absent [2]. As asserted by Jeffs and Smith [8], informal education offers choice not compulsion; freedom not order; empowerment not indoctrination. This makes the role of informal learning very significant given the wide use of social networking technologies in higher education. This paper therefore argues that the current formal education programmes can be enhanced through informal learning styles by the use of social networking technology.

3   Dimensions of Informal Learning

Michael Eraut [9] defined two dimensions within the informal learning domain from which this paper establishes informal learning scenarios which have been proposed as suitable e-learning strategies that can be adopted as a scaffold within a formal educational programme. This is discussed in detail in the subsequent sections. The first dimension Eraut introduced is level of intension to learn which to him presents a range of learning phenomena including implicit learning at one extreme ("bottom-top" process); the deliberative learning at the other extreme ("top-bottom" process) and the reactive learning in between.

Implicit learning (as defined by Reber [10]) is learning in which the acquisition of knowledge is independent of conscious attempts to learn and is in the absence of explicit knowledge about what is learned- there being no intention to learn and no awareness of learning at the time it takes place. Implicit learning is therefore non-episodic learning of complex information in an incidental manner, without awareness

Table 1. A typology of informal learning adopted from Eraut [9].

Time of stimulus	Implicit learning	Reactive learning	Deliberative learning
Past episode (s)	Implicit linkage of past memories with current experience	Brief near-spontaneous reflection on past episodes, communications, events, experiences	Review of past actions, communications, events' experiences. More systematic reflection
Current experience	A selection from experience enters the memory	Incidental noting of facts, opinions, impressions, ideas. Recognition of learning opportunities	Engagement in decision making, problem solving, planned informal learning
Future behaviour	Unconscious effect of previous experiences	Being prepared for emergent learning opportunities	Planned learning goals. Planned learning opportunities

of what has been learned. Although Seger [11] points out that implicit may require a certain minimal amount of attention and may depend on attentional and working memory mechanisms, it may be difficult for any learning output arising from this dimension of learning to be meaningfully measured.

Because this research is considering scaffolding formal educational programme, which requires some prior planning (in terms of learning activities and learning output measurement), the proposed strategies will not take in consideration the implicit learning dimension.

Reactive learning is near-spontaneous and unplanned, the learner is aware of it but the level of intentionality will vary and often be debatable. What is important here is that an environment can be set to ensure that the learner is stimulated through social networking environment to learn. Its articulation in explicit form could also be difficult without setting aside time for more reflection and thus becoming deliberative [9]. Therefore learning activities that involve reflection may be planned.

Deliberative learning is when learning appeals to the learner whereby a time is specifically set aside for that purpose. In other words, it is when one decides if it is worthwhile to learn something. When the educator plans goal oriented learning activities especially whilst exploiting the opportunities in the social collaborative environment, learners may get more motivated to deliberately learn. This research will therefore explore the adoption of these strategies in order to determine whether or not effective learning can be achieved.

The second dimension is the timing of the events providing the focus for the learning. These events can be from the past, something happening in the present or part of some possible future action. Eraut combined the two dimensions time of local event and level of intention to construct a typology of informal learning (Table 1) from which this paper draws the informal learning strategies discussed in the next section.

4 The Informal Learning Strategies within Formal Programme

Informal learning takes place anywhere including inside and outside of formal and non-formal educational institutions. However, the main discussion in this paper is centered on the informal learning strategies within the formal higher education courses, which may include on campus and off campus courses where some of the students may be within the formal institutional settings and others in the informal settings including those who may be attending other institutions.

This paper argues that the social interactions and collaboration play a very significant role in bridging the communication gap between those who work within the formal educational setting and their counterparts in the informal settings as well as promoting, creating and sharing knowledge between students and lecturers; and among students themselves. This is based on the hypothesis that informal learning occurs in online communities. There are various technologies that support online social interactions however, what is missing is the culture within the higher education setting to stimulate and promote informal learning practices. Without this being integrated in the current e-learning systems, formal learning will remain less motivating.

In the typology shown in Table 1 above, Eraut [9] highlights nine types of situations informal learning takes place. Based on this typology, this paper introduces six strategies for effective "measurable" informal learning in support of carefully designed formal learning programme. As mentioned in the previous section, scenarios which are completely implicit will not be considered. The following are the six scenarios considered appropriately planned:

(a) Reflection on own past episodes
(b) Opinion and facts expressions
(c) Self-directed emergent learning
(d) Review of past activities
(e) Engagement in current problems
(f) Goal setting

Reflection on own past episodes: Near-spontaneous reflection on the past episodes and communicating events and experiences as noted by Eraut [9] as reactive learning provides essential knowledge that can be utilized for one's formal learning. This is specifically important is reactive decision making in case of an emergency other than a normal decision making process that follows steps including defining the problem, collecting necessary information, developing options, devising a plan, executing and making following-up. When an emergency situation occurs in a similar way to the past episode, it becomes easy to make a correct reactive decision basing on reflection on own past episodes.

Opinion and facts expressions: Incidental noting of facts, ideas and expression of learning opportunities also describe reactive learning using current stimulus. When learners are given opportunity to express their opinion on an object which has close link to the main subject of study, the scope of the learning opportunities can be developed. Allowing students to freely express their opinion about any learning experience or material certainly promotes learning. When students sure that their opinions are not censured by people in authority over them, they are highly encouraged to interact with their peers and express their opinion.

Self-directed emergent learning: Megginson [12] used the term emergent to describe an alternative strategy to planning. Emergent learning strategy is focused on learning through experience to continually and effectively get ready cease learning opportunities. Most self-directed emergent strategy learners start the learning process with just an idea of the outcome they want and progress as more opportunities avail. This strategy was illustrated by Gear et al. [13] using Tough's [14] concept of learning project (an extended piece of learning with a particular idea in mind) whereby less than 20 % of their respondents claimed to have unequivocally followed a pre-determined plan. 80 % per cent had an idea of the outcome they wanted, but followed an emergent strategy which took advantage of learning opportunities as they arose. What is important here is that allowing learners to have exploratory facilities will aid them in self-directed learning.

Review of past activities: Review of past actions, communications, events and experiences demonstrates deliberative learning from past episodes. Activities such as story-telling and experience sharing with an aim of getting lessons can provide a very supportive environment for informal learning. This scenario can be carefully managed through experiential learning activities. Learning that took place in the past can be reviewed to give experience needed for present and future learning.

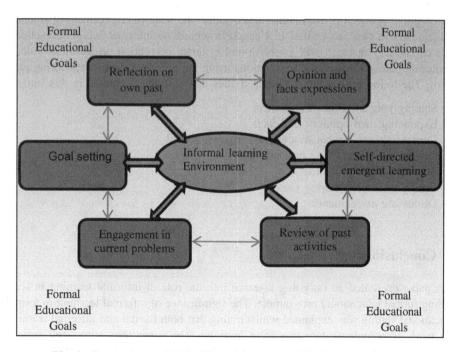

Fig. 1. Integration model for informal learning within formal programme

Engagement in current problems: Engagement with and aim of problem solving and decision making can promote informal learning. With the increased use of interactive media in education the focus of the teachers are more in engaging students, promoting independence and challenging learners. This can be done in a number of ways including: Using a wide range of tasks and resources, encouraging independent and small group research, allow presentation of results and encouraging different approaches to problem solving and judgment.

Goal setting: Planned learning goals and planned learning opportunities are commandingly used in facilitating deliberative learning for future achievements. For example if a teacher gives an assignment for the learners to learn how to cook a particular recipe. This task generates goals that will guide the learning in the future and make it easy to assess performance.

5 Involving Educators and Learners in Informal Interactions

With the increased use of social networking platforms in higher education institutions, students and their lectures are involved in informal interactions during and outside class time. This paper argues that the role of educators must therefore be flexible and change from formal to informal educators as argued by Jeffs and Smith [8]. When educators become informal instructors, they help learners to achieve learning outcomes, working in various styles and in informal settings. This can be achieved if the educators do understand and appreciate the significance of educational affordances of social networking and interactions offered by the social media platforms. One of the objectives of this on-going research is to establish and evaluate the level of engagement of students and lecturers in two universities in Uganda in regards to informal social interactions. This exploratory research will establish and evaluate perception on lecturers' role in promoting planned informal conversations using the common social networking platforms. The following are among key activities that will be considered in this study:

i. Sharing your own past experiences
ii. Expressing own opinions and facts
iii. Demonstration of what was learned by own accord
iv. Discussing or reviewing past activities
v. Solving current problems
vi. Setting goals and sharing them
vii. Discussing assignments.

6 Conclusions

This paper presented an on-going research into the role of informal learning in scaffolding formal educational programme. The significance of informal learning in formal educational setting was explained whilst noting that both formal and informal learning can work as complementary modes of learning. The paper also introduced various informal learning strategies that can be adopted using social networking technologies to scaffold e-learning. This can be achieved if educators' role can flexibly change from formal to informal learning whilst promoting greater conversations and interactions with learners. The implications of involving educators and learners in planned informal interactions was discussed whilst arguing that adopting the use of social networking services provides great opportunities to bridge the gap between informal learning and formal learning. The findings from this study will be useful in developing a framework to guide effective integration of social collaborative e-learning in higher education systems.

References

1. Schugurensky, D.: The forms of informal learning: towards a conceptualization of the field. WALL Working Paper, **19**. (2000)
2. Colley, H., Hodkinson, P., Janice, M.: Non-formal learning: mapping the conceptual terrain - a consultation report. Lifelong Learning Institute, University of Leeds, Leeds (2002)
3. Livingstone, D.W.: Adults' informal learning: definitions, findings, gaps and future research. NALL Working Paper (2001)
4. The EC: Progress towards the Common European Objectives in Education and Training: Indicators and benchmarks 2010/2011. In: Commission, T. E. (ed.) (2010)
5. Scribner, S., Cole, M.: Cognitive consequences of formal and informal education. Science Education **182**, 553–559 (1973)
6. Bernstein, B.: Class, Codes and Control. Routledge and Kegan Paul, London (1971)
7. Billett, S.: Critiquing workplace learning discourses: Participation and continuity at work. Stud. Educ. Adults **34**, 56–67 (2002)
8. Jeffs, T., Smith, M.K.: Informal Education – Conversation, Democracy & Learning, 2nd edn. Education Now Publishing, Ticknall (1999)
9. Eraut, M.: Non-formal learning and tacit knowledge in professional work. Br. J. Educ. Psychol. **70**, 113–136 (2000)
10. Reber, A.S.: Implicit learning and tacit knowledge: an essay on the cognitive unconscious. Oxford University Press, Oxford (1993)
11. Seger, C.A.: Implicit learning. Psychol. Bull. **115**, 163–196 (1994)
12. Megginson, D.: Planned and emergent learning: consequences for development. Manage. Learn. J Manag. Organ. Learn. **27**, 411–428 (1996)
13. Gear, J., McIntosh, A., Squires, G.: Informal learning in the professions (1994)
14. Tough, A.M.: The adult's learning projects. Ontario Institute for Studies in Education, Toronto (1971)

Virtual Labs Improve Student's Performance in a Classroom

Rakhi Radhamani[1], Hemalatha Sasidharakurup[1], Gopika Sujatha[1],
Bipin Nair[1], Krishnashree Achuthan[2], and Shyam Diwakar[1(✉)]

[1] Amrita School of Biotechnology, Amrita Vishwa Vidyapeetham
(Amrita University) Amritapuri, Clappana, Kollam 690525, India
shyam@amrita.edu
[2] Amrita School of Engineering (VALUE Centre), Amrita Vishwa
Vidyapeetham (Amrita University) Amritapuri, Clappana,
Kollam 690525, Kerala, India

Abstract. With the world wide acceptance of virtual educational technologies, it has been shown that they play a vital role in the scientific arena. The purpose of this paper was to analyze the role of Biotechnology virtual laboratories in integrating student's learning ability and introducing it as an effective instructional tool in biotechnology courses. A post-usage survey was conducted among the users and included questions about perceptions of virtual laboratories, its role in virtualization of sophisticated instruments. The survey suggested virtual labs usage enhanced autonomous and guided educational methods. Comparing groups on usage of virtual labs against a control (traditional lab), our studies suggest improved performance in students using virtual labs. Usage analysis and surveys indicated that biotechnology virtual labs are significant elements in adaptive learning process in blended classroom environment.

Keywords: Virtual labs · Biotechnology · Blended learning · Virtualization · Adaptive learning

1 Introduction

Information and Communication Technology (ICT)-based education is a new trend in gathering knowledge in the current educational scenario. The growth of web-based learning has massively influenced the present learning pedagogy [1]. A new model of computer-based learning was achieved by the introduction of Virtual laboratories in science education (http://vlab.co.in)] and also see MHRD Sakshat NMEICT mission document (http://www.sakshat.ac.in/PDF/Missiondocument.pdf). The virtual biotechnology laboratories focus on virtualizing wet-lab techniques has added a new dimension to the classroom education in Universities. This kind of educational technology supports an improved individualized learning that met rural and urban educational needs with high level of flexibility and reduced the concerns regarding time and space. Web tools have immensely influenced the current teaching and learning process [2]. Virtual labs offers diverse analysis of a concept through different components such as a close emulation of a real laboratory 'experience' through animations, which in turn

© Institute for Computer Sciences, Social Informatics and Telecommunications Engineering 2014
G. Vincenti et al. (Eds.): eLEOT 2014, LNICST 138, pp. 138–146, 2014.
DOI: 10.1007/978-3-319-13293-8_17

serves diagrammatic understanding of a concept or an experiment in an emphasized mode [3]. By simulating the key steps of an experiment, students may experience an alternative hands-on method of proceeding with the steps thereby promoting interaction with the laboratory scenario. This includes ways to reduce recurrence of mistakes as it cautions the user about the common errors one commits while handling equipment or while performing the experiment by resetting the experimental scene [4]. In current education prospect, computer-aided technologies provide special advantages for designing innovative biology course materials and developing highly interactive student-teacher relationship [5]. Modern web-based educational systems are distinct from the traditional educational models. Adapting to the web based educational systems requires certain qualities and different learning pedagogies. With this change in the education trend, many educational and research institutions widely employed such innovative technologies for teaching and learning purposes [6]. This user-friendly, interactive and problem-oriented methodology of instruction helps users to realize the concepts in a more precise manner.

Laboratory practices are fundamental in teaching and learning biotechnology courses [7]. There are lots of limitations to successfully carry out traditional labs mostly in developing countries [8]. Time constrains, shortage of equipment and reagents, insufficient laboratory protocol, issues in personal safety, inadequate technical support etc. are the most common reasons of setting up a proper laboratory condition in most Indian universities [9]. Online labs may be an asset to many universities which confront economic issues in maintaining equipment and other necessary conditions that need to be met for a good laboratory practice (Diwakar et al., submitted). Virtual labs are popularized as a visual tool that could add advantages to students and instructors towards reducing the laborious procedures in a more effective manner. Virtual labs offer diverse analysis through different components like user- interactive animations, simulations, remote-triggering of real laboratory equipment and haptic devices to employ productive online biotechnology laboratory [10]. The actual feel and visualization of a real laboratory can be delivered through graphical animations to a greater extent. Animations provide a diagrammatic understanding of the concepts of an experiment in a better way that cannot be easily conveyed through text based or passive illustrations. Visualization techniques employed in virtual labs allow the student to freely experience the virtual world to strive to make learning science fun [11]. In a traditional lab system, users may face certain problems such as limited access to laboratory facilities, equipment shortage, inadequate technical support, that may interfere with their curiosity for learning science. Virtual labs play a pivotal role in bridging the lack of lab facilities, and devising individual experience at a low cost and thus increase the chance of self-organized learning methods [12]. This ultimately imparts analytical thinking skills among the learners.

In this paper, we focus on the use of virtual biotechnology laboratory as a new pedagogy for promoting university student's learning experience. The study analyses the effect of virtual labs on student users thereby assessing the relationship between their cognitive and social presence in active learning.

2 Overview of Amrita Virtual Laboratories

To enhance University education in rural and urban areas, several national mission projects had been launched in the recent years. Sakshat Virtual Labs project (http://vlab.co.in) is a joint collaboration of several universities in India including the Indian Institutes of Technology and Amrita University amongst others. It is an initiative of

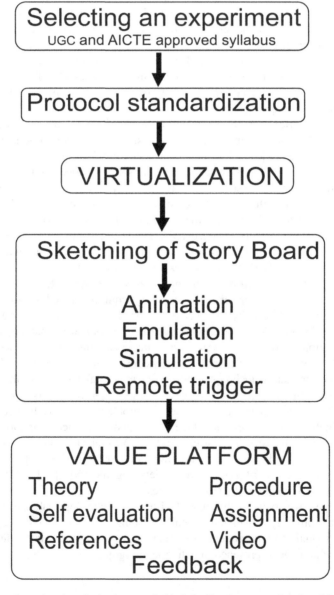

Fig. 1. Flow chart showing the basic steps behind the development of a virtual lab experiment

Ministry of Human Resource Department under National Mission on Education through ICT. The labs developed under Biotechnology and Biomedical Engineering Virtual Labs are freely available on the website http://amrita.vlab.co.in/. This covers about 23 disciplines of biotechnology course with a total of 211 experiments (8–10 experiments per lab). The experiments are virtualized after referring the syllabus (approved by the University Grants Commission (UGC) and All India Council for Technical Education (AICTE)) of different universities. The experimental protocol is first standardized by trial and error methods using different text book references and journal articles. The next step is the software development which includes a storyboard sketch, followed by animation, emulation (interactive animation) and simulation techniques. This virtualization steps helps to make the virtual laboratory with a close proximity to a traditional laboratory scenario. These classroom-based implementations as virtual laboratories were used as interactive textbooks and as tools for actual learning [13].

Apart from animation and simulation, for each experiment we added a theory section which explains the science behind the experiment, procedure which gives details of step- by step protocol performed in a real lab. The self evaluation icon helps to assess the user's knowledge on the experiment. The Assignment icon is provided with a set of questions that the user could answer as a part of laboratory examination. All additional information and reading materials for the experiment were linked in the Reference section. Recorded video of each experiments are also uploaded as an additional reference material. Feedback icon allows the users to post their comments and receive feedback on usage (See Fig. 1). It is a critical element that helps us to improve the quality of virtual lab exercises. Animation, Simulation and remote triggered experiments are accessible to the users through free registration using Google's Gmail id or an open-id. The id details are used only to keep track the number of users. All other components are openly available without any usage restrictions.

The remote-triggered laboratories are now adding a new venture to laboratory education. These labs are an excellent tool to provide access to costly lab equipment for users in places without such facilities. The advantage of using remote laboratory is that the user can effectively use the equipments such as light microscope and conduct experiments without being onsite [14]. VLCOP [15] in its full functionality was used as a platform for virtual labs. The animated or simulated experiments include the use of 2D Adobe Flash (AS3) which can run faster and reduces most server issues [16].

3 Methods

The evaluation of biotechnology virtual labs was performed via surveys to analyze whether virtual labs can bring a significant change in the learning process [14]. In order to evaluate the effect of virtual labs as an educational tool, we conducted a qualitative and quantitative analysis on students. The demonstration and hands on session were followed with a set of questionnaires to evaluate the students' adaptability in using virtual labs in their learning curriculum. The feedback survey included the following questions (See Table 1) with Likert-scale ratings (1- Poor, 2- Average, 3- Good, 4- Very

Table 1. Analysis on the adaptability of virtual labs in classroom learning

Sl No.	Questions for analysis
Q1	How do you rate the online performance of the experiment?
Q2	To what extent did you have control over the interactions?
Q3	To what degree was the actual lab environment simulated?
Q4	The measurement and analysis of data was found to be easy?
Q5	The manuals were found to be helpful?
Q6	The links provided were consistent with the objectives of the experiment?
Q7	Were the results of the experiment easily interpretable?
Q8	A clear understanding of the experiment and related topics was gained?

Table 2. Analysis on the overall performance of students when using virtual labs as a laboratory material

Sl No.	Questions for analysis
1	Name the primary stain used in the Gram staining procedure
2	Name the chamber in which Microbiology experiments are carried out
3	Name equipment used to transfer microorganism from a broth/agar to a slide
4	Name the critical step involved in the gram stain process
5	Specify the color of secondary stain used in the gram stain procedure
6	Specify the basic principle of gram staining
7	Name the instrument used to observe the gram stained organism
8	Name the counter stain used for gram stain
9	Identify the nature of *Staphylococcus aureus* under gram stain
10	Shape of *Escherichia coli* after gram stain

Good, 5- Excellent). The responses given by each user is then converted into corresponding percentage scales and plotted.

The effect of virtual labs on enhancing user perception and learning ability was the focus of this microbiology laboratory course-based case-study. The protocol followed includes survey-based analysis and assessment of student's theoretical and practical information on laboratory content. A total of 100 students, who were not previously introduced with concepts of microbiology laboratory practices were selected for this study. As a prior step, the 100 students were subjected for a questionnaire based pre-test having 10 questions regarding basics of gram staining. They were then allowed to perform the Gram stain experiment virtually to familiarize the basic laboratory concepts. After the virtual lab experience, a post-test was conducted with the same set of questions as in the pre-test. The performance level of students in each test was noted for further analysis. Virtual lab users were asked to respond to a pre and post-exercise survey (See Table 2).

4   Results

4.1   Student-Feedback Based Analysis Shows Easy Adaptation to Usage of Virtual Labs

The feedback data collected from the study participants of biotechnology virtual labs were used to determine the easy adoption to usage of the virtual labs in their learning process. About 45–50 % of the participants rated virtual labs as an excellent learning platform which compliments their laboratory education. User responses indicate that virtual labs are easily adaptable tools for students to improve their laboratory skills and thereby reduced common errors occurred while performing the experiment in the wet labs (see Fig. 2). Student users rate self-grading questions (Q1–Q4) with a lower mean value than information related questions (Q5–Q8) in the feedback.

The data was then analyzed by calculating the overall performance of the users based on the marks obtained from the examination and these were then converted to Percentage scale. The number of users scoring the respective percentage of marks was calculated and represented in a Pie chart (see Fig. 2).

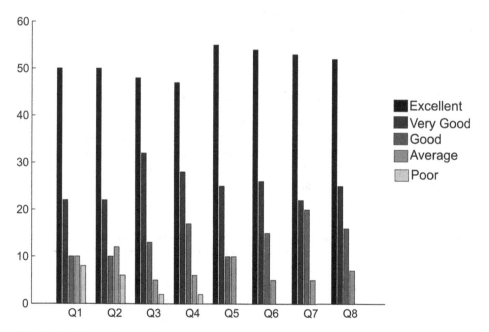

Fig. 2. Feedback of users. Each question was scored between 0–5 points on a Likert-scale. Questions for analysis on X-axis and percentage of users on Y-axis. Some values indicate information provided in virtual labs as easily readable ex. questions Q5–Q8 have a higher percentage (excellent) than other usage-related questions.

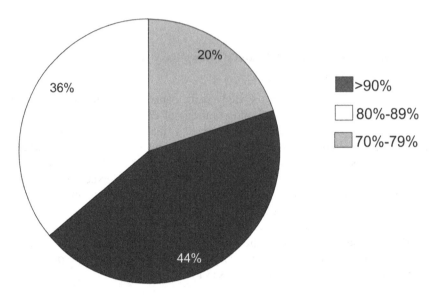

Fig. 3. Virtual labs improved student's performance rate (Post-test). The user performance was distributed according to the percentage scores from the examination. 44 % of the users scored above 90 % marks, 36 % of the users scored in the range of 80−89 and 20 % users scored above average scores in the range of 70−79 %.

4.2   Virtual Labs Augment Student's Performance in Classroom

The statistics shows 44 % of the users were able to score above 90 % marks in the post-test. The same users did not score as much in their pre-test evaluations. All participants scored above 70 % in the post-test, improving the class average from the pre-test scenario (see Fig. 3 and Table 3). This suggests the role of virtual labs as an augmented reality textbook for effective education.

Table 3. User performance rate in examination. Most students perform after using virtual labs as an interactive textbook (post-test) compared to traditional classroom learning (pre-test) and feedback shows improved performance post-test.

Percentage of marks	Pre-test evaluation (# or % users)	Post-test evaluation (# or % users)
>90	0	44
80−89	8	36
70−79	4	20
<70	88	0

5 Discussions

In this study, the effect of virtual biotechnology labs as an educational tool in supporting students to increase their active learning process was analyzed. The content-rich learning materials provided by the virtual laboratories help the users to understand the concepts of the experiments. The survey conducted amongst the students suggests virtual labs as a more effective learning material and usage ensured a better performance during evaluations. A student commented: "Since, most of the biology experiments are time consuming and requires high cost equipment it will limit individual practical experience. By getting experience from virtual laboratory, we students can avoid common mistakes such as improper handling of equipment in the traditional laboratory. Virtual laboratory experiments are direct to use, and also helpful in allowing students to gain the biological concepts, principles and procedure thoroughly". Studies on the incorporation of virtual labs in curriculum suggest that it has a greater impact in education due to its supplementary components. The study showed that students who has used virtual labs as an additional learning material understood the concepts of experiments even in the absence of an instructor.

The results of the study indicate virtual labs improve student's performance when virtual labs are used as a learning tool or as a textbook reference. From the preliminary studies on student performance, it was evident that virtual laboratory experiments are very effective when (a) the reagents and equipment are expensive (b) time requirement does not fit into the class room schedule (c) ethical concerns (d) Difficulty in result interpretation (e) handling of sophisticated instruments (f) Use of hazardous materials (data from student comments, not shown). Our study strongly supported that virtual labs serve as an alternative solution for some of the problems related to classroom laboratory environments, and thereby was effective in improving student performance in the classroom education. Although these initial results suggest virtual labs to be effective, the study is being extended to understand the interaction of social, cognitive and teaching presences in a virtual scene and within traditional blended learning environments.

Acknowledgements. This work derives direction and ideas from the Chancellor of Amrita University, Sri Mata Amritanandamayi Devi. Authors would like to thank Prof. Prema Nedungadi and Prof. Raghu Raman, Dr. Sanjay Pal, Dr. Nandhita Misra, Dr. Sobha V. Nair, Ms. Vidhya Prakash, Mr. Ajith Madhavan, Ms. Nijin Nizar and the whole of CREATE team of Amrita University for their contributions and support in developing this work. The work is supported by the Sakshat project of National Mission on Education through ICT, Department of Higher Education, Ministry of Human Resource Department and Government of India.

References

1. Muhamad, M., Zaman, H.B., Ahmad, A.: Virtual laboratory for learning biology – a preliminary investigation. World. Acad. Sci. Eng. Technol. **6**(71), 775–778 (2010)
2. Cook, D.A.: Web-based learning: pros, cons and controversies. Clin. Med. **7**, 37–42 (2007)
3. McCormick, B.H., DeFanti, T.A., Brown, M.D.: Visualization in scientific computing (1987)

4. Subramanian, R., Marsic, I.: ViBE: virtual biolog experiments (2001)
5. Diwakar, S., Parasuram, H., Medini, C., Raman, R., Nedungadi, P., Wiertelak, E., Srivastava, S., Achuthan, K., Nair, B.: Complementing neurophysiology education for developing countries via cost-effective virtual labs: case studies and classroom scenarios. J. Undergrad. Neurosci. Educ. **12**, A130–A139 (2014)
6. Angelino, H.: Distance education, virtual university and virtual laboratory: what opportunities for NII in the future? NII J. **4**, 37–47 (2005)
7. O'Donoghue, J., Singh, G., Dorward, L.: Virtual education in universities: a technological imperative. Br. J. Educ. Technol. **32**, 511–523 (2001)
8. Auer, M., Pester, A., Ursutiu, D., Samoila, C.: Distributed virtual and remote labs in engineering. In: Proceeding of IEEE International Conference on Industrial Technology, 2003, pp. 1208–1213. IEEE (2003)
9. Wentling, T.L., Park, J.-H.: Cost analysis of E-learning a case study of a university program. In: Proceedings of the AHRD, pp. 1–11. University of Illinois at Urbana-Champaign (2002)
10. Diwakar, S., Achuthan, K., Nedungadi, P., Nair, B.: Biotechnology virtual labs: facilitating laboratory access anytime-anywhere for classroom education. In: Agbo, E.C. (ed.) Innovations of Biotechnology. InTech, Rijeka (2012)
11. Huang, C.: Changing learning with new interactive and media-rich instruction environments: virtual labs case study report. Comput. Med. Imaging Graph. **27**, 64–157 (2003)
12. Mitra, S.: Self organising systems for mass computer literacy: findings from the "hole in the wall" experiments. Int. J. Dev. Issues **4**, 71–81 (2005)
13. Moore, D.S.: New pedagogy and new content: the case of statistics. Int. Stat. Rev. **65**, 123–137 (1997)
14. Nair, B., Krishnan, R., Nizar, N., Radhamani, R., Rajan, K., Yoosef, A.: Role of ICT-enabled visualization-oriented virtual laboratories in universities for enhancing biotechnology education – VALUE initiative: case study and impacts. FormaMente **7**(1-2), 1–18 (2012)
15. Raman, R., Nedungadi, P., Achuthan, K., Diwakar, S.: Integrating collaboration and accessibility for deploying virtual labs using VLCAP. Int. Trans. J. Eng. Manag. Appl. Sci. Technol. **2**(5), 547–560 (2011)
16. Diwakar, S., Achuthan, K., Nedungadi, P., Nair, B.: Enhanced facilitation of biotechnology education in developing nations via virtual labs: analysis, implementation and case-studies. Int. J. Comput. Theory Eng. **3**, 1–8 (2011)

Segmented and Interactive Modules
for Teaching Secure Coding: A Pilot Study

Sagar Raina$^{(\boxtimes)}$, Siddharth Kaza, and Blair Taylor

Department of Computer and Information Sciences, Towson University,
7800 York Road, Towson, MD, USA
{sraina,skaza,btaylor}@towson.edu

Abstract. Learners can experience content disorientation in web based learning modules. The security injection modules developed by Towson University have increased students' secure coding awareness and ability to apply secure coding principles, but feedback from instructors indicate that students tend to skim or skip the module contents and proceed directly to the laboratory assignment. In this paper, we describe the factors that cause cognitive overload in hypertext readers and address the pertinent issues and describe the process we used to enhance the effectiveness of the modules. Security Injections 2.0 incorporates principles of segmentation - breaking large module content into smaller sections and presenting each section one at a time, dialoguing - answering questions and receiving corrective or explanatory feedback, and controlling - reading and learning content at learners own pace. Segmentation, dialoguing, and controlling engage learners and retain concepts. Pilot study results indicate 77 % of the students scored above 70 % in concept retention assessment.

Keyword: Computers and education

1 Introduction

Addressing the crucial need for cybersecurity learning materials, the Security Injections@Towson project (towson.edu/securityinjections) has developed modules for Computer Science 0 (CS0), Computer Science 1 (CS1), Computer Science 2 (CS2) and Computer Literacy courses that target key secure coding concepts including integer error, buffer overflow, and input validation. Assessment results indicate that these modules have led to an increase in students' security awareness and their ability to apply secure coding principles [7, 15]. The modules, developed on the cognitive learning principles of Bloom's Taxonomy, adopt a uniform structure. Each module begins with a background section to describe the problem, including examples, followed by a code responsibly section which includes methods to avoid security issues, a laboratory assignment with a security checklist, and a discussion questions section. The module content is presented as hypertext on a single webpage [15]. The module structure is designed to help students to first *remember* and *understand* the problem through the background and code responsibly sections, *apply* the concepts learned through laboratory assignments and *analyze*, through discussion questions [15]. Students have to turn in the laboratory assignment and discussion question answers to their

© Institute for Computer Sciences, Social Informatics and Telecommunications Engineering 2014
G. Vincenti et al. (Eds.): eLEOT 2014, LNICST 138, pp. 147–154, 2014.
DOI: 10.1007/978-3-319-13293-8_18

instructors as text document to receive the grades and feedback. Over 160 instructors from various community colleges and universities are using security injection modules in CS0, CS1, CS2 and Computer Literacy courses. Although assessment results indicate significant improvement in students' secure coding awareness and their ability to apply secure coding principles, instructors using these modules have observed that students tend to skim or skip the module contents. The previous research suggests that skimming or skipping important content might hamper students' knowledge about the topic they are learning [6]. In this paper, we investigate this problem and propose a solution.

2   Literature Review

2.1   Hypertext Reading

The security injection modules are web-based, that is, students can access the modules as hypertext using a uniform resource locator (URL). Hypertext is defined as a document that contains a variety of media resources such as text, audio, video, graphics, presented in a non-linear fashion unlike printed textbooks. The media resources in hypertext, may link to other documents, giving flexibility to a reader to click any of the links and acquire knowledge [4, 9]. To acquire knowledge from hypertext, readers do not follow a specific reading order. Depending upon the readers' goals and interest, the hypertext readers may adopt a specific reading strategy [4, 8, 13]. The reading strategy allows readers to decide what to read and what to skim [13]. In addition, the amount of content presented on a screen is also considered as a deciding factor for skimming hypertext. Huge amount of hypertext on a screen may cause readers to skim the text in comparison to lesser amount of hypertext [5]. The readers, in skimming process, read the first half of the paragraphs and skip the rest if they think information gain is low and, start reading the next paragraph [5]. During this process, readers might skip important content [5, 13]. In addition, this selective reading might result in less in-depth reading, less concentration and less attention towards the content [9]. Overall, skimming content results negatively towards knowledge consumption [6]. In a study conducted among 113 participants, to observe their reading behavior, 78 % of participants reported they read more selectively because of the large amount of information available on web [9]. The process of selecting content to read hypertext requires readers to make decisions, which induces cognitive overload in a reader [4, 13]. There are several other factors that might induce cognitive overload in a reader including - lack of prior knowledge or domain knowledge about the content, complexity of the concept being taught, structure of the content, and lack of motivation to read the content [1]. Readers lacking prior knowledge or domain knowledge, have difficulty processing and understanding the content, thus inducing cognitive overload [4, 8, 12]. Additionally, if a concept itself is complex to teach and present, readers find it difficult to process and understand, resulting in cognitive overload in a reader. Well-structured hypertext is easy to process by human brains as compared to unstructured content. Unstructured content may distract readers while reading, and induce cognitive overload [1, 13]. Lack of motivation in a reader affects their cognitive ability to understand the content and thus inducing cognitive overload [1, 8]. Cognitive overload make reader's become disoriented and lose attention towards the content, resulting readers to skim or skip the content [2, 13, 16]. Also, because of the large amount of content presented on a single computer screen, readers scroll windows up and down, and during the process skip some lines of text and lose their place. In one study, which assessed 73 students reading on the web, 25 % of the students reported they skipped lines and lost their place while scrolling the window up and down on a computer screen [16]. In conclusion, there are several factors that induce cognitive overload in a reader while reading a hypertext, including domain knowledge/prior knowledge, concept complexity, content structure, amount of content presented on a single screen and lack of motivation. Cognitive overload cause readers to become disorient and inattentive towards the content, which results in skimming and skipping of content. In the next section, we discuss cognitive load theory.

2.2 Cognitive Load Theory

As discovered in the literature review section, one of the factors that might cause readers to skim or skip hypertext content is cognitive overload. According to cognitive load theory, cognitive load is the amount of information the working memory in a human brain can process at a given time [2, 4]. Human beings have a working memory which can hold or process a limited amount of new information at a given time [4, 10, 11]. When this working memory receives information to process beyond its limited capacity, it leads to cognitive overload in a human brain [11].

Working memory could be affected by different ways while processing information, resulting in different types of cognitive loads. If the working memory load is affected due to the complexity of the nature of learning task itself, it is called as intrinsic cognitive load. If the cognitive load is affected due to the way information is presented on the screen, it is called as extraneous cognitive load.

In order to avoid cognitive overload and induce learning in a reader, we need to either reduce the intrinsic or extraneous cognitive load or both [10, 11].

3 Proposed Solution

To improve the effectiveness of the secure coding modules, we analyzed the security injection modules for the factors that lead to cognitive overload in readers, which lead them to skip and skim the content. We found that domain knowledge/prior knowledge, concept complexity, and content structure are addressed by the security injection modules. The security injection modules did not address amount of content and lack of motivation factors. Section 3.1 provides detailed analysis of how we mapped cognitive overload factors with the security injection modules.

3.1 Mapping Cognitive Overload Factors with Security Injection Modules

1. *Amount of information presented on a single computer screen*: Security injection modules are presented on a single webpage which includes content related to background, and code responsibly information, laboratory assignments and

discussion questions. A single web page accommodates a large amount of information where students have to scroll window up and down for selecting any information. We believe there are higher chances that students might skim or skip the content because of large amount of text and scrolling phenomena.

2. *Domain Knowledge*: Security injection modules are given to students as a part of laboratory assignment. Before attempting the modules, students are taught basic programming concepts during lecture hours, for example: knowledge about data types, variables, arrays etc. Therefore, we assume students have enough domain knowledge to read and understand the security injection module content. Additionally, the modules are structured to provide foundational knowledge first.

3. *Complexity of content*: The security injection modules are designed based on the principles of Bloom's Taxonomy and are structured to help students methodically understand, remember and apply the concepts learned. The assumption is, by adhering to this taxonomy, content complexity is reduced.

4. *Structure of content*: The security injection modules follow a uniform format through all CS0, CS1, CS2 and Computer Literacy courses. Each module, across all courses, contains background, code responsibly, laboratory assignment and discussion questions sections. Each section has a heading and sub-heading that reader can easily process and understand.

5. *Lack of motivation*: The security injection modules are presented in a linear and non-interactive format and include a large amount of information on a single page. It is possible students are less interested and motivated to read the content because of little or no interactivity between the reader and the system.

3.2 Possible Solution

To increase their effectiveness in teaching secure coding content, the security injection modules need to address the amount of content and motivational factors to prevent students from skimming and skipping the content. The large amount of information presented at once can increase extrinsic cognitive load [11]. The research suggests, this type of cognitive load can be reduced by breaking large information into small chunks and present only one idea at a time on a single screen. This principle is called segmentation [1, 3, 12]. Segmentation improves processing of information in the working memory and makes recalling/retention of concepts easier [12].

Motivation can be increased by engaging learners or readers with the system they are interacting with. Engaging learners with the system can possibly be introduced by adding elements of interactivity within the learning system. The interactivity motivates learners to learn [12]. Interactivity in the context of learning is the "responsiveness to the learner's actions during learning" [12]. The types of interactivity in e-Learning environments include: *dialoguing*, *controlling*, *manipulating*, *searching* and *navigating* [12]. We focus on dialoguing and controlling types of interactivity, the remaining three are addressed by the platform where security injection modules are currently hosted. Dialoguing occurs when the learner answers questions and receives feedback to his/her input. Controlling means the learner can determine or control the pace of the presentation. Dialoguing help students to learn better, through the feedback provided by the learning environment [12]. Feedback reduces extraneous cognitive load in the working memory. Controlling also help students learn better by allowing them to control the pace of the presentation. Controlling reduces the extraneous load by allowing learners to process smaller chunks of information in the working memory at their own pace.

We propose to enhance the security injection modules by incorporating principles of segmentation and interactivity (dialoguing and controlling). We propose to implement segmentation by breaking the module content per section (background, code responsibly, laboratory assignment, discussion questions) and present each section one at a time on a computer screen. This way readers have to read small amount of content one at a time and there will be less processing load on the working memory, which will help readers to retain the concept's learned for the longer period [1, 3, 12, 14]. We propose to implement dialoguing by including a set of questions at the end of each section. Based on the student's response, they will receive both corrective and explanatory feedback. Feedback will increase student learning [12]. We propose to implement controlling by not allowing students to proceed to the next section until they answer all of the questions correctly, which might encourage students to refer back to the content, on answering incorrectly [3, 11, 12].

4 System Implementation

4.1 System Design

To implement the proposed solution, several solutions were considered (including writing the system from scratch) before determining that a modified version of Stanford University's class2go web-based application (https://github.com/Stanford-Online/class2go/) was most appropriate. Class2go is built using the django framework and is a well-tested open-source framework that provides core functionality including user registration, course creation, test administration, and components for auto-grading. The application creates modules and sections within those modules. Each section in a module is auto-graded using built-in functionality for text and multiple choice questions. Additional components were added to allow students to find and correct software vulnerabilities in code segments using security checklists until all questions are answered correctly (Refer Fig. 1).

4.2 Module Design

Applying the segmentation principle [1], the learning modules were organized into four subsections: background, code responsibly, laboratory assignment, and discussion questions. In the background and code responsibly sections, students are required to go through the content and answer a series of questions. Each question provides feedback upon submit, thus satisfying the dialoguing principle. The student cannot advance to the next section until all questions are answered correctly, which satisfies the controlling type of interactivity. In laboratory assignments and discussion questions, students answer text-based and multiple choice questions, and identify vulnerabilities based on a security checklist. The student is able to highlight portions of the code according to steps in the checklist. These are also auto-graded until completion.

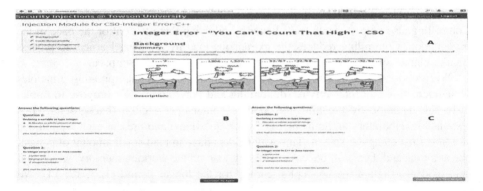

Fig. 1. The (a) security injection module, (b) content-based questions, (c) instant feedback.

5   Pilot Evaluation

5.1   Method

A pilot study was conducted with the newly built system using a C++ module focused on integer error in a CS0 class at Towson University. The class had 60 in-class undergraduate computer science students and 9 online students. The students were given security injections 2.0 module URL and were asked to follow the instructions. While in-class students were interacting with the newly built system, their behavior was observed by the instructors, giving an idea of students' engagement towards the system. A week later, a paper-based test was conducted to assess the students' retention of integer overflow concepts. Students in a paper-based test were asked to "Explain integer overflow". The students were evaluated on the scale out of 10 on the paper-based test.

5.2   Assessment

The data was evaluated for 43 students who took the post-test. The assessment results indicate that students scored an average of 7.7 out of 10 with a standard deviation (SD) of 3.18. Approximately 77 % of students scored 7 and above (falling on the higher end, on the scale of 0–10) in their post-test, reflecting their good understanding and retention of integer overflow concepts including 45 % students scoring 10 out of 10 and 25 % students scoring 8 out of 10 (Refer Fig. 2). We also assessed the correlation between the number of attempts student made to complete the module and their post-test scores to find out if increase in number of attempts improves learning and retention of integer overflow concepts. The results indicate weak pearson's correlation coefficient (-2.63), thus giving us a hint that multiple attempts does not contribute to learning and retention of concepts. We intend to study the data to further analyze this claim.

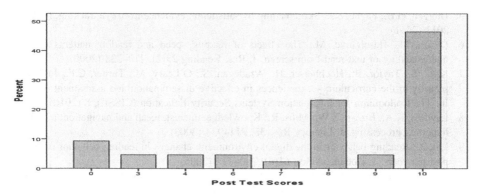

Fig. 2. Post-test scores versus students (percent)

6 Conclusion and Future Work

In this study, we addressed students' tendency to skip and skim content in order to improve the effectiveness of secure coding learning modules. We enhanced the modules by incorporating segmentation and interactivity principles to create segmented, feedback-oriented and self-paced modules to improve student learning by engaging them with content and increase their motivation. Assessment of the results indicated higher scores for the majority (77 %) of the students. Though the design of this study lacks a control group and has a small sample size, therefore, the results cannot be generalized to entire population, but, the descriptive statistics gives us an idea of students' good performance on security injections 2.0 modules. To further expand the study, we are designing an experiment and instruments which includes the deployment of multiple modules in CS0, CS1, and Computer Literacy to measure student learning, student concept retention and student engagement in two e-learning modalities (interactive modules and non-interactive modules) and plan to pilot them this summer. Future work will include auto-grading for full-text questions, which is currently limited to matching keywords. In addition, the system architecture requires modification to support large-scale dissemination and assessment.

References

1. Al-Samarraie, H., Teo, T., Abbas, M.: Can structured representation enhance students' thinking skills for better understanding of E-learning content? Comput. Educ. **69**, 463–473 (2013)
2. Chalmers, P.A.: The role of cognitive theory in human–computer interface. Comput. Hum. Behav. **19**(5), 593–607 (2003)
3. Clark, R.C., Mayer, R.E.: E-Learning and the Science of Instruction: Proven Guidelines for Consumers and Designers of Multimedia Learning (Google eBook). Wiley, New York (2011)
4. DeStefano, D., LeFevre, J.-A.: Cognitive load in hypertext reading: a review. Comput. Hum. Behav. **23**(3), 1616–1641 (2007)

5. Duggan, G.B., Payne, S.J.: Skim reading by satisficing: evidence from eye tracking. In: CHI 2011 (2011)
6. Dyson, M., Haselgrove, M.: The effects of reading speed and reading patterns on the understanding of text read from screen. J. Res. Reading **23**(2), 210–223 (2000)
7. Kaza, S., Taylor, B., Hochheiser, H., Azadegan, S., O'Leary, M., Turner, C.F.: Injecting security in the curriculum – experiences in effective dissemination and assessment design. In: The Colloquium for Information Systems Security Education (CISSE), 8 (2010)
8. Lawless, K.A., Brown, S.W., Mills, R.: Knowledge, interest, recall and navigation: a look at hypertext processing. J. Literacy Res. **35**, 911–934 (2003)
9. Liu, Z.: Reading behavior in the digital environment: changes in reading behavior over the past ten years. J. Documentation **61**(6), 700–712 (2005)
10. van Merrienboer, J.J.G., Ayres, P.: Research on cognitive load theory and its design implications for e-learning. Educ. Tech. Res. Dev. **53**(3), 5–13 (2005)
11. van Merrienboer, J.J.G., John, S.: Cognitive load theory in health professional education: design principles and strategies. Med. Educ. **44**, 85–93 (2010)
12. Moreno, R., Mayer, R.: Interactive multimodal learning environments. Educ. Psychol. Rev. **19**(3), 309–326 (2007)
13. Protopsaltis, A., Bouk, V.: Towards a hypertext reading/comprehension model. In: SIGDOC'05 (2005). http://delivery.acm.org/10.1145/1090000/1085349/p159-protopsaltis.pdf
14. Singh, A.-M., Marcus, N., Ayres, P.: The transient information effect: investigating the impact of segmentation on spoken and written text. Appl. Cogn. Psychol. **26**(6), 848–853 (2012)
15. Taylor, B., Kaza, S.: Security injections: modules to help students remember, understand, and apply secure coding techniques. In: Proceedings of the 16th Annual Joint Conference on Innovation and Technology in Computer Science Education. **99**, 3–7, ACM (2011)
16. Tseng, M.: The difficulties that EFL learners have with reading text on the web. Internet TESL J. **14**(2) (2008). Available at http://iteslj.org/Articles/Tseng-TextOnTheWeb.html

From the First Generation of Distance Learning to Personal Learning Environments: An Overall Look

Andrea Santo-Sabato[(✉)] and Marta Vernaleone

Mediasoft Research, Via Sonzini 25, Galatina, Italy
{andrea.santosabato,
marta.vernaleone}@mediasoftonline.com

Abstract. This article aims to confront how e-learning models have evolved over time from the characteristics of the web 1.0 to those of 2.0 looking briefly at the CMS, LMS, LCMS and PLE platforms and how it is essential to carefully first consider the constructivist pedagogical theories so as to comprehend the present situation, as well as that of the forthcoming future.

1 Introduction

Defining "E-Learning" is arduous, but of great benefit. Even today, scientific literature has not been able to produce an unequivocal, exhaustive and complete definition that encapsulates not only the complexity of the phenomena being examined, but also the variables that characterize experiences linked to Distance Learning and E-learning. Every attempt has therefore only partially achieved the fixed goal [1].

Fixing a definition means carrying out what it actually defines, and the difficulty lies exactly in this: how can one "maieutically" define the field of "E Learning" without falling into the trap of recursive, auto referential and tautological defining processes? This difficulty also stems from the conception that "teaching" is the "transmission of knowledge" linked to a solely anthropological view of humankind that has become engraved over the course of millennia [2]. We therefore pass from an "instructor centered" to a "learner and learning centered" model [3].

A rare attempt that succeeded was by the ANEE Observatory who in 2004 defined the phenomenon of E Learning.[1]

---

[1] Eletti V. (a cura di), Che cos'è l'e-learning, Carocci, 2002: "E-learning is a method of teaching and learning that involves both the product and the training process. Product training is any type of material or content made available in digital format through media or network. Training process is meant instead to manage the entire learning process that involves the aspects of supply, use, interaction, assessment. In this dimension, the real added value of e-learning emerges in support services and tutoring, in both synchronous and asynchronous modes of interaction, sharing and collaboration at the level of the community. Peculiarities of e-learning is the high flexibility afforded to the learner by the availability of anytime, anywhere learning content, which enables the self-management and self-determination of their own learning; remains of paramount importance scanning of the training process, according to an agenda that empowers forming and trainer in order to achieve the educational objectives set."

© Institute for Computer Sciences, Social Informatics and Telecommunications Engineering 2014
G. Vincenti et al. (Eds.): eLEOT 2014, LNICST 138, pp. 155–158, 2014.
DOI: 10.1007/978-3-319-13293-8_19

We therefore deduce that together with the use of new educational paradigms that are intrinsically linked to the rapid diffusion and propagation of new technologies, E-Learning changes the way in which educational processes are managed, in which learning is obtained and provided, and in which educational content is organized, managed and designed [4].

The role of the user becomes fundamental and of central importance. It is the conception of a learning system that from now on is based on the web and separate from space and time [5]. It is now the student who decides how to approach study methods via collaborative, active and pro-active learning in complete autonomy. As underlined by Ganino [6], in order to be categorized within the phenomenological field of "E-learning", the processes of "digital provision of learning" must have the following essential characteristics :

• Interactivity with teaching materials, the tutors, the teachers and other students
• Multimedia exposition
• Independence from temporal and physical limitations
• The valorisation of the social and collaborative dimensions of learning
• The constant monitoring of the learning level via self-evaluation and evaluation
• The access to platforms via the web and technological devices
• The synchronous or asynchronous interaction of the processes

The role and experience of the User/Student now becomes "fundamental" and decisive. Learning becomes a social process, that gives an active role to the user who becomes a member of a community on which "the whole learning process" is linked to a "horizontal" sharing of knowledge.

2 From DL to E-Learning

Perhaps Isaac Pitman, the English inventor of the phonographic system for the stenograph, would not have believed that his idea of "teaching" via correspondence course would in time have revolutionized the paradigm of the centrality of teaching between teacher/student. Without digressing in interesting historical and historical evolutionary opinions, let us see how e-learning has passed from the perspective of closed environments based on the provision of structured and rigid content to the centrality of the person who is learning and participates in the shared construction of their knowledge. The introduction of web 2.0, has revolutionized teaching models, methodologies and tools. From now on the "Leitmotiv" is "Participation and Sharing": it is now the individual subject who produces knowledge and becomes the creator and propagator of contents on-line. "Multimedia and multi-channel availability" are the technological basis of this new approach. This new paradigm of proactive learning leads to the growth of the individual within objectives shared by a group: from now on one "learns together" and individual learning is the result of a collective process. Shared knowledge is created, new virtual learning communities are born and individuals learn through areas of interest in which they can communicate in an interactive way. The technological matrixes behind this new phase are supported by: video/audio conferences, chat groups, forums, instant messaging, podcasts etc.

This is the new "Digital Learning" model in which being proactive takes on a key-role for growth and development. This phase is characterized by and stands out for the retrieval and valorization of spontaneous and informal ways of using the web. From now on the Web is the spontaneous "educational setting" that integrates both what is formal and informal. This conception is supported by Paulsen's [7] hexagon theory and Vigotsky theories on intersubjectivity and learned behavior, in which the environment (technology) is a guide and "scaffolding" for the development of knowledge and capabilities.

As mentioned, this phase commenced with the launch of Web 2.0. In parallel, there was a decisive evolution of e-learning in which new technologies substituted "Virtual Learning Environments" based exclusively on CMS (Content Management System), LMS (Learning Management System), and LCMS (Learning Content Management System) platforms, with the more communicative and agile PLEs "Personal learning Environments". Every individual can create their own personal learning environment so as to manage and organize their own personal resources in complete autonomy. Now that the web is more interactive and dynamic, it is the users rather than technology that add value to the services that the web has to offer. Using PLEs, with their participative architecture, each individual becomes a player and author of content, according to participative and collaborative models. These are therefore environments that are based on people, that are able to support both informal and formal educational elements that are based on consolidated schemes outlined on the web by e-learning platforms. On PLE platforms the rules that Ravitz described in his 4P model apply [8].

The aim is to overcome the problems in traditional education by overcoming the "informal/formal" dichotomy (via the assumption of constructivist pedagogical theories): this aim can be reached passing from a static vertical type of education to a conception of the autonomy of an individual within a group.

The user is now the beneficiary and creator, as conscious designer of their own learning. We pass from "closed" and one-directional spaces to shared interconnected spaces that place the student ever more and the teacher of the course ever less at the centre of the learning process: through the possibility offered by these new platforms, the user can autonomously choose the ways of receiving knowledge and enlarge the content itself through their own experience, thus propagating new shared experiences for the group or class they belong to. Via interactivity, courses are "learned centered" and "cooperative learned". Learning is no longer based on vertical "educational" provision, but starts and develops in a network of already founded relations.

An interesting aspect is the possibility to join virtual communities that are interested in discussing and working on the same topics, sharing experiences and activities. The centrality of relational aspects is clear: knowledge is built in a new, interactive and collaborative way.

The concept of community is of central importance: in the community education is a social event, that doesn't end with receiving operations but generates a "continuum" propagated by informal ties of the student with the group and the student with the teacher.

We are therefore witnessing a migration towards new horizons of e-learning, both from the theoretical and practical points of view, where new technologies heavily linked to the Web 2.0, are little by little overtaking the "old" virtual learning environments (identifiable in the various LMS or LCMS platforms) with the more flexible and communicative PLEs. One begins to talk about Web 2.0.

The first to talk about 2.0 e-learning was Stephen Downes, a researcher for the National Research Council of Canada and one of the leading e-learning experts on a global scale. In an article published on the eLearn Magazine, Downes first theorized the link between e-learning and Web 2.0, providing the basis of a discussion that in time gradually became of global scale and is very likely to become the future of electronic learning.

PLEs are therefore to be considered the environment for learning in the future since they encapsulate the "learner student centered" paradigm in an incisive way by integrating E-portfolios as a structural element.

Within this superior penetration of PLE platforms, one must consider Blackall's more radical vision who states that the web itself is a PLE system and that a specific intermediate system is therefore not necessary.

3 Conclusions

In the near future we will no longer talk about transmission "media", platforms or paradigms but of "environments" and "systems" in which information, content and "knowledge" will be assembled according to personal taste with regards to main necessities and interests. Applications and platforms will bow out to interconnected "environments", in which importance will not only be given to the information "deposited" but also to how they are conveyed.

We are therefore moving towards the so-called "ubiquitous computing". Learning and real-life will merge indiscernibly.

References

1. Banzato, M.: Apprendere in rete. Modelli e strumenti per l'e-learning. Utet, Torino (2006)
2. Aleandri, G.: Educazione permanente nelle prospettive del lifelong e lifewide learning. Armaldo Editore, Roma (2011)
3. Bonfiglio, A.: E-Learning, Podcasting: una didattica collaborativa in rete
4. Eletti, V.: Che cos'è l'E.Learning, p. 65. Carocci Editore, Roma (2002)
5. Trentin, G.: Insegnare e apprendere in rete, pp. 120–123. Zanichelli, Bologna (1998)
6. Ganino, G.: Immagini per la didattica. Metodologie e Tecnologie dell'audiovisivo digitale, pp. 60–61. Anicia, Roma (2009)
7. Paulsen, M.F.: The Exagon of cooperative freedom: adistance education theory ayyuned to computer conferencing. In: DEOSNEWS, vol. 3, no. 2
8. Ravitz, J.: Building online communities and ID model

Inter-University International Collaboration for an Online Course: A Case Study

Claudia Igbrude[1], John O'Connor[1], and Dudley Turner[2(✉)]

[1] Dublin Institute of Technology, Dublin, Ireland
claudia00l@gmail.com,
john.oconnor@dit.ie
www.dit.ie
[2] University of Akron, Akron, USA
dbturne@uakron.edu
www.uakron.edu

Abstract. This paper is a practical account of the experience of collaboration between two international partners – one in Europe and the other in the United States. This collaboration experience is a lens through which the authors outline the origin, design and implementation of an inter-university teaching experience. The processes, strengths and difficulties are outlined and the rationale for utilising a virtual world is given, along with the participants' perspectives of the experience. No institutional changes or formal agreements were needed.

The same course was validated and accredited by each institution and designed to address the requirements of each with the responsibility for participant progress and assessment remaining with the home institution. The paper discusses issues of coordination and makes recommendations for developing similar collaborations.

Keywords: Virtual learning environments VLEs · Virtual worlds · Second life · Communities of practice · Collaborative learning · Globalization · Student exchange

1 Introduction

As employers become more globalised the expectations of students coming into higher education include a culturally diverse and internationally focused experience. In addition, the growing numbers and diversity of students requires that education transcend local restrictions. This has resulted in a particular challenge to Higher Education Institutions (HEIs) in considering how to meet the needs of students and their future workplaces. One way for European students to access international experience has been the Erasmus Programme that funds student-exchange arrangements between European HEIs. While this programme has shown increased participation every year since its inception in 1987 [1], HEIs still face challenges in encouraging students to take advantage of the opportunity. In the United States K-12 and HEIs have an emphasis on global literacy but a significant issue has been the cost of sending students overseas to get an international perspective [2].

© Institute for Computer Sciences, Social Informatics and Telecommunications Engineering 2014
G. Vincenti et al. (Eds.): eLEOT 2014, LNICST 138, pp. 159–166, 2014.
DOI: 10.1007/978-3-319-13293-8_20

Collaboration between institutions, particularly international collaborations such as inter-university teaching, allow both students and staff the opportunity to engage with alternative viewpoints in both practice and learning, as well as providing an opportunity for exposure to a globally diverse experience. Online Virtual Learning Environments (VLEs) such as learning management systems, web-conferencing platforms, and virtual worlds provide viable and cost effective ways to facilitate global collaborative learning experiences.

In 2008 a five-credit module (under the European Credit Transfer and Accumulation System) of one semester duration and titled *Virtual Environments: Is one life enough?* – developed by John O'Connor and Claudia Igbrude for delivery entirely in the online virtual environment Second Life[1] – was undertaken as a pilot by academic staff interested in eLearning at the Dublin Institute of Technology (DIT). The following year it was offered to full time art and design undergraduate students on an elective basis. Delivery has continued each semester and more than ten student groups have successfully completed to date. The module has received two major awards for innovation in learning and teaching.[2] Since 2010 additional places have been offered to members of the wider Second Life community on a Continuing Professional Development (CPD) basis in partnership with Dublin Virtually Live.[3] These participants joined the undergraduates to create a richer learning experience for all.[4] Some were academics interested in exploring virtual education and this led to Dudley Turner proposing a collaborative offering between DIT and the University of Akron (UA) to deliver the course to a group made up of undergraduate students from both institutions in 2014. Each institution maintained responsibility for its own students, keeping control of the administration and examination processes, while the teaching, assessment and feedback were shared. This flexible approach supported the opportunity to test the viability of virtual collaboration while keeping to a minimum the inter-institutional bureaucracy that might normally slow down such collaborative ventures – the only requirement being a formal validation of the module by UA.

2   Communities, Relationships and Networking

Virtual Environments: Is one life enough? addresses the need for undergraduate students to be digitally literate and understand the potential for creating and managing their online identities. It introduces participants to collaborative online working in a practical way by scheduling classes in the widely available virtual world Second Life. Simple to

---

[1] www.secondlife.com [accessed 22 May 2014].

[2] In 2010 the module received the annual Jennifer Burke Award for Innovation in Learning and Teaching presented in Dublin by the Irish Learning and Teaching Association http://www. jenniferburkeaward.ie/winners10.html [accessed on 22 May 2014]. In 2012 it won the Learning Without Frontiers Award for Further and Higher Education presented at the LWF12 Conference and Festival in London http://virtualenvironmentsmodule.com/2012/01/26/winner/ [accessed on 22 May 2014].

[3] Teaching is delivered in various locations around a virtual model of Dublin in Second Life that already hosts a well-established community of residents with broad creative and cultural interests. http://dublin.readyhosting.com/index.php [accessed 23 May 2014].

[4] Participants from locations across Europe and the US began taking the course.

use, Second Life provides a realistic environment for learning and is easily accessible globally. Lecturers and participants meet for a ninety-minute weekly class throughout the semester where they interact via a voice enabled avatar in a classroom-like setting. The syllabus includes lectures, class discussion based on reading material given in advance, student presentations, and guest speakers who share experiences and lead virtual field trips to other locations in Second Life. Participants are required to write a blog in which they reflect on their learning throughout the semester. From the beginning of the semester they are divided into small groups to work on a collaborative project. The lecturers maintain a module blog[5] where a summary of each class and activities to be completed for the next class are posted. The blog also contains support material such as reading lists, tutorials, technical support and so on. Student feedback is given in Second Life outside scheduled class time and through email. All engagement between lecturers and participants takes place online thereby supporting globally dispersed participants.

The module has six learning objectives describing what the participants will be able to do on completion of the course:

1. Access online virtual environments and networking communities to carry out specific activities;
2. Create and manage their presence online;
3. Establish and maintain virtual relationships;
4. Explain how the regulations and conventions operating in online virtual environments and networking communities support the creation and management of content;
5. Describe the potential outcomes from creating content;
6. Apply this knowledge to create and exploit original content for online virtual environments and networking communities.

2.1 Participant Background

Undergraduate students taking the module come from a variety of disciplines such as computer science, engineering, art and design, accountancy, dance and across a range of levels in their study, from first year to final year. They are all active users of web 2.0 media – particularly Facebook and YouTube. Those taking the class on a CPD basis are more experienced professionals with a specific interest in developing their skills in online collaborative project work. Many are teachers and lecturers, artists and designers. Most have been active in Second Life before joining the class and some have gone on to develop classes in the virtual world with their own institutions. The partnership developed by the authors between DIT and UA is the first to have emerged from the module.

3 Module Design and Delivery

3.1 Building a Learning Community

Much current thinking around learning communities has been influenced by observing the 'virtual communities' that develop in MMOGs (massively multiplayer online

---

[5] www.virtualenvironmentsmodule.com [accessed 17 July 2014].

games) such as EverQuest and World of Warcraft. Writing specifically on this topic Galarneau highlights Seely Brown's suggestion that these provide an entirely new kind of social learning experience:

> Understanding the social practices and constructivist ecologies being created around open source and massively multiplayer games will provide a glimpse into new kinds of innovation ecologies and some of the ways that meaning is created for these kids – ages 10 to 40. Perhaps our generation focused on information, but these kids focus on meaning – how does information take on meaning? [3]

An environment such as Second Life also provides the opportunity for learners to engage in peripheral activities that support a deeper engagement and results in greater understanding and retention. Lave and Wenger suggest that 'the way to maximize learning is to perform, not to talk about it' in a community context [4]. Wenger has since elaborated on the concept of 'communities of practice' (now commonly known in academic circles as 'learning communities') describing them as characterised by 'joint enterprise', 'mutual engagement' and a 'shared repertoire' of community resources where learners must have 'broad access to arenas of mature practice' and are engaged not only in learning activity, but in 'productive activity', in order to participate [5].

Very little amendment was required to prepare *Virtual Environments: Is one life enough?* for joint delivery between DIT and UA. The objectives for both groups differed slightly but the content and contexts remained the same. To coordinate the planning, lecturers used a wiki. Information about weekly objectives, activities and guest lecturers was all put into the wiki, reviewed and edited by all lecturers, then if issues arose that needed discussion or decision, they would meet in Second Life to resolve them. These meeting were typically after the class meetings. Use of the wiki facilitated asynchronous communication allowing for efficient time management in planning and conducing the module, particularly as lecturers operated in different time zones.

For DIT participants, the continuation of the module offered the same benefit as the original offering, that is, the opportunity to work collaboratively in an online context and begin the process of developing an online identity. For UA participants, the benefits of offering the class included learning about virtual worlds and what they had to offer. For both groups of participants the opportunity for interaction, collaboration and networking between participants and lecturers from different disciplines, institutions and cultures is a significant attraction.

3.2   An Alternative to Student Exchange

In the twenty-first century workplace the ability to work with globally distributed teams is a valuable skill for employees. Junior Year Abroad programmes, the *Erasmus* programme, summer courses or work experience are usually the vehicles through which students experience other cultures and environments. However, due to time and cost constraints, it is not possible for all students to avail of these opportunities in face to face settings. Collaboration in the online virtual space, as experienced in this class, was designed to give students – and indeed, lecturers – the benefits of such an experience without the cost. Morgado, et al. [6] highlight virtual worlds as providing potential for learning contexts where students and teachers 'interact cooperatively, immersed in context-rich situations'.

An online learning environment that brings together people of all ages and cultures around common goals and interests and is 'openly networked', using online platforms and digital tools to make learning resources available to everybody can play an important part in widening opportunity [7].

The use of the *Flipped Classroom* – where students are given pre-class work to watch and read to facilitate later discussion in class [8] – with guest speakers who would normally not have been available to participants provides for a diverse and engaging learning environment. The advantage of the virtual world over the video conferencing in this particular module is that it allows the participants to assume a character through which they can explore the learning objectives of the module. The use of the virtual world platform Second Life as a learning environment allowed for approaches that helped integrate the participants' experiences in real and virtual contexts and supported global, social learning. Second Life, as other 3D virtual worlds, has the possibility for 'immersive learning experience and a safe environment to facilitate remote interactions' and 'offer a more personal experience than more conventional communication technologies' and may 'evoke a much stronger sense of presence … particularly when participants are involved in collaborative activities or group work' [9]. This is evidenced in the use of tools to support the learning and collaboration, including blogs, wikis, instant messages and so on.

3.3 Delivery and Assessment

Classes are structured to follow relevant themes or topics each week. Videos, blog posts, articles and academic papers are assigned for study in advance of class meetings. These form the stimulus for discussion in class around the topic of the week. Participants are encouraged to link what they read and discussed to their own contexts for study and personal interest. By the third week they are assigned to groups (combined of DIT and UA students) comprising five participants to work on a collaborative project.

The assessment of learning for the module is based on the reflective blog kept by each participant and the collaborative group work. The blog consists a series of reflective written texts posted each week and initially based on prompts given by the lecturers. The group work assessment was not based entirely on the artefact produced but on the process of collaboration that led to it. Participants evidence this through their reflective writing in the blog, class discussion and presentation of the project. The project is merely a vehicle to engage participants in the dynamic of working collaboratively with a group in an online context and to record their individual contributions while also reflecting critically on the process.

They are also assessed on how they applied what they learn each week in their group task. The emphasis was not on the end product but the process and how they captured evidence of the process using online tools.

After class each week the lecturers review the progress of the participants against the lesson plan and make adjustments to the outline for the following week based on what worked, didn't work and participant feedback. This type of responsive implementation allowed for deeper involvement and engagement with the participants. Given that these were online participants, this was a valuable way to keep track of where there might have been challenges. This interaction has been recorded in an online wiki maintained by the lecturers since the commencement of the module and it provides a valuable record of the development.

4   Feedback from Students

4.1   Methods of Feedback

Feedback from participants was received in a variety of ways. Weekly evaluation through informal conversations proved a valuable way to get feedback on an ongoing basis. The time for this is built into the schedule and the lecturers remained after class to meet participants individually and ask specific questions such as: 'how is your work going?'; 'why is your blog not up to date?'; 'is there any way we can help you meet your targets for the week?' or a simple 'is everything going well?'. This approach meant that it was possible to catch any conflicts that arose before they had gone too far, but participants could also be given reassurance that they were on the right track, especially important as there was no real life face-to-face contact.

Additionally, the participants' own reflective blogs were designed to provide a window into what they were doing, their rationale for their decisions, their reactions to readings and guest speakers, and their perception of their own progress. Prompts were given to encourage reflection and writing, and clear guidelines were given as to what was required in the written work.

4.2   Student Comments

Being able to interact with others on a global scale, flexibility of the lecturers, and team-working were the key aspects participants appreciated in the module.

> 'The dissolving of boundaries. Our "class" was composed of students not just from all over Ohio but from across the ocean as well.'
> 'I appreciate the very different approach that deviates from normal classrooms. I liked that it was more about discussion and current events.'

While a few participants were either not sure of what skills they might use in the future or felt that it was an elementary class for them, most were able to identify direct relevance of the module to their future careers. Some participants appreciated that it was:

> 'extremely hard to coordinate and communicate in groups without face to face or voice interaction', and that
> 'everyone has their own schedule and you must make the best you can to adhere to each other's timeframes.'

Most importantly, they came to an understanding of the importance of taking ownership of their digital identities or online presence and being digitally literate while being online. Some participants said that the lectures on virtual identities and the impacts on things posted online will remain with them forever. Others said that the information about personal branding and creating online presence will be very useful in their future careers. Many also highlighted that they learned about how to convey their ideas online and that online etiquette and appearance are as important as in face-to-face interactions. Considering that most of these are third level students, the fact that these were the learning points that stood out for them indicates the need for such education.

Previously to this module, only one US participant had any international experience. Nearly half of the participants (45 %) felt that they would be more confident about working on an international project after their experience on this module. Some felt they were already prepared or had confidence enough (e.g., 'They [students from the other institution] really weren't that different'). However, many felt that they had learned lessons both in terms of what worked and didn't work, and what to watch out for. For example,

> 'I would feel more confident because this module allowed me to see some of the big problems with international projects – timing, dialect, backgrounds – so that I will be better able to handle these in the future.'

4.3   Technical Framework

It is important to remember that as has been pointed out there is a varied cohort on this course so it has been important to stress that it is not a technical requirement so as not to deter any potential students. This has meant that the technical framework used allows for the participation of a range of abilities. The framework adopted has involved a scaffolded approach with links to community-based support while encouraging peer support as well as independence and self accountability.

Prior to the start of the pilot, it was discovered that the ports used by Second Life were blocked by default on the Institutional network. This was addressed in conjunction with the Information services department (IS). Second Life was also installed in designated computer labs, but students were generally encouraged to work on their own computers where possible. This ensured that they were responsible for their own computers and own technical support, and could attend the class from anywhere. However, it was necessary to ensure that they could use the institutional infrastructure to get online while on campus and in this respect, we continue to work with the IS departments. As far as use of the Virtual Space-(Second Life) is concerned, students are encouraged to support each other rather than seeking to use class time for technical issues. This approach ensures that the class discussions are beyond the scope of technical support issues. As the DIT is based in a virtual community –Virtual Dublin, members of this community have also been part of the support structure for students.

5   Conclusion

Feedback from the participants confirms the need for this module both for international experience and for virtual understanding. If the purpose of higher education is to prepare students for a life beyond the confines of the institution, then, being able to manage their online identities and being digitally literate is an essential aspect of their education.

Additionally, collaboration between the two universities has involved negotiation and cooperation, but also buy-in from senior management. By offering the module using each institution's pre-existing course structure, the need for any extensive paperwork and approval process was eliminated. Collaboration between the lecturers helps assure that the needs of participants for their degree requirements can be achieved while providing this valuable international experience. Use of Web 2.0 tools by lecturers not only helps reach these goals in planning and implementing the course, but also can be used as an illustration of international collaboration in itself. All tools are widely available at little or no cost and supported by a range of platforms. They are easy to use requiring little technical ability beyond basic digital competence.

It is important to get initial buy-in or support from local IS services, however, also get students to take the responsibility for their own technical support. Using this as a "teachable moment" is a useful way to highlight the benefits of accessing online communities.

Building on this experience, it is expected that the module will be offered beyond UA and DIT in the following terms.

References

1. A Statistical Overview of the ERASMUS Programme in 2011–12. Directorate-General for Education and Culture, European Commission, Brussels (2013)
2. Barker, C.M.: Education for International Understanding and Global Competence. Carnegie Corporation Convention, New York (2000)
3. Galarneau, L.: Spontaneous communities of learning: learning ecosystems in massively multiplayer online gaming environments. In:Proceedings of DiGRA 2005 Conference: Changing Views – Worlds in Play (2005)
4. Lave, J., Wenger, E.: Situated Learning: Legitimate Peripheral Participation. Cambridge University Press, Cambridge (1991)
5. Wenger, E.: Communities of practice: learning as a social system. Syst. Think. 9(5), 2–3 (1998)
6. Morgado, L., Varajão, J., Coelho, D., Rodrigues, C., Sancin, C., Castello, V.: The attributes and advantages of virtual worlds for real world training. J. Virtual Worlds Educ. 1(1), 15–36 (2010)
7. Schaffhauser, D.: Research: education could use more 'connected learning'. T.H.E. Journal (2013). http://thejournal.com/articles/2013/01/17/research-education-could-use-more-connected-learning.aspx. Accessed 27 May 2014
8. Tucker, B.: The flipped classroom. Educ. Next 12(1), 82–83 (2012)
9. Rapanotti, L., Minocha, S., Barroca, L., Boulos, M.N., Morse, D.R.: 3D virtual worlds in higher education. In: Olofsson, A.D., Lindberg, J.O. (eds.) Informed Design of Educational Technologies in Higher Education: Enhanced Learning and Teaching, pp. 212–240. IGI Global, Hershey (2012)

Smart e-Learning as a Student-Centered Biotechnical System

Vladimir Uskov[1(✉)], Andrey Lyamin[2], Lubov Lisitsyna[2],
and Bhuvana Sekar[1]

[1] Department of Computer Science and Information Systems,
Bradley University, 1501 West Bradley Avenue, Peoria, IL 61625, USA
`{uskov,bsekar}@mail.bradley.edu`
[2] Department of Computer Educational Technology, ITMO University,
Kronvrkskiy pr. 49, Saint Petersburg 197101, Russia
`{lyamin,lisizina}@mail.ifmo.ru`

Abstract. The Smart e-Learning System (SeLS) should be designed and developed as a smart student-centered biotechnical system with certain features of smart systems (sensing, transmission, big data processing, activation of actuators) and levels of "smartness" (adaptation, sensing, inferring, learning, anticipation, self-organization). In order to provide higher efficiency of learning process in general, and, SeLS, in particular, SeLS should use multiple parameters of student psychophysiological state.

Keywords: e-Learning · Smart system · Student psychophysiological state

1 Introduction

A combination of smart systems with e-learning – Smart e-Learning – is a nascent area that potentially can combine the features and advantages of both areas, and, as a result, in the future provide learners and instructors with non-existing functionality and features.

1.1 Smart Systems for Learning: Examples

Various smart systems for learning have been designed and developed recently; relevant examples include but are not limited to the following ones: Smart Classroom based on Reconfigurable Context - Sensitive Middleware (RCSM) [1], Context Aware Smart Classroom [2], Open Smart Classroom [3], Smart Classroom for Tele-education [4], smart environments for learning [5], and other.

The performed analysis of [1–5] as well as multiple additional publications shows that currently the developed prototypes of smart systems with applications in eduction and/or learning are predominantly technical systems with a major focus on software-hardware solutions, components, mobile devices and machine-to-machine data exchange protocols. However, based on authors' active involvement into e-learning from 1994, multiple completed research projects and gained experience, the Smart e-Learning Systems (SeLS), first of all, should be considered as biotechnical systems.

G. Vincenti et al. (Eds.): eLEOT 2014, LNICST 138, pp. 167–175, 2014.
DOI: 10.1007/978-3-319-13293-8_21

In those systems a human being - a student or a learner with particular abilities to read, write, understand, learn, process data, make logical conclusions, retain knowledge - should be placed into a center. Secondly, as a smart system, SeLS should demonstrate certain smart features and levels of "smartness".

1.2   Research Project Goal and Objectives

The main goals of ongoing research project are (1) to define various types of smart entities relevant to education and/or learning, (2) to define levels of "smartness" of those entities, (3) to identify features and characteristics of smart systems for education and/or learning, (4) identify student/learner psychophysiological characteristics that should be actively used by advanced SeLS. Those aspects are important for advanced and sophisticated SeLS successful design, development and highly effective use by both learners and instructors.

2   Smart e-Learning: Smart Entities

The above-mentioned examples of smart systems with applications in education and/or learning as well as numerous additional examples of smart entities could be classified using the "systems thinking" approach, i.e. in terms of "system = objects + activities + technology/services" software architectural hierarchical model:

(1) level of systems: examples of smart systems in education/learning may include but are not limited to smart classroom, smart lab, smart e-learning system, smart university, smart school, etc.;
(2) level of smart objects (as components of smart systems): SeLS user/learner, smart phones, smart video cameras, smart sensors (transducers), smart mobile devices, etc.;
(3) level of smart activities/processes (as components of smart systems): smart curriculum, smart teaching, smart learning, smart testing, smart compilation of learning modules into courses and curriculum based on student/learner specific – in some cases, limited - psychophysiological parameters, etc.;
(4) level of smart technology/services (as components of smart systems): smart computing, smart sensor technology, smart grid technology, Internet-of-Things, etc.

This proposed classification of smart entities, particularly, enables designers and/or users to identify the "maturity" level of proposed and/or to-be-developed or existing SeLS in terms of smart objects, processes and technologies.

Despite a great variety of known and emerging smart entities, their scopes are defined by main features of smart systems [6]; the proposed adjusted and extended version of that classification is presented in Table 1.

Based on the ideas of "intelligence" levels that were introduced in [7], and in order to categorize smart systems based on their "smartness" maturity level, the improved and detailed classification of "smartness" levels of a smart system (including SeLS) is given in Table 2.

Table 1. Classification of general features of a smart entity

Feature	Goal	Components
Acquisition (sensing) of real-world raw data, and, possibly, a local pre-processing of raw data	To collect raw data needed for an appropriate sensing, and, thus, monitor a situation, condition, object, system, environment, etc.	Sensors, smart phones, smart devices, transducers, machine-to-machine communication, etc.
Transmission of raw data and/or pre-processed sensory information	To transmit the sensor raw or pre-processed data to the local and/or central control unit	Smart phones, smart devices, transmitters, wide area network, Internet, etc.
Big data processing and smart analytics at central control units	To manage and control the entire system	Central processing unit (CPU), invariant analysis systems, big data storage units, etc.
Transmission of instructions	To transmit the decisions made and the associated instructions to actuators	Smart phones, smart devices, transmitters, wide area network, Internet, etc.
Activation (triggering) of physical and/or virtual actuators (devices)	To initiate or perform activities to provide system's reaction on received raw data	Actuators, smart devices

Table 2. Classification of "smartness" levels of a smart system

Ability to	Details	Who/what is involved
Adapt	Ability to modify characteristics to fit the environment or better survive in it	SeLS, adaptive hyper media
Sense	Ability to identify, recognize, understand and/or become aware of process, action, object, etc.	SeLS user, sensors, software/hardware intelligent agents
Infer	Ability to make logical conclusion(s) on the basis of raw data, processed information, observations, evidence, assumptions, rules, and reasoning	SeLS user, reasoning systems, inference engines
Learn	Ability to acquire new or modify existing knowledge, experience, behavior to improve performance, effectiveness, skills, etc.	SeLS user, software intelligent agents, genetic programming
Anticipate	Ability of thinking or reasoning to predict what is going to happen or what to do next	SeLS user, intelligent tutoring systems
Self-organize	Ability of a system to change its internal structure (components), in purposeful (non-random) manner under appropriate conditions but without an external agent/entity	SeLS, smart technology and objects at the cellular or nano-technology level

The proposed classification in Table 2 clearly shows a difference between (a) existing prototypes of smart systems for education and/or learning that are pure technical software/hardware systems with their only smart abilities "to adapt", "to anticipate", and "to self-organize", and (b) advanced SeLS as student-centered biotechnical systems with their additional important smart abilities "to sense", "to infer", and "to learn".

3   Smart e-Learning: Student Psychophysiological Parameters

A student/learner is a key component of advanced SeLS; he/she has specific abilities to read, write, sense, understand process and/or data, infer, make logical conclusions, learn, and retain and use knowledge. The optimization of those activities involves obtaining maximum learning outcomes in a minimal time period with the highest retention factor possible. However, this process can be effective and optimal under the condition that student psychophysiological functional state is optimal [8].

3.1   Learner's Mental Working Capacity

The learning load and intensity should not lead to a reduction of student's psychophysiological functional state, including learner's mental working capacity (MWC). In order to predict it, it is necessary to distinguish the following MWC phases and corresponding activities:

(1)   getting started (i.e. forming a new functional system focused on achieving identified outcomes); a certain tension of regulatory mechanisms is needed;
(2)   optimal MWC (in this case, the tension level of physiological systems corresponds to mental stress);
(3)   full productivity (with possible initial signs of tiredness but without decrease of MWC);
(4)   unstable productivity (with clear signs of tiredness and decrease of MWC);
(5)   progressive decrease of MWC with fast increase of tiredness and obvious decrease of efficiency of learning.

These identified phases fit well into a classification of degrees of regulatory mechanisms' tension, specifically (a) tension and/or stress, (b) overload or burden, and (c) tiredness.

In order to evaluate learner's MWC we actively use the Heart Rate Variability (HRV) method.

3.2   Heart Rate Variability (HRV) Method

The HRV method is focused on monitoring of learner's regulator mechanisms (a) before, (b) during, and (c) after learning experience. This method is based on (a) recognition and measurement of RR-intervals between the high-amplitude peaks of electrocardiogram (R-peak), (b) construction of time series of RR-intervals between two neighboring peaks, and (c) numerical analysis of obtained R-peak data [9–11]. The most informative parameters of the HRV method are (1) Heart Rate (*HR*), (2) Stress Index (*SI*), and (3) Centralization Index (*IC*).

The *SI* parameter is calculated based on the RR-intervals' histogram:

$$SI = \frac{Amo \cdot 100\%}{2 \cdot Mo \cdot MxDMn} \tag{1}$$

where *Mo* – mode, *AMo* – mode's amplitude, *MxDMn* – variation range. The *SI* parameter is sensitive to increased sympathetic nervous system tone; as a result, a small physical, emotional or mental overload may increase *SI* values by 1.5–2 times.

The *IC* parameter is associated with psycho-emotional stress and the functional state of brain; it is calculated as follows:

$$IC = \frac{VLF + LF}{HF} \tag{2}$$

where *VLF* – spectral density of RR-intervals in a very low frequency range, *LF* - in the range of low frequency, *HF* - in the high frequency range.

3.3 The Varikard Software/Hardware System

In order to actually calculate all designated parameters of the HRV method, and, therefore, monitor learner's MWC, the Varikard software/hardware system – the Varikard system - has been used in performed experiments; its Web-based graphic user interface is presented at Fig. 1.

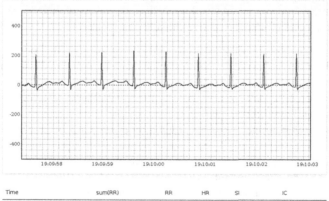

Fig. 1. The web-based graphic user interface of the Varikard system

Its main functions include but are not limited to:

(1) obtaining learner's functional state and health related signals,
(2) signals' filtering using various applied algorithms,
(3) identification of R-peaks,
(4) identification of RR-intervals,
(5) mathematical formation of dynamic series of RR-intervals,
(6) calculation of numeric values of *HR, SI, IC* parameters,
(7) direct transfer of obtained data to learning management system,
(8) visualization of processed data.

An example of the Varikard system in action – i.e. RR-intervals, and values of calculated parameters *HR, SI,* and *IC* - is presented on Fig. 1.

4 Experimental Data Obtained and Research Outcomes

In order to test the effectiveness of proposed approach – i.e. a consideration of SeLS system as a biotechnical system which effectiveness significantly depends on learner's functional state including MWC – we randomly selected and divided first-year students into two groups:

(1) experimental group EG of 46 students – a group of students who used the SeLS system for learning and testing, whose psychophysiological functional states were carefully measured, collected, processed and analyzed during learning process;
(2) regular group RG of 23 students – a group of students who also used the SeLS system for learning and testing; however, students in this group were not informed about the fact that their *IC* parameter "crossed the border" in terms of elevated *IC* parameter values; it was expected that due to complexity of learning content and to-be-taken comprehensive exams, tiredness, stress, and individual psychophysiological characteristics some of students probably would not be able to effectively learn, understand and retain new knowledge, i.e. values of their *IC* parameters will "cross the border" and stay above the allowed highest level of *IC* = 9.5 (Fig. 2).

Students in both groups were asked to take a 4-week long "Methods of Information Coding" online course using a learning management system. Course main topics included but were not limited to mathematical methods of data encoding/decoding, data transmission protocols, data processing algorithms, methods of information storage, data structures and algorithms, etc.

Each class in that online course included a set of tests and/or quizzes for (a) a new course topic, and, if necessary, (b) revised assignments for a previous topic in case *IC* parameter "crossed the border" and was above the recommended maximum one (*IC* = 9.5) for a particular student during previous test/quiz (Fig. 2).

Students of both groups took pre-course and post-course comprehensive exams. Each exam contained 45 problems and was 45 min long. Multiple experimental data have been obtained using the HRV method and the Varikard system; those data precisely reflected student psychophysiological state during both designated exams.

A summary of obtained experimental data is presented in Table 3.

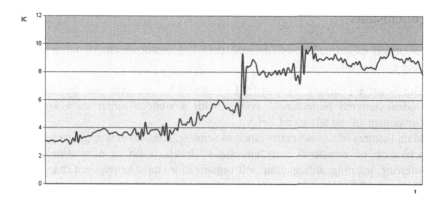

Fig. 2. The Varikard system: *IC* parameter values "crossed the border" case (with *IC* > 9.5)

Table 3. Obtained experimental data.

	Student groups	
	Experimental group (EG) with 46 students	Regular group (RG) with 23 students
Pre-course online exam		
Average score	42 %	42 %
Average IC	4.9	4.9
Post-course online exam		
Average score	86 %	79 %
Average IC	4.5	5.1

Outcome # 1. Students of both EG and RG groups had the same average scores (42 %) and average values of *IC* parameter (4.9) during a pre-course exam. However, during a post-course comprehensive exam EG students demonstrated better average scores (86 % in EG group versus 79 % in RG group) and smaller values of *IC* parameter – 4.5 in EG group versus 5.1 in RG group (as on Fig. 2, smaller value of *IC* is better). As a result, in general, an average student in EG group used fewer psychophysiological resources to achieve better learning outcomes than an average student in RG group; these obtained data strongly support the proposed approach.

Outcome # 2. Based on (a) obtained specific values of HRV method's indicators for a particular student for a particular learning assignment, and (b) range of "normal" HRM method values for this type of students, the SeLS system will get additional useful criteria to smartly compile an individual e-learning trajectory for a particular student. In other words, it will be able to automatically generate an individual sequence of reusable information and learning objects and atoms, pre- and post-tests, learning modules, learning assignments, types of problems in tests/quizzes to be taken, etc. in order to provide maximum efficiency of student learning outcomes [12].

5   Conclusions

The performed experiments and obtained data and outcomes enable us to make the following conclusions:

(1) The Smart e-Learning System (SeLS) should be designed and developed as a student-centered biotechnical system with a student/learner as a key central component in the advanced SeLS.

(2) Main features of a smart entity (such as sensing, transmission, big data processing, activation of actuators) and "smartness" levels (such as adaptation, sensing, inferring, learning, anticipation, self-organization) must be required characteristics of advanced SeLS.

(3) Multiple parameters of student psychophysiological state should be actively used in advanced SeLS for higher efficiency of (a) SeLS usability, (b) student learning process, and (c) student learning outcomes and knowledge retention factor.

References

1. Yau, S., Guppta, S., et al.: Smart classroom: enhancing collaborative learning using pervasive computing technology. In: Proceedings of the 2003 ASEE Annual Conference and Exposition, Nashville, TN, 23–25 June 2003
2. O'Driscoll, C., Mithileash, et al.: Deploying a context aware smart classroom. In: International Technology, Education and Development Conference INTED (2008)
3. Yue Suo, Y., Miyata, N., et al.: Open smart classroom: extensible and scalable learning system in smart space using Web service technology. IEEE Trans. Knowl. Data Eng. 21(6), 814–828 (2009)
4. Shi, Y., Xie, W., et al.: The smart classroom: merging technologies for seamless tele-education. Pervasive Comput. 2(2), 45–55 (2003). IEEE
5. Das, S.K., Cook, D.J.: Designing and modeling smart environments. In: World of Wireless. Mobile and Multimedia Networks, WoWMoM (2006)
6. Akhras, G.: Smart materials and smart systems for the future. Can. Mil. J. http://www.revue.forces.gc.ca/vol1/no3/doc/25-32-eng.pdf
7. Derzko, W.: Smart Technologies (2006). http://archives.ocediscovery.com/discovery2007/presentations/Session3WalterDrezkoFINAL.pdf
8. Lisitsyna, L., Lyamin, A., Skshidlevsky, A.: Estimation of student functional state in learning management system by heart rate variability method. In: Proceedings of the First International Conference on Smart Technology Based Education and Training, Crete, Greece, June 2014
9. Maraes, V., Carreiro, D., Barbosa, N.: Study of heart rate variability of university trained at rest and exercise. In: 2013 Pan American Health Care Exchanges (PAHCE), Medellin (2013)
10. Karthikeyan, P., Murugappan, M., Yaacob, S.: A study on mental arithmetic task based human stress level classification using discrete wavelet transform. In: Proceedings of the 2012 IEEE Conference on Sustainable Utilization and Development in Engineering and Technology (STUDENT), Kuala Lumpur, pp. 77–81, October 2012

11. Wu, W., Lee, J.: Improvement of HRV methodology for positive/negative emotion assessment. In: Proceedings of the 5th International Conference on Collaborative Computing: Networking, Applications and Worksharing, Washington, DC, 11–14 Nov 2009
12. Uskov, V., Uskova, M.: Reusable learning objects approach to web-based education. In: Proceedings of the 5th International Conference on Computers and Advanced Technology in Education CATE-2002, Cancun, Mexico, 20–22 May, pp. 165–170 (2002)

Author Index